# THE TRAGEDY

OF

# HAMLET

## PRINCE OF DENMARK

EDITED BY

### E. K. CHAMBERS, B.A.

SOMETIME SCHOLAR OF CORPUS CHRISTI COLLEGE, OXFORD
EDITOR OF "MACBETH"

1895

# GENERAL PREFACE.

In this edition of SHAKESPEARE an attempt is made to present the greater plays of the dramatist in their literary aspect, and not merely as material for the study of philology or grammar. Criticism purely verbal and textual has only been included to such an extent as may serve to help the student in the appreciation of the essential poetry. Questions of date and literary history have been fully dealt with in the Introductions, but the larger space has been devoted to the interpretative rather than the matter-of-fact order of scholarship. Aesthetic judgments are never final, but the Editors have attempted to suggest points of view from which the analysis of dramatic motive and dramatic character may be profitably undertaken. In the Notes likewise, while it is hoped that all unfamiliar expressions and allusions have been adequately explained, yet it has been thought even more important to consider the dramatic value of each scene, and the part which it plays in relation to the whole. These general principles are common to the whole series ; in detail each Editor is alone responsible for the play or plays that have been intrusted to him.

Every volume of the series has been provided with a Glossary, an Essay upon Metre, and an Index ; and Appendices have been added upon points of special interest, which could not conveniently be treated in the Introduction or the Notes. The text is based by the several Editors on that of the *Globe* edition : the only omissions made are those that are unavoidable in an edition likely to be used by young students.

By the systematic arrangement of the introductory matter, and by close attention to typographical details, every effort has been made to provide an edition that will prove convenient in use.

BOSTON, *August*, 1895.

# CONTENTS.

# INTRODUCTION.

## 1. LITERARY HISTORY OF THE PLAY.

THE early history of *Hamlet* affords one of the most difficult problems with which Shakespearian scholarship has to
deal. Three printed versions of the text have The critical
come down to us. These present remarkable problem.
variations from each other, and one of them in particular,
the earliest, appears to be fundamentally different from the
other two. The most probable explanation is that the play
underwent a process of revision after it was originally written
and acted. If, then, we could determine the exact relation in
which the three forms stand to one another, we should learn
a good deal about Shakespeare's dramatic method as shown
in the deliberate modification of his first ideas. Unfortu-
nately this is not so easy. Scholars still disagree hopelessly
as to the exact nature of the earliest version; and the whole
question is complicated by the probable existence of a pre-
Shakespearian *Hamlet*, which may have had a considerable
influence upon the later play. So that for the present one
must be content to bring together the facts, to indicate the
conditions of the problem, and to suggest the most likely
hypothesis for its solution.

The Registers of the Stationer's Company for The Stationers'
1602, amongst other entries of books 'allowed Registers.
to be printed', contain the following:—

### xxvj<sup>to</sup> Julij

James Robertes. Entered for his copie vnder the handes
of master **Pasfield** and master **Waterson** warden, A
booke called '*the Revenge of HAMLETT Prince* [*of*] *Denmarke*' *as y<sup>t</sup> was latelie Acted by the Lord Chamberleyne his
seruantes.* . . . . . . . . . vj<sup>d.</sup>

No edition is known to have been published in 1602, but in 1603 appeared the perplexing First Quarto (Q 1). In the interval the Lord Chamberlain's players had passed under the direct patronage of James the First, and they are therefore entitled 'his Highness' servants' upon the title-page, which runs:—

*The First Quarto of 1603 (Q 1).*

> THE | Tragicall Hiftorie of ¦ HAMLET | *Prince of Denmarke* | By William Shakefpeare. | As it hath beene diverfe times acted by his Highneffe fer- | vants in the Cittie of London: as alfo in the two V- | niverfities of Cambridge and Oxford, and elfe-where | [*Vignette*] | At London printed for N. L. and Iohn Trundell. | 1603.

James Roberts' name is not here mentioned; but he may have printed the book for the publisher N[icholas] L[ing], whose device forms the vignette. At any rate he appears to have done this in the case of the Second Quarto (Q 2), which was published in 1604, with the following title-page:—

*The Second Quarto of 1604 (Q 2).*

> THE | Tragicall Hiftorie of | HAMLET, | *Prince of Denmarke.* | By William Shakefpeare. | Newly imprinted and enlarged to almoft as much againe as it was, according to the true and perfect | Coppie | [*Vignette*] | AT LONDON, | Printed by I. R. for N. L. and are to be fold at his fhoppe vnder Saint Dunfton's Church in | Fleet ftreet. 1604.

The First Quarto stands by itself; the later Quartos follow the second; but an independent text is afforded by the First Folio (F 1) edition of the collected plays issued after Shakespeare's death in 1623. Here *Hamlet* is entitled a Tragedy, and no longer a Tragical History. In the order of the plays it follows *Julius Cæsar* and *Macbeth*, and immediately precedes *King Lear*.

*The First Folio of 1623 (F 1).*

The modern text of *Hamlet* is based upon a combination of the Second Quarto and the First Folio, and it is therefore necessary briefly to compare the two with each other, and both with the First Quarto.

The editors of the First Folio claim to have provided care-

fully corrected texts of all plays whereof 'stolen and surreptitious copies' had been in circulation before. To Comparison of
a certain extent this is justified as to *Hamlet.* Q 2 and F 1.
The Second Quarto is very ill printed; it is disfigured by
obvious mistakes and confusions;[1] the punctuation is chaotic.
The First Folio is not faultless in these respects, but it is a
great improvement. Many of the errors of the Quarto have
been avoided, and the minor details of presswork, the
commas and colons, have been carefully attended to. Moreover the Folio adds a few passages which are not found in
the Quarto.[2] But these advantages are more than compen-
sated for by considerable and important omissions, especially in the soliloquies.[3] The Second Quarto was evidently
printed from a longer and more complete manuscript than
the Folio, and where divergencies of reading occur, and the
compositor is not in fault, it generally provides the better
sense.[4]

The relation of the First Quarto to the later versions is a
much more difficult matter. Most critics are agreed that,
whatever may have been the case with the Character of
Second Quarto, the First, like the First Quarto Q 1.
of *Romeo and Juliet*, was fairly to be put down by the editors
of the 1623 folio as a 'stolen and surreptitious copy'. The
publication of it was doubtless due rather to the enterprise
of a piratical bookseller than to the wish of Shakespeare
or his company. And in all probability it was founded upon
hasty notes, taken in shorthand or otherwise, by some agent
of this bookseller's during a performance at the theatre.
This would account for the extreme shortness of the text, for
its mutilated character, for the obvious gaps in the sense,

---

[1] See notes on i. 3. 74, 76; i. 4. 36; i. 5. 56; ii. 2. 73; iii. 2. 373; iii. 4. 169;
iv. 7. 22; v. 2. 283, &c.

[2] See notes to ii. 2. 215, 244, 335, 352; iii. 2. 277; iv. 2. 32; iv. 5. 161; v. 1. 37,
115; v. 2. 68; together with Appendix D and Mr. Furnivall's introduction to
Griggs' facsimile of Q 2.

[3] See notes to i. 1. 108; i. 2. 58; i. 4. 18, 75; iii. 4. 168; iv. 4. 9; iv. 7. 69; v. 2. 203.

[4] See notes to i. 1. 65, 163; i. 2. 129, 248; ii. 1. 39; ii. 2. 52, 442, 580; iv. 5. 145;
v. 1. 255, 269, &c. Sometimes F 1 substitutes a less archaic or unusual word for
that in Q 2; now and then it may contain a finishing touch (*e.g. inurned* for
*interred* in i. 4. 49).

for the number of imperfect and wrongly arranged lines, and of misheard words and phrases.  Some scholars have held that the note-taker's materials were pieced out, either from a sight of the prompter's copy or the actors' parts, or by the pen of a hack poet.  But if this had been the case to any considerable extent, the defects would hardly have been so glaring as they are.  I do not think that more has been done than just to transcribe the careless and incomplete notes, and perhaps here and there to fill up a line by the addition of a few words.  In any case the printed copy is very far from reproducing the dialogue of the play as it was presented upon the stage.

But now comes the point which is still the subject of the keenest controversy.  Supposing that this dialogue had been *The question* reproduced with absolute accuracy, would the *of revision.* result have closely resembled the Second Quarto? In other words, was the play as acted when the note-taker went to the theatre practically identical with the play as acted and printed in 1604; or did it undergo alteration and revision in the interval?  Scholars of great authority have declared on both sides, but the weight of evidence appears to me to be in favour of the theory that there was a considerable and important revision.  The order of the scenes in the First Quarto is not quite that of the second.  Some of the characters, notably that of Gertrude, are differently conceived; the great soliloquies are almost entirely omitted; the dialogue is less subtle and elaborate, as might well be the case in a first sketch.  There are passages which make very good sense and not bad poetry as they stand, where there is no sign that the reporter has gone far wrong, but which have apparently been rewritten and improved throughout for the Second Quarto.  And finally, the names of the characters are not quite the same in the two versions: the Polonius and Reynaldo of the Second Quarto replace the Corambis and Montano of the First.  In all probability, then, the First Quarto is an exceedingly corrupt text of a first sketch of *Hamlet*; the Second Quarto represents much more accurately a revised form of the same play.

It has been asked—Was this first sketch of *Hamlet* Shakespeare's throughout, or did it contain parts by an earlier writer, which in the revision Shakespeare cut out and replaced by his own work? One cannot suppose Shakespeare's masterpiece of tragedy to have *The pre-Shakespearian Hamlet.* been written in the sixteenth century; but there certainly was a play of *Hamlet* in existence as early as 1589 or possibly 1587. There are several allusions to this play in contemporary literature,[1] notably in Nash's prefatory epistle to Greene's *Menaphon*. And in the diary of Henslowe the manager there is a record of a performance of it, not as a 'new enterlude', on June 9, 1594. It was acted by the Lord Chamberlain's company, who were then playing for about ten days under Henslowe's management at Newington Butts. It has been suggested with some plausibility that this early *Hamlet* was written by Thomas Kyd, author of *The Spanish Tragedy*. In any case, seeing that it had come into the hands of the Lord Chamberlain's company by 1594, there can be little doubt that Shakespeare used it as a starting-point, when he wrote his own play on the same subject for the same company. Probably he kept the framework of the plot, including the ghost, the play within a play, and the somewhat bloodthirsty final scene. Shakespeare was never careful to invent his own plots; his art lay rather in using old bottles to contain his quite new wine. But the dialogue, the characters, the psychological motive—these are his and his alone, and it is in these that the greatness of *Hamlet* lies. The only question is whether this process of adaptation was complete in the first sketch, or whether fragments of the earlier author's writing are still embedded in the text. The Clarendon Press editors adopt the second alternative. They believe that the First Quarto represents Shakespeare's remodelling of an old play "after it had been retouched by him to a certain extent, but before his alterations were complete", and they go on to say: "In the earlier form it appears to us that Shakespeare's modification of the play had not gone much beyond the second act". I am obliged to dissent

---

[1] For early allusions to the pre-Shakespearian *Hamlet* see Appendix B.

entirely from this theory. It ascribes a great deal too much to the older writer. Tentative as the First Quarto is, it still contains the essential outlines of the perfected play; and if the bulk of it is not Shakespeare's, then there was another Elizabethan dramatist as great as Shakespeare himself, who has left no other sign of his existence. If there are any traces of the older play left in the first sketch, I am pretty sure they are very slight, and I rather think they are retained in the revised version also.

There is another source from which it has been suggested that we may perhaps get some idea of what the pre-Shake-spearian *Hamlet* was like. This is the German version, known as *Der bestrafte Brudermord*, or *Fratricide Punished*. The existing text dates only from 1710, but in the opinion of some scholars it is a degenerate form of a play, written not later than 1589.[1] Several companies of English actors visited Germany at the end of the sixteenth and the beginning of the seventeenth centuries, and there is a record of a performance of *Hamlet a Prince in Dennemarck* by 'the English actors' at the court of Dresden in 1626. It is not at all unlikely that the MS. of an early *Hamlet*, by Kyd or another, was carried by Leicester's players to Denmark in 1585, and thence to Saxony in 1586. Or it may have been written, appropriately enough, for performance in Denmark. Three of these players, Will (Kempe?), George Bryan, and Thomas Pope, had joined the Chamberlain's (then Lord Strange's) company by 1593, and thus the play would have come into Shakespeare's hands. *Fratricide Punished* is very short—a mere dramatic sketch; but it contains the outlines of *Hamlet*, without the Shakespearian psychology or the Shakespearian style. These are replaced by coarse humour and a good deal of bathos and commonplace. Something of this may be due to German influences; but on the whole the difference is just what one would expect to find between a popular drama of 1585 and a Shakespearian drama based upon it. Some of the *dramatis personæ* bear other names than those in *Hamlet*, and it is

The German version: *Fratricide Punished.*

[1] See Appendix C.

noteworthy that Polonius is represented by Corambus. It must be remembered, however, that the German play cannot be proved to date from the sixteenth century. The MS. belongs to the eighteenth, and the resemblances to *Hamlet* may be due to the fact that the author was simply adapting a copy of the First Quarto which had drifted to Germany.

*Hamlet*, then, is probably based upon an older play of the crude 'revenge' type. To what dates are we to ascribe the various stages of Shakespeare's treatment of the theme? The revised version may fairly be put at about 1603-4, between the date of the publi- *The question of Date, 1601-1603.* cation of the Second Quarto and the visit of the surreptitious note-taker to the theatre. The first sketch cannot be later than the entry in the Stationers' Registers for 26th July, 1602. And it cannot well be earlier than 1598, as it is not mentioned in the list of Shakespeare's plays given by Francis Meres in his *Palladis Tamia* of that year. Internal evidence appears to fix 1601 as the most likely date. We know from the title-page of the First Quarto that it was acted when Shakespeare and his fellows were touring in the provinces; and this being so, we may fairly find in what is said about the players in act ii. sc. 2 an allusion to the fortunes of the Chamberlain's company. Two reasons are there given for the 'travelling' of the actors; one, an 'inhibition', due to a 'late innovation'; the other, the popularity of a rival company, an 'eyrie of children', who had 'be-rattled the common stages'.[1] No other year fits these references so well as 1601. The Chamberlain's company were 'inhibited' from giving their customary court performances at the Christmas of that year, on account of their connection with Essex's attempt at political 'innovation'. We know that they 'travelled', for they are found at Aberdeen in October, and there are also traces of a possible visit to Cambridge at about this time. In 1601, moreover, Jonson's satirical plays, in which he attacked most of the rival dramatists, were being produced by the Chapel children at Blackfriars. This sufficiently explains the allusion to the 'eyrie of children'. It is also worth noting that at

[1] On these allusions see Appendix D.

this period William Kempe, the famous actor of clowns, was not a member of the Chamberlain's company. He left them in 1599, and probably returned in 1602. This explains why the hit at him in iii. 2. 41 is so much more elaborate in the first than in the Second Quarto.[1] There is yet one more consideration which points to this date of 1601. It brings the play into close connection with *Julius Cæsar* and *Macbeth*, both of which belong to just this period, the period of the earliest tragedies. And it is noteworthy that the same dramatic motive is used in all three plays—the contrast, namely, between the active and the speculative temperament.[2]

I may sum up this discussion by a brief sketch of what I conceive to have taken place. I may add that for this I am largely indebted to the suggestive work of Mr. Fleay. I think, then, that ever since 1594 the Chamberlain's company had possessed the manuscript of the old 'revenge' play of *Hamlet*. While they were on tour in 1601, Shakespeare used this as a basis for a hasty drama on the same subject. When they returned to London in 1602 they continued to perform this, and it was pirated by James Roberts. In the meantime, however, Shakespeare had revised his work, and the new version was put upon the stage in 1603. Then Roberts or Ling came to terms with the company, and was allowed to publish a second and authorized edition from the poet's manuscript. Thus the Second Quarto represents the completest form of the drama, as performed in 1604. But it nearly always happens that when a play has been on the boards some little time, it requires 'cutting' and altering in detail for stage purposes. It was so with *Hamlet*. In particular, some of the soliloquies proved too long. And in the same way, a few new passages were from time to time introduced. These alterations would naturally be inserted in the stage-copy, and from this stage-copy the First Folio was printed in 1623. A good deal of this sketch is merely hypothesis, but at least it is an hypothesis which

*Summary.*

[1] See note ad loc.
[2] Cf. Professor Dowden, *Shakspere: his Mind and Art*; preface to Third Edition.

gives an intelligible theory of the relation between the various versions.

The distinction between the Quarto and Folio text was maintained throughout the seventeenth century. The Folios of 1632 (F 2), 1664 (F 3), and 1685 (F 4) all repro- *The later Folios and Quartos.* duce in the main the text of 1623. Quarto editions were published during the poet's lifetime in 1605 (Q 3) and 1611 (Q 4). The date of Q 5, which follows Q 4, is unknown. Then come the Quarto of 1637 (Q 6), and what are called the Players' Quartos of 1676, 1683, and 1703. All of these follow the Second Quarto, with certain emendations of their own.

The first actor of the part of Hamlet was doubtless Richard Burbage. A record of his performance is pre- *The Actors of Hamlet.* served in an elegy upon his death, written perhaps in 1619.[1] The lines run as follows :—

> "He 's gone, and with him what a world are dead
> [Which he reviv'd, to be revived so
> No more: young Hamlet, old Hieronimo,
> Kind Leir, the grieved Moor, and more beside,
> That liv'd in him, have now for ever died.]
> Oft have I seen him leap into the grave,
> Suiting the person, that he seem'd to have,
> Of a sad lover, with so true an eye,
> That there I would have sworn he meant to die.
> Oft have I seen him play this part in jest,
> So lively, that spectators and the rest
> Of his sad crew, while he but seemed to bleed,
> Amazed thought ev'n then he died indeed."

Burbage was succeeded by Joseph Taylor, and from Taylor the tradition of the part was handed down to Thomas Betterton, the famous actor of the Restoration.

## 2. SOURCE OF THE PLOT.

Hamlet first appears in the *Historia Danica* of Saxo Grammaticus. This chronicler lived at the end of the twelfth

---

[1] On the various versions of this Elegy, and their authenticity, see Ingleby, *Shakespere: the Man and the Book*, Part II. The four bracketed lines are probably spurious.

century, and his work was first printed at Paris in 1514. The story of Hamlet or Amlethus is contained in the third and fourth books, under the reign of King Röricus. Grytha, the daughter of Röricus, was Hamlet's mother. From Saxo the story passed into European literature. Hans Sachs wrote a doggerel German version of it in 1558; and in 1570 it was included in the fifth volume of Francis de Belleforest's *Histoires Tragiques*, a collection in which the history of Romeo and Juliet is also found. The French version may have come under Shakespeare's notice, and an English translation of the *Historie of Hamblet* is in existence. But the only known edition of this was printed for Thomas Pavier in 1608. And though there may have been earlier issues, it is noticeable, as Elze has pointed out, that the translation diverges from the French original in one or two places, and that in these the influence of the play is plainly apparent. In any case only the outlines of Shakespeare's plot are to be found in the novel. "The murder of Hamlet's father", says Mr. Furness, "the marriage of his mother with the murderer, Hamlet's pretended madness, his interview with his mother, and his voyage to England, are nearly the only points in common." With the exception of Amleth and Geruth, the very names are different. In all probability Shakespeare only had before him the earlier play on the subject already referred to.

Numerous attempts have been made to identify the characters of the play with actual men and women of the Elizabethan age. One critic holds that Hamlet is throughout a satire on the famous essayist Michel de Montaigne. Another believes that the whole tragedy is a veiled picture of the relations between Mary Queen of Scots, Darnley, Bothwell, and James the First. Yet other theorists interpret Hamlet as Sir Philip Sidney; Polonius, Laertes, and Ophelia as Lord Burleigh, Robert and Anne Cecil, Claudius as Sir Nicholas Bacon, Horatio as Hubert Languet; Marcellus, Bernardo, and Lamond as Fulke Greville, Edward Dyer, and Sir Walter Raleigh. The want of definite evidence for these conjectures makes it unnecessary to discuss them at length. They are suggestive to the imagination rather than to the reason, and from the imaginative point of view I have ventured to say a word on one of them at the close of this Introduction.

## 3. CRITICAL APPRECIATION.

The criticism of *Hamlet* is apt to centre round the question, 'Was Hamlet mad?' The problem is not merely insoluble; it cannot even be propounded in an intelligible guise. Psychology knows no rigid dividing line between the sane and the insane. The alleged madness of Hamlet. The pathologist, indeed, may distinguish certain abnormal conditions of brain-areas, and call them diseased; or the lawyer may apply practical tests to determine the point where restraint of the individual liberty becomes necessary in the public interest. But beyond this you cannot go; you cannot, from any wider point of view, lay your finger upon one element here or there in the infinite variety of human character and say, 'That way madness lies'. Of this, however, we may be sure. Shakespeare did not mean Hamlet to be mad in any sense which would put his actions in a quite different category from those of other men. That would have been to divest his work of humanity and leave it meaningless. For the tragedy of *Hamlet* does not lie in the fact that it begins with a murder and ends with a massacre; it is something deeper, more spiritual than that. The essential tragedy. The most tragic, the most affecting thing in the world is the ruin of a high soul. This is the theme of *Hamlet*; it is a tragedy of failure, of a great nature confronted with a low environment, and so, by the perversity of things, made ineffective and disastrous through its own greatness. Keeping, then, this central idea in mind, let us attempt an analysis of the play in which it is set forth.

Hamlet is presented to us as a man of sensitive temperament and high intellectual gifts. He is no ordinary prince; his spirit has been touched to finer issues; his wit is keen-edged and dipped in irony; his delicacy of moral insight is unusual among the ruder Danes. He is no longer in his

first youth when the play opens, but up to that moment his
life has been serene and undisturbed. His
father's unexpected death has called him back
from the University of Wittenberg, where his
time has been spent in an atmosphere of studious
calm and philosophic speculation. His tastes are those of
the scholar; he loves to read for hours together, and, like
most literary men, he takes great delight in the stage, with
whose theory and practice he is familiar. He is no recluse;
he has the genius for friendship and for love; when at
Elsinore he has been conspicuous in the gallant exercises of
the age. He is the darling of the court and beloved by the
people. But his real interest is all in speculation, in the play
of mind around a subject, in the contemplation of it on all
sides and from every point of view. Such a training has not
fitted him to act a kingly part in stirring times; the intellectual element in him has come to outweigh the practical; the
vivid consciousness of many possible courses of conduct
deters him from the strenuous pursuit of one; so that he has
lost the power of deliberate purposeful action, and, by a
strange paradox, if this thoughtful man acts at all, it must be
from impulse.

*Analysis of the play. The character of Hamlet.*

Quite suddenly the dreamer finds himself face to face with
a thing to be done. According to the ethics of the day it
becomes his imperative duty to revenge his
father's murder; a difficult task, and one whose
success might well seem doubtful. But Hamlet
does not shrink at first from recognizing the obligation; it
is 'cursed spite' that the burden of setting the world
straight should have fallen upon him, but he will not refuse
to shoulder it. Only the habits of a lifetime are not to be
thrown off so easily. As the excitement of the ghost's revelation passes away, the laws of character begin to reassert
themselves. The necessity of 'thinking it over' is potent
with Hamlet. Instead of revealing all to his friends and
enlisting their assistance, he binds them to secrecy and forms
the plan of pretending madness that he may gain time to
consider his position. Let us consider it with him.

*The Apparition: a call for action.*

In the first place, he is absolutely alone.  The court at Elsinore is filled with quite ordinary people, none of whom can understand him, to none of whom he can  The court of look for help.  This note of contrast between  Elsinore. Hamlet and his surroundings is struck again and again. They are of another world than his, limited, commonplace, incapable of ideals.  His motives and feelings, his scruples and hesitations, are hopelessly beyond their comprehension. And therefore—this is the irony of it—most of them are far more fitted to deal with a practical crisis in life than this high-strung idealist of a prince.  There are 'the good king and queen'; Claudius, shrewd and ready for an emergency, one who has set foot in the paths of villany and will not turn back, for all the dim visitings of momentary remorse; Gertrude, a slave to the stronger nature, living in the present, unable to realize her own moral degradation.  There is Horatio, a straightforward upright soldier, one whom Hamlet intensely respects, comes even to envy, but who is not subtle enough to be of much use to him.  There is Polonius, a played-out state official, vain and slow-witted, pattering words of wisdom which he does not understand and cannot put into practice.  There are his son and daughter, Laertes and Ophelia : Laertes, a shallow vigorous young noble, quick with a word, and quick with a blow, but demoralized by the *esprit Gaulois*; Ophelia, a timid conventional girl, too fragile a reed for a man to lean upon.  Hamlet loves her, and she loves Hamlet, but it is not a love that will bear him through the deep waters of affliction.  The rest of the court are typi- fied by Osric the waterfly, and by Guildenstern and Rosen- crantz, of whom if you say Rosencrantz and Guildenstern it makes no difference; echoes, nonentities.  With Hamlet on one side and these on the other, the elements of a tragedy are complete; the problem can work out to no satisfactory conclusion.

Once Hamlet has shrunk from immediate action, the possibilities of delay exercise an irresistible fas-  The course of cination over him.  The ingenuity of his intellect  the tragedy. exhausts itself in the discovery of obstacles; he takes every

turn and twist to avoid the fatal necessity for action. At
first he turns to Ophelia, the well-beloved. She will give
him strength to accomplish his mission; but the scene in her
closet, and still more the lie which she tells when her father
is behind the arras, confess her weakness and compel him to
renunciation. In the meantime he continues the assumption
of madness. It serves a double purpose: he is free from the
intolerable burden of keeping on good terms with Claudius
and the rest; he can fight out the battle with himself in
peace, while he mocks them with the ironies congenial to his
mood. And what is more, he can let himself go; the strain
of his overwrought mind relieves itself in bursts of an
extravagance only half affected. He plays the madman to
prevent himself from becoming one. But all the while he is
no nearer the end. He has turned the whole matter over
and cannot decide. His thoughts slip away from the plain
issue and lose themselves in a bitter criticism of all created
things. In this the speculative temper infallibly betrays
itself; the interest of the universal, not of the particular, is
always dominant with Hamlet; not his mother's sin, but the
frailty of women, is his natural theme. And so it is with a
pang that he constantly recalls himself to the insistent actual
life, from the world in which he is a past-master to that
wherein he gropes ineffectively. Of course he is fully aware
of his own weakness; a deficiency of self-analysis is not
likely to be one of his failings; but this does not give
him power to throw it off, nor help him from his maze of
recurring dilemmas. More than once he is on the point of
cutting the knot by death, but even for that he has not the
resolution.

At last the crisis comes. Hamlet has resolved that the
play-scene shall decide once for all the question of the king's
guilt. That guilt is made most manifest, and
the opportunity for revenge is offered him. He
does not take it. Covering his weakness with unreal reasons,
he passes into the queen's chamber. After that it is too late.
The impetuous murder of Polonius is the first link in a chain
of calamities. Moreover it gives Claudius his chance. The

king has never been wholly deceived by Hamlet's madness; he is sent to England, and only escapes that trap to fall into another. True, in the end the king dies by one impulsive stroke; but that cannot repair the ruin which Hamlet's want of purpose has caused. The infinitely sad fate of Ophelia; the deaths of Polonius, Laertes, Gertrude, Rosencrantz, Guildenstern; for all their faults, all these are a sacrifice on the altar of his infirmity. Only for Hamlet himself was the fatal blow 'a consummation devoutly to be wished'.

The ineffectiveness of the speculative intellect in a world of action, that is the key-note of the play. In Hamlet, as in Brutus, the idealist gets the worst of it, and *The contrast* we are left to wonder at the irony of things *to Hamlet.* by which it is so. And just as the figure of Brutus is set between the two triumphant Philistines, Cæsar and Antony, so Shakespeare is careful to provide a similar contrast for Hamlet. Partly this is to be found in Horatio and Laertes, but still more in the Norwegian, Fortinbras. The very existence of Fortinbras and the danger with which he threatens the state show the need for an iron hand in Denmark; Hamlet's reflections on his meeting with the Norwegian soldiers emphasizes the same point, and the final appearance of Fortinbras and his selection by Hamlet as the true saviour of society is fully significant. It is the lesson of *Henry V.*, the lesson of the 'still strong man in a blatant land'. Only in Hamlet it is the other side that is apparent; not the political principle, but the human tragedy, the ruin of the great soul because it is not strong, practical.

It would be an interesting task to estimate how far the genius of Shakespeare has been impaired for a modern reader by the change in sentiments which the lapse of *The modernity* three crowded centuries has brought about. An *of Hamlet.* Elizabethan dramatist could appeal with confidence to sympathies which are evanescent to-day. *The Merchant of Venice*, for instance, in spite of all its beauty and all its wit, yet bears an air of unreality to us, because its leading motive, that of the *Judenhetze*, no longer finds an echo outside the limits of Whitechapel. Probably Mr. Irving's histrionic

instinct was right when it led him to convert a villain into a
hero, and to present the play as an apology for toleration,
though this was an idea foreign to Shakespeare and impossible on the boards of the Theatre. It is remarkable, however, that there is one tragedy at least in which the normal
law is reversed, and which is more vivid, more intelligible
to us than it could have been to our Elizabethan ancestors.
Modern civilization has indeed discarded the ethics of the
*vendetta*; the moral sentiment which holds revenge for a
father's murder to be a binding duty upon the son no longer
appears obvious and natural. An effort of the historic imagination is required to grasp its importance as a leading idea
in the drama of *Hamlet*. But with the dominant figure, with
Hamlet himself, it is otherwise. A prolonged study of the
character leaves one with the startling sense that out of the
plenitude of his genius Shakespeare has here depicted a type
of humanity which belongs essentially not to his age but to
our own. There was, we know, an older *Hamlet*, a popular
revenge-play, pulsating, no doubt, like *Titus Andronicus*,
with blood and fire. Into the midst of such a story the poet
has deliberately set this modern born out of due time, this
high-strung dreamer, who moves through it to such tragic
issues. The key-note of Hamlet's nature is the over-cultiva-
tion of the mind. He is the academic man, the philosopher
brought suddenly into the world of strenuous action. The
fatal habit of speculation, fatal at Elsinore, however proper
and desirable at Wittenberg, is his undoing. Cursed with the

> "craven scruple
> Of thinking too precisely on the event",

he is predestined to practical failure, failure from which no
delicacy of moral fibre, no truth and intensity of feeling, can
save him. It is surely no mere accident that so many
features in the portrait of Hamlet are reproduced in Mrs.
Ward's Edward Langham. The worship of intellect, the ab-
sorbing interest in music and the theatre, the nervous excita-
bility, the consciousness of ineffectiveness taking refuge in

irony and sarcasm, these and countless other points stamp them as temperaments of kindred mould. And in both lives the tragic woof is the same; it is the tragedy of spiritual impotence, of deadened energies and paralysed will, the essential tragedy of modernity. Hamlet fascinates us, just as Langham fascinates us, because we see in him ourselves; we are all actual or potential Hamlets.

Was Shakespeare, then, a prophet, or how came he to hit upon a conception so alien to the 'form and pressure' of the time? One thinks of Elizabethan England as vigorous and ardent, flushed with youth and hope, little vexed with intellectual subtleties. Laertes is its type, not Hamlet. Perhaps the *Sonnets*, with the personal insight they give us into the poet's temper, help to solve the problem. Shakespeare was not Hamlet, but he touched him on many sides. The maker, like the puppet, had his moments of world-weariness, and breathed his sigh for ' restful death'. But there is another than Shakespeare himself in whom we would willingly recognize in some measure the original of Hamlet. It is not needful to commit ourself to the growing modern theory that the dramas of Shakespeare, comedies and tragedies alike, are largely Aristophanic in their intent, filled with topical sketches and allusions, to which in many cases the clue is now lost. But it is difficult not to think it probable that in this particular the poet gathered some hints from the noticeable personality of Sir Philip Sidney. Sidney is curiously lacking in the characteristic Elizabethan blitheness; he looks by preference on the gloomy side of things; the pessimistic note comes out no less in his letters than in the bitter mockery of the famous dirge. And, like Hamlet, he was a scholar and an idealist, set in an uncongenial environment and always striving ineffectually to escape from it into the life of action. The lingering and futility of his later years were due in great measure to the force of external circumstance, yet something in them may also be traced, clearly enough, to Hamlet's irresolution and impotence of will. Nor can one fail to be struck by the parallel between the language common

*(margin note: Sir Philip Sidney.)*

o the wits and poets of Elizabeth's court in speaking of 'ı
president of noblesse and of chivalry' and the lament
Ophelia over the unstrung nerves of her lover :—

> " Oh, what a noble mind is here o'erthrown !
> The courtier's, soldier's, scholar's, eye, tongue, sword,
> The expectancy and rose of the fair state,
> The glass of fashion and the mould of form,
> The observed of all observers, quite, quite down !"

E. K. C.

*Nov. 9th, 1893.*

# HAMLET,

## PRINCE OF DENMARK.

# DRAMATIS PERSONÆ.

CLAUDIUS, king of Denmark.

HAMLET, son to the late, and nephew to the present king.

POLONIUS, lord chamberlain.

HORATIO, friend to Hamlet.

LAERTES, son to Polonius.

VOLTIMAND,
CORNELIUS,
ROSENCRANTZ,
GUILDENSTERN,  } courtiers.
OSRIC,
A Gentleman,

A Priest.

MARCELLUS,
BERNARDO,  } officers.

FRANCISCO, a soldier.

REYNALDO, servant to Polonius

Players.

Two clowns, grave-diggers.

FORTINBRAS, prince of Norway.

A Captain.

English Ambassadors.

GERTRUDE, queen of Denmark, and mother to Hamlet.

OPHELIA, daughter to Polonius.

Lords, Ladies, Officers, Soldiers, Sailors, Messengers, and other Attendants.

Ghost of Hamlet's Father.

SCENE: *Denmark.*

# HAMLET,

## PRINCE OF DENMARK.

---

### ACT I.

SCENE I. *Elsinore. A platform before the castle.*

FRANCISCO *at his post. Enter to him* BERNARDO.

*Ber.* Who's there?
*Fran.* Nay, answer me: stand, and unfold yourself.
*Ber.* Long live the king!
*Fran.* Bernardo?
*Ber.* He.
*Fran.* You come most carefully upon your hour.
*Ber.* 'T is now struck twelve; get thee to bed, Francisco
*Fran.* For this relief much thanks: 't is bitter cold,
And I am sick at heart.
*Ber.* Have you had quiet guard?
*Fran.*                         Not a mouse stirring. 10
*Ber.* Well, good night.
If you do meet Horatio and Marcellus,
The rivals of my watch, bid them make haste.
*Fran.* I think I hear them. Stand, ho! Who's there?

*Enter* HORATIO *and* MARCELLUS.

*Hor.* Friends to this ground.
*Mar.*                         And liegemen to the Dane.
*Fran.* Give you good night.
*Mar.*   .                    O, farewell, honest soldier:
Who hath relieved you?
*Fran.*                 Bernardo has my place.
Give you good night.                        [*Exit.*
*Mar.*              Holla! Bernardo!
*Ber.*                             Say,
What, is Horatio there?
*Hor.*                  A piece of him.
*Ber.* Welcome, Horatio: welcome, good Marcellus.   20

*Hor.* What, has this thing appear'd again to-night?
*Ber.* I have seen nothing.
*Mar.* Horatio says 't is but our fantasy,
And will not let belief take hold of him
Touching this dreaded sight, twice seen of us:
Therefore I have entreated him along
With us to watch the minutes of this night;
That if again this apparition come,
He may approve our eyes and speak to it.
*Hor.* Tush, tush, 't will not appear.
*Ber.*                                    Sit down awhile;        30
And let us once again assail your ears,
That are so fortified against our story
What we have two nights seen.
*Hor.*                               Well, sit we down,
And let us hear Bernardo speak of this.
*Ber.* Last night of all,
When yond same star that's westward from the pole
Had made his course to illume that part of heaven
Where now it burns, Marcellus and myself,
The bell then beating one,—

*Enter* Ghost.

*Mar.* Peace, break thee off; look, where it comes again!
*Ber.* In the same figure, like the king that's dead.       41
*Mar.* Thou art a scholar; speak to it, Horatio.
*Ber.* Looks it not like the king? mark it, Horatio.
*Hor.* Most like: it harrows me with fear and wonder.
*Ber.* It would be spoke to.
*Mar.*                               Question it, Horatio.
*Hor.* What art thou that usurp'st this time of night,
Together with that fair and warlike form
In which the majesty of buried Denmark
Did sometimes march? by heaven I charge thee, speak!
*Mar.* It is offended.
*Ber.*                          See, it stalks away!                50
*Hor.* Stay! speak, speak! I charge thee, speak!
                                              [*Exit Ghost.*
*Mar.* 'T is gone, and will not answer.
*Ber.* How now, Horatio! you tremble and look pale:
Is not this something more than fantasy?
What think you on 't?
*Hor.* Before my God, I might not this believe
Without the sensible and true avouch
Of mine own eyes.

*Mar.*          Is it not like the king?
*Hor.* As thou art to thyself:
Such was the very armour he had on                    60
When he the ambitious Norway combated;
So frown'd he once, when, in an angry parle,
He smote the sledded pole-axe on the ice.
'T is strange.
  *Mar.* Thus twice before, and jump at this dead hour,
With martial stalk hath he gone by our watch.
  *Hor.* In what particular thought to work I know not;
But in the gross and scope of my opinion,
This bodes some strange eruption to our state.
  *Mar.* Good now, sit down, and tell me, he that knows, 70
Why this same strict and most observant watch
So nightly toils the subject of the land,
And why such daily cast of brazen cannon,
And foreign mart for implements of war;
Why such impress of shipwrights, whose sore task
Does not divide the Sunday from the week;
What might be toward, that this sweaty haste
Doth make the night joint-labourer with the day:
Who is 't that can inform me?
  *Hor.*                    That can I;
At least, the whisper goes so.  Our last king,      80
Whose image even but now appear'd to us,
Was, as you know, by Fortinbras of Norway,
Thereto prick'd on by a most emulate pride,
Dared to the combat; in which our valiant Hamlet—
For so this side of our known world esteem'd him—
Did slay this Fortinbras; who, by a seal'd compact,
Well ratified by law and heraldry,
Did forfeit, with his life, all those his lands
Which he stood seized of, to the conqueror:
Against the which, a moiety competent             90
Was gaged by our king; which had return'd
To the inheritance of Fortinbras,
Had he been vanquisher; as, by the same covenant,
And carriage of the article design'd,
His fell to Hamlet.  Now, sir, young Fortinbras,
Of unapproved mettle hot and full,
Hath in the skirts of Norway here and there
Shark'd up a list of lawless resolutes,
For food and diet, to some enterprise
That hath a stomach in 't; which is no other—     100
As it doth well appear unto our state—

But to recover of us, by strong hand
And terms compulsatory, those foresaid lands
So by his father lost: and this, I take it,
Is the main motive of our preparations,
The source of this our watch and the chief head
Of this post-haste and romage in the land.
  *Ber.* I think it be no other but e'en so:
Well may it sort that this portentous figure
Comes armed through our watch; so like the king      110
That was and is the question of these wars.
  *Hor.* A mote it is to trouble the mind's eye.
In the most high and palmy state of Rome,
A little ere the mightiest Julius fell,
The graves stood tenantless and the sheeted dead
Did squeak and gibber in the Roman streets:
As stars with trains of fire and dews of blood,
Disasters in the sun; and the moist star
Upon whose influence Neptune's empire stands
Was sick almost to doomsday with eclipse:      120
And even the like precurse of fierce events,
As harbingers preceding still the fates
And prologue to the omen coming on,
Have heaven and earth together demonstrated
Unto our climatures and countrymen.—
But soft, behold! lo, where it comes again!

### *Re-enter* Ghost.

I'll cross it, though it blast me.   Stay, illusion!
If thou hast any sound, or use of voice,   [*It spreads its arms.*
Speak to me:
If there be any good thing to be done,      130
That may to thee do ease and grace to me,
Speak to me:
If thou art privy to thy country's fate,
Which, happily, foreknowing may avoid,
O, speak!
Or if thou hast uphoarded in thy life
Extorted treasure in the womb of earth,
For which, they say, you spirits oft walk in death,
                                        [*The cock crows.*
Speak of it: stay, and speak!   Stop it, Marcellus.
  *Mar.* Shall I strike at it with my partisan?      140
  *Hor.* Do, if it will not stand.
  *Ber.*                        'T is here!
  *Hor.*                                'T is here!

*Mar.* 'T is gone!                         [*Exit Ghost.*
We do it wrong, being so majestical,
To offer it the show of violence;
For it is, as the air, invulnerable,
And our vain blows malicious mockery.
   *Ber.* It was about to speak, when the cock crew.
   *Hor.* And then it started like a guilty thing
Upon a fearful summons.  I have heard,
The cock, that is the trumpet to the morn,          150
Doth with his lofty and shrill-sounding throat
Awake the god of day; and, at his warning,
Whether in sea or fire, in earth or air,
The extravagant and erring spirit hies
To his confine: and of the truth herein
This present object made probation.
   *Mar.* It faded on the crowing of the cock.
Some say that ever 'gainst that season comes
Wherein our Saviour's birth is celebrated,
The bird of dawning singeth all night long:          160
And then, they say, no spirit dare stir abroad
The nights are wholesome; then no planets strike,
No fairy takes, nor witch hath power to charm,
So hallow'd and so gracious is the time.
   *Hor.* So have I heard and do in part believe it.
But, look, the morn, in russet mantle clad,
Walks o'er the dew of yon high eastward hill:
Break we our watch up; and by my advice,
Let us impart what we have seen to-night
Unto young Hamlet; for, upon my life,          170
This spirit, dumb to us, will speak to him.
Do you consent we shall acquaint him with it,
As needful in our loves, fitting our duty?
   *Mar.* Let's do't, I pray; and I this morning know
Where we shall find him most conveniently.       [*Exeunt.*

##### SCENE II.  *A room of state in the castle.*

*Enter* CLAUDIUS King of Denmark, GERTRUDE the Queen,
   HAMLET, POLONIUS, LAERTES and his sister OPHELIA,
   Lords Attendant.

   *King.* Though yet of Hamlet our dear brother's death
The memory be green, and that it us befitted
To bear our hearts in grief and our whole kingdom
To be contracted in one brow of woe,

Yet so far hath discretion fought with nature
That we with wisest sorrow think on him,
Together with remembrance of ourselves.
Therefore our sometime sister, now our queen,
The imperial jointress to this warlike state,
Have we, as 't were with a defeated joy,—          10
With an auspicious and a dropping eye,
With mirth in funeral and with dirge in marriage,
In equal scale weighing delight and dole,—
Taken to wife: nor have we herein barr'd
Your better wisdoms, which have freely gone
With this affair along.   For all, our thanks.
Now follows, that you know, young Fortinbras,
Holding a weak supposal of our worth,
Or thinking by our late dear brother's death
Our state to be disjoint and out of frame,          20
Colleagued with the dream of his advantage,
He hath not fail'd to pester us with message,
Importing the surrender of those lands
Lost by his father, with all bonds of law,
To our most valiant brother.   So much for him.
Now for ourself and for this time of·meeting:
Thus much the business is: we have here writ
To Norway, uncle of young Fortinbras,—
Who, impotent and bed-rid, scarcely hears
Of this his nephew's purpose,—to suppress          30
His further gait herein; in that the levies,
The lists and full proportions, are all made
Out of his subject: and we here dispatch
You, good Cornelius, and you, Voltimand,
For bearers of this greeting to old Norway;
Giving to you no further personal power
To business with the king, more than the scope
Of these delated articles allow.
Farewell, and let your haste commend your duty.
     *Cor.* ⎫
     *Vol.* ⎭  In that and all things will we show·our duty.     40
     *King.* We doubt it nothing: heartily farewell.
                    [*Exeunt Voltimand and Cornelius.*
And now, Laertes, what 's the news with you?
You told us of some suit; what is 't, Laertes?
You cannot speak of reason to the Dane,
And lose your voice: what wouldst thou beg, Laertes,
That shall not be my offer, not thy asking?
The head is not more native to the heart,

The hand more instrumental to the mouth,
Than is the throne of Denmark to thy father.
What wouldst thou have, Laertes?
 *Laer.*       My dread lord,  50
Your leave and favour to return to France;
From whence though willingly I came to Denmark,
To show my duty in your coronation,
Yet now, I must confess, that duty done,
My thoughts and wishes bend again toward France
And bow them to your gracious leave and pardon.
 *King.* Have you your father's leave? What says Polonius?
 *Pol.* He hath, my lord, wrung from me my slow leave
By laboursome petition, and at last
Upon his will I seal'd my hard consent:  60
I do beseech you, give him leave to go.
 *King.* Take thy fair hour, Laertes; time be thine,
And thy best graces spend it at thy will!
But now, my cousin Hamlet, and my son,—
 *Ham.* [*Aside*] A little more than kin, and less than kind.
 *King.* How is it that the clouds still hang on you?
 *Ham.* Not so, my lord; I am too much i' the sun.
 *Queen.* Good Hamlet, cast thy nighted colour off,
And let thine eye look like a friend on Denmark.
Do not for ever with thy vailed lids  70
Seek for thy noble father in the dust:
Thou know'st 't is common; all that lives must die,
Passing through nature to eternity.
 *Ham.* Ay, madam, it is common.
 *Queen.*      If it be,
Why seems it so particular with thee?
 *Ham.* Seems, madam! nay, it is; I know not 'seems'.
'T is not alone my inky cloak, good mother,
Nor customary suits of solemn black,
Nor windy suspiration of forced breath,
No, nor the fruitful river in the eye,  80
Nor the dejected 'haviour of the visage,
Together with all forms, moods, shows of grief,
That can denote me truly: these indeed seem,
For they are actions that a man might play:
But I have that within which passeth show;
These but the trappings and the suits of woe.
 *King.* 'T is sweet and commendable in your nature, Hamlet,
To give these mourning duties to your father:
But, you must know, your father lost a father;
That father lost, lost his, and the survivor bound  90

In filial obligation for some term
To do obsequious sorrow: but to persever
In obstinate condolement is a course
Of impious stubbornness; 't is unmanly grief;
It shows a will most incorrect to heaven,
A heart unfortified, a mind impatient,
An understanding simple and unschool'd:
For what we know must be and is as common
As any the most vulgar thing to sense,
Why should we in our peevish opposition          100
Take it to heart?  Fie! 't is a fault to heaven,
A fault against the dead, a fault to nature,
To reason most absurd; whose common theme
Is death of fathers, and who still hath cried,
From the first corse till he that died to-day,
' This must be so'.  We pray you, throw to earth
This unprevailing woe, and think of us
As of a father: for let the world take note,
You are the most immediate to our throne;
And with no less nobility of love          110
Than that which dearest father bears his son,
Do I impart toward you.  For your intent
In going back to school in Wittenberg,
It is most retrograde to our desire:
And we beseech you, bend you to remain
Here, in the cheer and comfort of our eye,
Our chiefest courtier, cousin, and our son.
     *Queen.* Let not thy mother lose her prayers, Hamlet
I pray thee, stay with us; go not to Wittenberg.
     *Ham.* I shall in all my best obey you, madam.          120
     *King.* Why, 't is a loving and a fair reply:
Be as ourself in Denmark.  Madam, come ;
This gentle and unforced accord of Hamlet
Sits smiling to my heart: in grace whereof,
No jocund health that Denmark drinks to-day,
But the great cannon to the clouds shall tell,
And the king's rouse the heavens shall bruit again,
Re-speaking earthly thunder.  Come away.
                    [*Exeunt all but Hamlet.*
     *Ham.* O, that this too too solid flesh would melt,
Thaw and resolve itself into a dew!          130
Or that the Everlasting had not fix'd
His canon 'gainst self-slaughter!  O God! God!
How weary, stale, flat and unprofitable,
Seem to me all the uses of this world!

Fie on 't! ah fie! 't is an unweeded garden,
That grows to seed; things rank and gross in nature
Possess it merely.   That it should come to this!
But two months dead: nay, not so much, not two:
So excellent a king; that was, to this,
Hyperion to a satyr; so loving to my mother          140
That he might not beteem the winds of heaven
Visit her face too roughly.   Heaven and earth!
Must I remember? why, she would hang on him,
As if increase of appetite had grown
By what it fed on: and yet, within a month—
Let me not think on 't—Frailty, thy name is woman!—
A little month, or ere those shoes were old
With which she follow'd my poor father's body,
Like Niobe, all tears:—why she, even she—
O God! a beast, that wants discourse of reason,      150
Would have mourn'd longer—married with my uncle,
My father's brother, but no more like my father
Than I to Hercules: within a month:
Ere yet the salt of most unrighteous tears
Had left the flushing in her galled eyes,
She married.   O, most wicked speed, to post
With such dexterity to incestuous sheets!
It is not nor it cannot come to good:
But break, my heart; for I must hold my tongue.

    *Enter* HORATIO, MARCELLUS, *and* BERNARDO.

  *Hor.* Hail to your lordship!
  *Ham.*                     I am glad to see you well:
Horatio,—or I do forget myself.                      161
  *Hor.* The same, my lord, and your poor servant ever.
  *Ham.* Sir, my good friend; I 'll change that name with you:
And what make you from Wittenberg, Horatio? Marcellus?
  *Mar.* My good lord—
  *Ham.* I am very glad to see you.   Good even, sir.
But what, in faith, make you from Wittenberg?
  *Hor.* A truant disposition, good my lord.
  *Ham.* I would not hear your enemy say so,         170
Nor shall you do mine ear that violence,
To make it truster of your own report
Against yourself: I know you are no truant.
But what is your affair in Elsinore?
We 'll teach you to drink deep ere you depart.
  *Hor.* My lord, I came to see your father's funeral.
  *Ham.* I pray thee, do not mock me, fellow-student;

I think it was to see my mother's wedding.
*Hor.* Indeed, my lord, it follow'd hard upon.
*Ham.* Thrift, thrift, Horatio! the funeral baked meats 180
Did coldly furnish forth the marriage tables.
Would I had met my dearest foe in heaven
Or ever I had seen that day, Horatio!
My father!—methinks I see my father.
*Hor.* Where, my lord?
*Ham.* In my mind's eye, Horatio.
*Hor.* I saw him—once; he was a goodly king.
*Ham.* He was a man, take him for all in all,
I shall not look upon his like again.
*Hor.* My lord, I think I saw him yesternight.
*Ham.* Saw? who? 190
*Hor.* My lord, the king your father.
*Ham.* The king my father!
*Hor.* Season your admiration for a while
With an attent ear, till I may deliver,
Upon the witness of these gentlemen,
This marvel to you.
*Ham.* For God's love, let me hear.
*Hor.* Two nights together had these gentlemen,
Marcellus and Bernardo, on their watch,
In the dead waste and middle of the night,
Been thus encounter'd. A figure like your father,
Armed at point exactly, cap-a-pe, 200
Appears before them, and with solemn march
Goes slow and stately by them: thrice he walk'd
By their oppress'd and fear-surprised eyes,
Within his truncheon's length; whilst they, distill'd
Almost to jelly with the act of fear,
Stand dumb and speak not to him. This to me
In dreadful secrecy impart they did;
And I with them the third night kept the watch:
Where, as they had deliver'd, both in time,
Form of the thing, each word made true and good, 210
The apparition comes: I knew your father;
These hands are not more like.
*Ham.* But where was this?
*Mar.* My lord, upon the platform where we watch'd.
*Ham.* Did you not speak to it?
*Hor.* My lord, I did;
But answer made it none: yet once methought
It lifted up it head and did address
Itself to motion, like as it would speak;

But even then the morning cock crew loud,
And at the sound it shrunk in haste away,
And vanish'd from our sight.
　　*Ham.*　　　　　　　'T is very strange.　　　　220
　　*Hor.* As I do live, my honour'd lord, 't is true;
And we did think it writ down in our duty
To let you know of it.
　　*Ham.* Indeed, indeed, sirs, but this troubles me.
Hold you the watch to-night?
　　*Mar.* ⎫
　　*Ber.* ⎬　　　We do, my lord.
　　*Ham.* Arm'd, say you?
　　*Mar.* ⎫
　　*Ber.* ⎬　Arm'd, my lord.
　　*Ham.* From top to toe?
　　*Mar.* ⎫
　　*Ber.* ⎬　　　My lord, from head to foot.
　　*Ham.* Then saw you not his face?
　　*Hor.* Oh, yes, my lord; he wore his beaver up.　　230
　　*Ham.* What, look'd he frowningly?
　　*Hor.* A countenance more in sorrow than in anger.
　　*Ham.* Pale or red?
　　*Hor.* Nay, very pale.
　　*Ham.*　　　　　And fix'd his eyes upon you?
　　*Hor.* Most constantly.
　　*Ham.*　　　　　I would I had been there.
　　*Hor.* It would have much amazed you.
　　*Ham.* Very like, very like.　Stay'd it long?
　　*Hor.* While one with moderate haste might tell a hundred.
　　*Mar.* ⎫
　　*Ber.* ⎬　Longer, longer.
　　*Hor.* Not when I saw 't.
　　*Ham.*　　　　　His beard was grizzled,—no? 240
　　*Hor.* It was, as I have seen it in his life,
A sable silver'd.
　　*Ham.*　　　I will watch to-night;
Perchance 't will walk again.
　　*Hor.*　　　　　I warrant it will.
　　*Ham.* If it assume my noble father's person,
I 'll speak to it, though hell itself should gape
And bid me hold my peace.　I pray you all,
If you have hitherto conceal'd this sight,
Let it be tenable in your silence still;
And whatsoever else shall hap to-night,
Give it an understanding, but no tongue:　　　　250

I will requite your loves.  So, fare you well:
Upon the platform, 'twixt eleven and twelve,
I'll visit you.
 *All.*   Our duty to your honour.
 *Ham.* Your loves, as mine to you: farewell.
       [*Exeunt all but Hamlet.*
My father's spirit in arms! all is not well;
I doubt some foul play: would the night were come!
Till then sit still, my soul: foul deeds will rise,
Though all the earth o'erwhelm them, to men's eyes.  [*Exit.*

SCENE III. *A room in Polonius' house.*

*Enter* LAERTES *and* OPHELIA.

 *Laer.* My necessaries are embark'd: farewell:
And, sister, as the winds give benefit
And convoy is assistant, do not sleep,
But let me hear from you.
 *Oph.*    Do you doubt that?
 *Laer.* For Hamlet and the trifling of his favour,
Hold it a fashion and a toy in blood,
A violet in the youth of primy nature,
Forward, not permanent, sweet, not lasting,
The perfume and suppliance of a minute;
No more.
 *Oph.* No more but so?
 *Laer.*    Think it no more:   10
For nature, crescent, does not grow alone
In thews and bulk, but, as this temple waxes,
The inward service of the mind and soul
Grows wide withal.  Perhaps he loves you now,
And now no soil nor cautel doth besmirch
The virtue of his will: but you must fear,
His greatness weigh'd, his will is not his own;
For he himself is subject to his birth:
He may not, as unvalued persons do,
Carve for himself; for on his choice depends  20
The safety and health of this whole state;
And therefore must his choice be circumscribed
Unto the voice and yielding of that body
Whereof he is the head.  Then if he says he loves you,
It fits your wisdom so far to believe it
As he in his particular act and place
May give his saying deed; which is no further

Than the main voice of Denmark goes withal.
Then weigh what loss your honour may sustain,
If with too credent ear you list his songs,                    30
Or lose your heart, or your chaste treasure open
To his unmaster'd importunity.
Fear it, Ophelia, fear it, my dear sister,
And keep you in the rear of your affection,
Out of the shot and danger of desire.
The chariest maid is prodigal enough,
If she unmask her beauty to the moon:
Virtue itself 'scapes not calumnious strokes:
The canker galls the infants of the spring,
Too oft before their buttons be disclosed,                     40
And in the morn and liquid dew of youth
Contagious blastments are most imminent.
Be wary then; best safety lies in fear:                    ·
Youth to itself rebels, though none else near.
   *Oph.* I shall the effect of this good lesson keep,
As watchman to my heart.   But, good my brother,
Do not, as some ungracious pastors do,
Show me the steep and thorny way to heaven;
Whiles, like a puff'd and reckless libertine,
Himself the primrose path of dalliance treads,                 50
And recks not his own rede.
   *Laer.*                    O, fear me not.
I stay too long: but here my father comes.

                    *Enter* POLONIUS.

A double blessing is a double grace;
Occasion smiles upon a second leave.
   *Pol.* Yet here, Laertes! aboard, aboard, for shame!
The wind sits in the shoulder of your sail,
And you are stay'd for.   There; my blessing with thee!
And these few precepts in thy memory
See thou character.   Give thy thoughts no tongue,
Nor any unproportion'd thought his act.                        60
Be thou familiar, but by no means vulgar.
Those friends thou hast, and their adoption tried,
Grapple them to thy soul with hoops of steel;
But do not dull thy palm with entertainment
Of each new-hatch'd, unfledged comrade.   Beware
Of entrance to a quarrel, but being in,
Bear't that the opposed may beware of thee.
Give every man thy ear, but few thy voice;
Take each man's censure, but reserve thy judgement.

Costly thy habit as thy purse can buy,                    70
But not express'd in fancy; rich, not gaudy;
For the apparel oft proclaims the man,
And they in France of the best rank and station
Are of a most select and generous choice in that.
Neither a borrower nor a lender be;
For loan oft loses both itself and friend,
And borrowing dulls the edge of husbandry.
This above all: to thine own self be true,
And it must follow, as the night the day,
Thou canst not then be false to any man.                    80
Farewell: my blessing season this in thee!
   *Laer.* Most humbly do I take my leave, my lord.
   *Pol.* The time invites you; go; your servants tend.
   *Laer.* Farewell, Ophelia; and remember well
What I have said to you.
   *Oph.*        'T is in my memory lock'd,
And you yourself shall keep the key of it.
   *Laer.* Farewell.                              [*Exit.*
   *Pol.* What is 't, Ophelia, he hath said to you?
   *Oph.* So please you, something touching the Lord Hamlet.
   *Pol.* Marry, well bethought:                    90
'T is told me, he hath very oft of late
Given private time to you; and you yourself
Have of your audience been most free and bounteous:
If it be so, as so 't is put on me,
And that in way of caution, I must tell you,
You do not understand yourself so clearly
As it behoves my daughter and your honour.
What is between you? give me up the truth.
   *Oph.* He hath, my lord, of late made many tenders
Of his affection to me.                                   100
   *Pol.* Affection! pooh! you speak like a green girl,
Unsifted in such perilous circumstance.
Do you believe his tenders, as you call them?
   *Oph.* I do not know, my lord, what I should think.
   *Pol.* Marry, I 'll teach you: think yourself a baby;
That you have ta'en these tenders for true pay,
Which are not sterling. Tender yourself more dearly;
Or—not to crack the wind of the poor phrase,
Running it thus—you 'll tender me a fool.
   *Oph.* My lord, he hath importuned me with love       110
In honourable fashion.
   *Pol.* Ay, fashion you may call it; go to, go to.
   *Oph.* And hath given countenance to his speech, my lord,

With almost all the holy vows of heaven.
   *Pol.* Ay, springes to catch woodcocks.   I do know,
When the blood burns, how prodigal the soul
Lends the tongue vows: these blazes, daughter,
Giving more light than heat, extinct in both,
Even in their promise, as it is a-making,
You must not take for fire.   From this time      120
Be somewhat scanter of your maiden presence;
Set your entreatments at a higher rate
Than a command to parley.   For Lord Hamlet,
Believe so much in him, that he is young,
And with a larger tether may he walk
Than may be given you: in few, Ophelia,
Do not believe his vows; for they are brokers,
Not of that dye which their investments show,
But mere implorators of unholy suits,
Breathing like sanctified and pious bonds,      130
The better to beguile.   This is for all:
I would not, in plain terms, from this time forth,
Have you so slander any moment leisure,
As to give words or talk with the Lord Hamlet.
Look to 't, I charge you: come your ways.
   *Oph.* I shall obey, my lord.          [*Exeunt.*

SCENE IV.   *The platform.*

*Enter* HAMLET, HORATIO, *and* MARCELLUS.

   *Ham.* The air bites shrewdly; it is very cold.
   *Hor.* It is a nipping and an eager air.
   *Ham.* What hour now?
   *Hor.*             I think it lacks of twelve.
   *Mar.* No, it is struck.
   *Hor.* Indeed?   I heard it not: then it draws near the
      season
Wherein the spirit held his wont to walk.
    [*A flourish of trumpets, and ordnance shot off, within.*
What does this mean, my lord?
   *Ham.* The king doth wake to-night and takes his rouse,
Keeps wassail, and the swaggering up-spring reels;
And, as he drains his draughts of Rhenish down,      10
The kettle-drum and trumpet thus bray out
The triumph of his pledge.
   *Hor.*            Is it a custom?
   *Ham.* Ay, marry, is 't:

But to my mind, though I am native here
And to the manner born, it is a custom
More honour'd in the breach than the observance.
This heavy-headed revel east and west
Makes us traduced and tax'd of other nations:
They clepe us drunkards, and with swinish phrase
Soil our addition; and indeed it takes         20
From our achievements, though perform'd at height,
The pith and marrow of our attribute.
So, oft it chances in particular men,
That for some vicious mole of nature in them,
As, in their birth—wherein they are not guilty,
Since nature cannot choose his origin—
By the o'ergrowth of some complexion,
Oft breaking down the pales and forts of reason,
Or by some habit that too much o'er-leavens·
The form of plausive manners, that these men,    30
Carrying, I say, the stamp of one defect,
Being nature's livery, or fortune's star,—
Their virtues else—be they as pure as grace,
As infinite as man may undergo—
Shall in the general censure take corruption
From that particular fault: the dram of eale
Doth all the noble substance of a doubt
To his own scandal.
    *Hor.*              Look, my lord, it comes!

             *Enter* Ghost.

    *Ham.* Angels and ministers of grace defend us!
Be thou a spirit of health or goblin damn'd,    40
Bring with thee airs from heaven or blasts from hell,
Be thy intents wicked or charitable,
Thou comest in such a questionable shape
That I will speak to thee: I'll call thee Hamlet,
King, father, royal Dane: O, answer me!
Let me not burst in ignorance; but tell
Why thy canonized bones, hearsed in death,
Have burst their cerements; why the sepulchre,
Wherein we saw thee quietly inurn'd,
Hath oped his ponderous and marble jaws,    50
To cast thee up again. What may this mean,
That thou, dead corse, again in complete steel
Revisit'st thus the glimpses of the moon,
Making night hideous; and we fools of nature
So horridly to shake our disposition

With thoughts beyond the reaches of our souls?
Say, why is this? wherefore? what should we do?

*[Ghost beckons Hamlet.*

*Hor.* It beckons you to go away with it,
As if it some impartment did desire
To you alone.
 *Mar.*  Look, with what courteous action  60
It waves you to a more removed ground:
But do not go with it.
 *Hor.*     No, by no means.
 *Ham.* It will not speak; then I will follow it.
 *Hor.* Do not, my lord.
 *Ham.*    Why, what should be the fear?
I do not set my life at a pin's fee;
And for my soul, what can it do to that,
Being a thing immortal as itself?
It waves me forth again: I 'll follow it.
 *Hor.* What if it tempt you toward the flood, my lord,
Or to the dreadful summit of the cliff  70
That beetles o'er his base into the sea,
And there assume some other horrible form,
Which might deprive your sovereignty of reason
And draw you into madness? think of it:
The very place puts toys of desperation,
Without more motive, into every brain
That looks so many fathoms to the sea
And hears it roar beneath.
 *Ham.*    It waves me still.
Go on; I 'll follow thee.
 *Mar.* You shall not go, my lord.
 *Ham.*    Hold off your hands. 80
 *Hor.* Be ruled; you shall not go.
 *Ham.*    My fate cries out,
And makes each petty artery in this body
As hardy as the Nemean lion's nerve.
Still am I call'd. Unhand me, gentlemen.
By heaven, I 'll make a ghost of him that lets me.
I say, away! Go on; I 'll follow thee.

*[Exeunt Ghost and Hamlet.*

 *Hor.* He waxes desperate with imagination.
 *Mar.* Let 's follow; 't is not fit thus to obey him.
 *Hor.* Have after. To what issue will this come?
 *Mar.* Something is rotten in the state of Denmark. 90
 *Hor.* Heaven will direct it.
 *Mar.*    Nay, let 's follow him. (*Exeunt.*

SCENE V. *Another part of the platform.*

*Enter* GHOST *and* HAMLET.

*Ham.* Where wilt thou lead me? speak; I'll go no further.
*Ghost.* Mark me.
*Ham.*          I will.
*Ghost.*          My hour is almost come,
When I to sulphurous and tormenting flames
Must render up myself.
     *Ham.*          Alas, poor ghost!
     *Ghost.* Pity me not, but lend thy serious hearing
To what I shall unfold.
     *Ham.*          Speak; I am bound to hear.
     *Ghost.* So art thou to revenge, when thou shalt hear.
*Ham.* What?
     *Ghost.* I am thy father's spirit,
Doom'd for a certain term to walk the night,          10
And for the day confined to fast in fires,
Till the foul crimes done in my days of nature
Are burnt and purged away. But that I am forbid
To tell the secrets of my prison-house,
I could a tale unfold whose lightest word
Would harrow up thy soul, freeze thy young blood,
Make thy two eyes, like stars, start from their spheres,
Thy knotted and combined locks to part
And each particular hair to stand an end,
Like quills upon the fretful porpentine:          20
But this eternal blazon must not be
To ears of flesh and blood. List, list, O, list!
If thou didst ever thy dear father love—
     *Ham.* O God!
     *Ghost.* Revenge his foul and most unnatural murder.
     *Ham.* Murder!
     *Ghost.* Murder most foul, as in the best it is;
But this most foul, strange and unnatural.
     *Ham.* Haste me to know't, that I, with wings as swift
As meditation or the thoughts of love,          30
May sweep to my revenge.
     *Ghost.*          I find thee apt;
And duller shouldst thou be than the fat weed
That roots itself in ease on Lethe wharf,
Wouldst thou not stir in this. Now, Hamlet, hear:
'T is given out that, sleeping in my orchard,
A serpent stung me; so the whole ear of Denmark

Is by a forged process of my death
Rankly abused: but know, thou noble youth,
The serpent that did sting thy father's life
Now wears his crown.
    *Ham.*                    O my prophetic soul!          40
My uncle!
    *Ghost.*  Ay, that incestuous, that adulterate beast,
With witchcraft of his wit, with traitorous gifts,—
O wicked wits and gifts, that have the power
So to seduce!—won to his shameful lust
The will of my most seeming-virtuous queen:
O Hamlet, what a falling-off was there!
From me, whose love was of that dignity
That it went hand in hand even with the vow
I made to her in marriage, and to decline          50
Upon a wretch whose natural gifts were poor
To those of mine!
But virtue, as it never will be moved,
Though lewdness court it in a shape of heaven,
So lust, though to a radiant angel link'd,
Will sate itself in a celestial bed,
And prey on garbage.
But, soft! methinks I scent the morning air;
Brief let me be.  Sleeping within my orchard,
My custom always of the afternoon,          60
Upon my secure hour thy uncle stole,
With juice of cursed Hebona in a vial,
And in the porches of my ears did pour
The leperous distilment; whose effect
Holds such an enmity with blood of man
That swift as quicksilver it courses through
The natural gates and alleys of the body,
And with a sudden vigour it doth posset
And curd, like eager droppings into milk,
The thin and wholesome blood: so did it mine;          70
And a most instant tetter bark'd about,
Most lazar-like, with vile and loathsome crust,
All my smooth body.
Thus was I, sleeping, by a brother's hand
Of life, of crown, of queen, at once dispatch'd:
Cut off even in the blossoms of my sin,
Unhousel'd, disappointed, unaneled,
No reckoning made, but sent to my account
With all my imperfections on my head: .
O, horrible! O, horrible! most horrible!          80

If thou hast nature in thee, bear it not;
Let not the royal bed of Denmark be
A couch for luxury and damned incest.
But, howsoever thou pursuest this act,
Taint not thy mind, nor let thy soul contrive
Against thy mother aught: leave her to heaven
And to those thorns that in her bosom lodge,
To prick and sting her.  Fare thee well at once!
The glow-worm shows the matin to be near,
And 'gins to pale his uneffectual fire:                    90
Adieu, adieu!  Hamlet, remember me.          [*Exit*.
  *Ham.*  O all you host of heaven!  O earth! what else?
And shall I couple hell?  ☛O, fie!  Hold, hold, my heart;
And you, my sinews, grow not instant old,
But bear me stiffly up.  Remember thee!
Ay, thou poor ghost, while memory holds a seat
In this distracted globe.  Remember thee!
Yea, from the table of my memory
I 'll wipe away all trivial fond records,
All saws of books, all forms, all pressures past,      100
That youth and observation copied there;
And thy commandment all alone shall live
Within the book and volume of my brain,
Unmix'd with baser matter: yes, by heaven!
O most pernicious woman!
O villain, villain, smiling, damned villain!
My tables,—meet it is I set it down,
That one may smile, and smile, and be a villain;
At least I 'm sure it may be so in Denmark:      [*Writing*.
So, uncle, there you are.  Now to my word;          110
It is 'Adieu, adieu! remember me'.
I have sworn 't.
   *Mar.* ⎱ [*Within*] My lord, my lord,—
   *Hor.* ⎰
   *Mar.*                        [*Within*] Lord Hamlet,—
   *Hor.*                        [*Within*] Heaven secure him!
  *Ham.* So be it!
  *Hor.* [*Within*] Hillo, ho, ho, my lord!
  *Ham.* Hillo, ho, ho, boy! come, bird, come.

    *Enter* HORATIO *and* MARCELLUS.

  *Mar.* How is 't, my noble lord?
  *Hor.*                        What news, my lord?
  *Ham.* O, wonderful!
  *Hor.*               Good my lord, tell it.

*Ham.* No; you'll reveal it.

*Hor.* Not I, my lord, by heaven.

*Mar.*                           Nor I, my lord.     120

*Ham.* How say you, then; would heart of man once think
  it?

But you'll be secret?

*Hor.*  )
*Mar.*  }          Ay, by heaven, my lord.

*Ham.* There's ne'er a villain dwelling in all Denmark
But he's an arrant knave.

*Hor.* There needs no ghost, my lord, come from the grave
To tell us this.

*Ham.*           Why, right; you are i' the right;
And so, without more circumstance at all,
I hold it fit that we shake hands and part:
You, as your business and desire shall point you;
For every man has business and desire,          130
Such as it is; and for mine own poor part,
Look you, I 'll go pray.

*Hor.* These are but wild and whirling words, my lord.

*Ham.* I 'm sorry they offend you, heartily;
Yes, 'faith, heartily;

*Hor.*                 There 's no offence, my lord.

*Ham.* Yes, by Saint Patrick, but there is, Horatio,
And much offence too.  Touching this vision here,
It is an honest ghost, that let me tell you:
For your desire to know what is between us,
O'ermaster 't as you may.  And now, good friends,     140
As you are friends, scholars and soldiers,
Give me one poor request.

*Hor.* What is 't, my lord? we will.

*Ham.* Never make known what you have seen to-night.

*Hor.*  )
*Mar.*  } My lord, we will not.

*Ham.*                         Nay, but swear 't.

*Hor.*                                 In faith,
My lord, not I.

*Mar.*         Nor I, my lord, in faith.

*Ham.* Upon my sword.

*Mar.*                 We have sworn, my lord, already.

*Ham.* Indeed, upon my sword, indeed.

*Ghost.* [*Beneath*] Swear.

*Ham.* Ah, ha, boy! say'st thou so? art thou there, truepenny?                                           150
Come on—you hear this fellow in the cellarage—

Consent to swear.
    *Hor.*          Propose the oath, my lord.
    *Ham.* Never to speak of this that you have seen,
Swear by my sword.
    *Ghost.* [*Beneath*] Swear.
    *Ham.* Hic et ubique? then we'll shift our ground.
Come hither, gentlemen,
And lay your hands again upon my sword:
Never to speak of this that you have heard,
Swear by my sword.                                                    160
    *Ghost.* [*Beneath*] Swear.
    *Ham.* Well said, old mole! canst work i' the earth so fast?
A worthy pioner! Once more remove, good friends.
    *Hor.* O day and night, but this is wondrous strange!
    *Ham.* And therefore as a stranger give it welcome.
There are more things in heaven and earth, Horatio,
Than are dreamt of in our philosophy.
But come;
Here, as before, never, so help you mercy,
How strange or odd soe'er I bear myself,                              170
As I perchance hereafter shall think meet
To put an antic disposition on,
That you, at such times seeing me, never shall,
With arms encumber'd thus, or this head-shake,
Or by pronouncing of some doubtful phrase,
As 'Well, well, we know', or 'We could, an if we would',
Or 'if we list to speak', or 'There be, an if they might',
Or such ambiguous giving out, to note
That you know aught of me: this not to do,
So grace and mercy at your most need help you,                       180
Swear.
    *Ghost.* [*Beneath*] Swear.
    *Ham.* Rest, rest, perturbed spirit! [*They swear.*] So,
        gentlemen,
With all my love I do commend me to you:
And what so poor a man as Hamlet is
May do, to express his love and friending to you,
God willing, shall not lack. Let us go in together;
And still your fingers on your lips, I pray.
The time is out of joint: O cursed spite,
That ever I was born to set it right!                                190
Nay, come, let's go together.                          [*Exeunt.*

## ACT II.

SCENE I.  *A room in Polonius' house.*

*Enter* POLONIUS *and* REYNALDO.

*Pol.* Give him this money and these notes, Reynaldo.
*Rey.* I will, my lord.
*Pol.* You shall do marvellous wisely, good Reynaldo,
Before you visit him, to make inquire
Of his behaviour.
*Rey.*            My lord, I did intend it.
*Pol.* Marry, well said; very well said.   Look you, sir,
Inquire me first what Danskers are in Paris;
And how, and who, what means, and where they keep,
What company, at what expense; and finding
By this encompassment and drift of question              10
That they do know my son, come you more nearer
Than your particular demands will touch it.
Take you, as 't were, some distant knowledge of him;
As thus, 'I know his father and his friends,
And in part him': do you mark this, Reynaldo?
*Rey.* Ay, very well, my lord.
*Pol.* 'And in part him; but' you may say 'not well:
But, if 't be he I mean, he 's very wild;
Addicted so and so': and there put on him
What forgeries you please; marry, none so rank           20
As may dishonour him; take heed of that;
But, sir, such wanton, wild and usual slips
As are companions noted and most known
To youth and liberty.
*Rey.*            As gaming, my lord.
*Pol.* Ay, or drinking, fencing, swearing, quarrelling,
Drabbing: you may go so far.
*Rey.* My lord, that would dishonour him.
*Pol.* 'Faith, no; as you may season it in the charge.
You must not put another scandal on him,
That he is open to incontinency;                         30
That 's not my meaning: but breathe his faults so quaintly
That they may seem the taints of liberty,
The flash and outbreak of a fiery mind,
A savageness in unreclaimed blood,
Of general assault.
*Rey.*            But, my good lord,—
*Pol.* Wherefore should you do this?

*Rey.*                              Ay, my lord,
I would know that.
    *Pol.*                    Marry, sir, here's my drift;
And, I believe, it is a fetch of warrant:
You laying these slight sullies on my son,
As 't were a thing a little soil'd i' the working,          40
Mark you,
Your party in converse, him you would sound,
Having ever seen in the prenominate crimes
The youth you breathe of guilty, be assured
He closes with you in this consequence;
'Good sir', or so, or 'friend', or 'gentleman',
According to the phrase or the addition
Of man and country.
    *Rey.*                  Very good, my lord.
    *Pol.* And then, sir, does he this—he does—what was I
about to say? By the mass, I was about to say something:
where did I leave?                                          51
    *Rey.* At 'closes in the consequence', at 'friend or so', and
'gentleman'.
    *Pol.* At 'closes in the consequence', ay, marry;
He closes thus: 'I know the gentleman;
I saw him yesterday, or t' other day,
Or then, or then; with such, or such; and, as you say
There was a' gaming; there o'ertook in 's rouse;
There falling out at tennis': or perchance,
'I saw him enter such a house of sale',                     60
Videlicet, a brothel, or so forth.
See you now;
Your bait of falsehood takes this carp of truth:
And thus do we of wisdom and of reach,
With windlasses and with assays of bias,
By indirections find directions out:
So by my former lecture and advice,
Shall you my son. You have me, have you not?
    *Rey.* My lord, I have.
    *Pol.*                    God be wi' you; fare you well.
    *Rey.* Good my lord!                                 70
    *Pol.* Observe his inclination in yourself.
    *Rey.* I shall, my lord.
    *Pol.* And let him ply his music.
    *Rey.*                    Well, my lord.
    *Pol.* Farewell!                          [*Exit Reynaldo.*

*Enter* OPHELIA.

How now, Ophelia! what 's the matter?
*Oph.* O, my lord, my lord, I have been so affrighted!
*Pol.* With what, i' the name of God?
*Oph.* My lord, as I was sewing in my closet,
Lord Hamlet, with his doublet all unbraced;
No hat upon his head; his stockings foul'd,
Ungarter'd, and down-gyved to his ancle;          80
Pale as his shirt; his knees knocking each other;
And with a look so piteous in purport
As if he had been loosed out of hell
To speak of horrors,—he comes before me.
    *Pol.* Mad for thy love?
    *Oph.*                    My lord, I do not know;
But truly, I do fear it.
    *Pol.*                    What said he?
    *Oph.* He took me by the wrist and held me hard;
Then goes he to the length of all his arm;
And, with his other hand thus o'er his brow,
He falls to such perusal of my face          90
As he would draw it.   Long stay'd he so;
At last, a little shaking of mine arm
And thrice his head thus waving up and down,
He raised a sigh so piteous and profound
As it did seem to shatter all his bulk
And end his being: that done, he lets me go:
And, with his head over his shoulder turn'd,
He seem'd to find his way without his eyes;
For out o' doors he went without their helps,
And, to the last, bended their light on me.          100
    *Pol.* Come, go with me: I will go seek the king.
This is the very ecstasy of love,
Whose violent property fordoes itself
And leads the will to desperate undertakings
As oft as any passion under heaven
That does afflict our natures.   I am sorry.
What, have you given him any hard words of late?
    *Oph.* No, my good lord, but, as you did command,
I did repel his letters and denied
His access to me.
    *Pol.*                    That hath made him mad.          110
I am sorry that with better heed and judgement
I had not quoted him: I fear'd he did but trifle,
And meant to wreck thee; but, beshrew my jealousy!

By heaven, it is as proper to our age
To cast beyond ourselves in our opinions
As it is common for the younger sort
To lack discretion.   Come, go we to the king:
This must be known; which, being kept close, might move
More grief to hide than hate to utter love.        [*Exeunt.*

SCENE II.   *A room in the castle.*

*Enter* KING, QUEEN, ROSENCRANTZ, GUILDENSTERN,
*and* Attendants.

   *King.* Welcome, dear Rosencrantz and Guildenstern!
Moreover that we much did long to see you,
The need we have to use you did provoke
Our hasty sending.   Something have you heard
Of Hamlet's transformation; so call it,
Since nor the exterior nor the inward man
Resembles that it was.   What it should be,
More than his father's death, that thus hath put him
So much from the understanding of himself,
I cannot dream of: I entreat you both,                     10
That, being of so young days brought up with him,
And since so neighbour'd to his youth and humour,
That you vouchsafe your rest here in our court
Some little time: so by your companies
To draw him on to pleasures, and to gather,
So much as from occasion you may glean,
Whether aught, to us unknown, afflicts him thus,
That, open'd, lies within our remedy.
   *Queen.* Good gentlemen, he hath much talk'd of you;
And sure I am two men there are not living             20
To whom he more adheres.   If it will please you
To show us so much gentry and good will
As to expend your time with us awhile,
For the supply and profit of our hope,
Your visitation shall receive such thanks
As fits a king's remembrance.
   *Ros.*                         Both your majesties
Might, by the sovereign power you have of us,
Put your dread pleasures more into command
Than to entreaty.
   *Guil.*               But we both obey,
And here give up ourselves, in the full bent           30
To lay our service freely at your feet,

To be commanded.

*King.* Thanks, Rosencrantz and gentle Guildenstern.

*Queen.* Thanks, Guildenstern and gentle Rosencrantz:
And I beseech you instantly to visit
My too much changed son.   Go, some of you,
And bring these gentlemen where Hamlet is.

*Guil.* Heavens make our presence and our practices
Pleasant and helpful to him!

*Queen.*                      Ay, amen!

[*Exeunt Rosencrantz, Guildenstern, and some
Attendants.*

*Enter* POLONIUS.

*Pol.* The ambassadors from Norway, my good lord,    40
Are joyfully return'd.

*King.* Thou still hast been the father of good news.

*Pol.* Have I, my lord?   I assure my good liege,
I hold my duty, as I hold my soul,
Both to my God and to my gracious king:
And I do think, or else this brain of mine
Hunts not the trail of policy so sure
As it hath used to do, that I have found
The very cause of Hamlet's lunacy.

*King.* O, speak of that; that do I long to hear.    50

*Pol.* Give first admittance to the ambassadors;
My news shall be the fruit to that great feast.

*King.* Thyself do grace to them, and bring them in.
[*Exit Polonius.*
He tells me, my dear Gertrude, he hath found
The head and source of all your son's distemper.

*Queen.* I doubt it is no other but the main;
His father's death, and our o'erhasty marriage.

*King.* Well, we shall sift him.

*Re-enter* POLONIUS, *with* VOLTIMAND *and* CORNELIUS.

Welcome, my good friends!
Say, Voltimand, what from our brother Norway?

*Volt.* Most fair return of greetings and desires.    60
Upon our first, he sent out to suppress
His nephew's levies; which to him appear'd
To be a preparation 'gainst the Polack;
But, better look'd into, he truly found
It was against your highness: whereat grieved,
That so his sickness, age and impotence
Was falsely borne in hand, sends out arrests
On Fortinbras; which he, in brief, obeys;

Receives rebuke from Norway, and in fine
Makes vow before his uncle never more          70
To give the assay of arms against your majesty.
Whereon old Norway, overcome with joy,
Gives him three thousand crowns in annual fee,
And his commission to employ those soldiers,
So levied as before, against the Polack:
With an entreaty, herein further shown,          [*Giving a paper.*
That it might please you to give quiet pass
Through your dominions for this enterprise,
On such regards of safety and allowance
As therein are set down.
    *King.*          It likes us well;          80
And at our more consider'd time we 'll read,
Answer, and think upon this business.
Meantime we thank you for your well-took labour:
Go to your rest; at night we 'll feast together:
Most welcome home!     [*Exeunt Voltimand and Cornelius.*
    *Pol.*        This business is well ended.
My liege, and madam, to expostulate
What majesty should be, what duty is,
Why day is day, night night, and time is time,
Were nothing but to waste night, day and time.
Therefore, since brevity is the soul of wit,          90
And tediousness the limbs and outward flourishes,
I will be brief: your noble son is mad:
Mad call I it; for, to define true madness,
What is 't but to be nothing else but mad?
But let that go.
    *Queen.*     More matter, with less art.
    *Pol.* Madam, I swear I use no art at all.
That he is mad, 't is true: 't is true 't is pity;
And pity 't is 't is true: a foolish figure;
But farewell it, for I will use no art.
Mad let us grant him, then: and now remains          100
That we find out the cause of this effect,
Or rather say, the cause of this defect,
For this effect defective comes by cause:
Thus it remains, and the remainder thus.
Perpend.
I have a daughter—have while she is mine—
Who, in her duty and obedience, mark,
Hath given me this: now gather, and surmise.          [*Reads.*
'To the celestial and my soul's idol, the most beautified
    Ophelia',—          110

That's an ill phrase, a vile phrase; 'beautified' is a vile
phrase: but you shall hear. Thus:          [*Reads.*
'In her excellent white bosom, these, *&c.*'
  *Queen.* Came this from Hamlet to her?
  *Pol.* Good madam, stay awhile; I will be faithful. [*Reads.*
          'Doubt thou the stars are fire;
            Doubt that the sun doth move;
            Doubt truth to be a liar;
            But never doubt I love.          119
  'O dear Ophelia, I am ill at these numbers; I have not art
to reckon my groans: but that I love thee best, O most best,
believe it.  Adieu.
              'Thine evermore, most dear lady, whilst this
                    machine is to him, HAMLET.'
This, in obedience, hath my daughter shown me,
And more above, hath his solicitings,
As they fell out by time, by means and place,
All given to mine ear.
  *King.*          But how hath she
Received his love?
  *Pol.*          What do you think of me?
  *King.* As of a man faithful and honourable.          130
  *Pol.* I would fain prove so.  But what might you think,
When I had seen this hot love on the wing—
As I perceived it, I must tell you that,
Before my daughter told me—what might you,
Or my dear majesty your queen here, think,
If I had play'd the desk or table-book,
Or given my heart a winking, mute and dumb,
Or look'd upon this love with idle sight;
What might you think?  No, I went round to work,
And my young mistress thus I did bespeak:          140
'Lord Hamlet is a prince, out of thy star;
This must not be': and then I prescripts gave her,
That she should lock herself from his resort,
Admit no messengers, receive no tokens.
Which done, she took the fruits of my advice;
And he, repulsed—a short tale to make—
Fell into a sadness, then into a fast,
Thence to a watch, thence into a weakness,
Thence to a lightness, and, by this declension,
Into the madness wherein now he raves,          150
And all we mourn for.
  *King.*          Do you think 't is this?
  *Queen.* It may be, very likely.

*Pol.* Hath there been such a time—I 'd fain know that—
That I have positively said "'T is so',
When it proved otherwise?
    *King.*                Not that I know.
    *Pol.* [*Pointing to his head and shoulder*] Take this from
        this, if this be otherwise:
If circumstances lead me, I will find
Where truth is hid, though it were hid indeed
Within the centre.
    *King.*        How may we try it further?
    *Pol.* You know, sometimes he walks four hours together
Here in the lobby.
    *Queen.*       So he does indeed.         161
    *Pol.* At such a time I 'll loose my daughter to him:
Be you and I behind an arras then;
Mark the encounter: if he love her not
And be not from his reason fall'n thereon,
Let me be no assistant for a state,
But keep a farm and carters.
    *King.*           We will try it.
    *Queen.* But, look, where sadly the poor wretch comes
    reading.
    *Pol.* Away, I do beseech you, both away:
I 'll board him presently.
        [*Exeunt King, Queen, and Attendants.*

    *Enter* HAMLET, *reading.*

             O, give me leave:     170
How does my good Lord Hamlet?
    *Ham.* Well, God-a-mercy.
    *Pol.* Do you know me, my lord?
    *Ham.* Excellent well; you are a fishmonger.
    *Pol.* Not I, my lord.
    *Ham.* Then I would you were so honest a man.
    *Pol.* Honest, my lord!
    *Ham.* Ay, sir; to be honest, as this world goes, is to be
one man picked out of ten thousand.
    *Pol.* That's very true, my lord.     180
    *Ham.* For if the sun breed maggots in a dead dog, being a
god kissing carrion,—Have you a daughter?
    *Pol.* I have, my lord.
    *Ham.* Let her not walk i' the sun: conception is a blessing:
but not as your daughter may conceive. Friend, look to 't.
    *Pol.* [*Aside*] How say you by that? Still harping on my
daughter: yet he knew me not at first; he said I was a fish-

monger: he is far gone, far gone: and truly in my youth I
suffered much extremity for love; very near this. I 'll speak
to him again. What do you read, my lord?

*Ham.* Words, words, words.

*Pol.* What is the matter, my lord?

*Ham.* Between who?

*Pol.* I mean, the matter that you read, my lord.

*Ham.* Slanders, sir: for the satirical rogue says here that
old men have grey beards, that their faces are wrinkled, their
eyes purging thick amber and plum-tree gum and that they
have a plentiful lack of wit, together with most weak hams:
all which, sir, though I most powerfully and potently believe,
yet I hold it not honesty to have it thus set down, for yourself, sir, should be old as I am, if like a crab you could go
backward.

*Pol.* [*Aside*] Though this be madness, yet there is method
in 't. Will you walk out of the air, my lord?

*Ham.* Into my grave.                                      210

*Pol.* Indeed, that is out o' the air. [*Aside*] How pregnant
sometimes his replies are! a happiness that often madness
hits on, which reason and sanity could not so prosperously
be delivered of. I will leave him, and suddenly contrive the
means of meeting between him and my daughter.—My honourable lord, I will most humbly take my leave of you.

*Ham.* You cannot, sir, take from me any thing that I will
more willingly part withal: except my life, except my life,
except my life.                                            221

*Pol.* Fare you well, my lord.

*Ham.* These tedious old fools!

*Enter* ROSENCRANTZ *and* GUILDENSTERN.

*Pol.* You go to seek the Lord Hamlet; there he is.

*Ros.* [*To Polonius*] God save you, sir! [*Exit Polonius.*

*Guil.* My honoured lord!

*Ros.* My most dear lord!

*Ham.* My excellent good friends! How dost thou, Guildenstern? Ah, Rosencrantz! Good lads, how do ye both?

*Ros.* As the indifferent children of the earth.           231

*Guil.* Happy, in that we are not over-happy;
On fortune's cap we are not the very button.

*Ham.* Nor the soles of her shoe?

*Ros.* Neither, my lord.

*Ham.* Then you live about her waist, or in the middle of
her favours? What 's the news?                             240

*Ros.* None, my lord, but that the world's grown honest.

*Ham.* Then is doomsday near: but your news is not true. Let me question more in particular: what have you, my good friends, deserved at the hands of fortune, that she sends you to prison hither?

*Guil.* Prison, my lord!

*Ham.* Denmark's a prison.

*Ros.* Then is the world one. 250

*Ham.* A goodly one; in which there are many confines, wards and dungeons, Denmark being one o' the worst.

*Ros.* We think not so, my lord.

*Ham.* Why, then, 'tis none to you; for there is nothing either good or bad, but thinking makes it so: to me it is a prison.

*Ros.* Why then, your ambition makes it one; 'tis too narrow for your mind. 259

*Ham.* O God, I could be bounded in a nut-shell and count myself a king of infinite space, were it not that I have bad dreams.

*Guil.* Which dreams indeed are ambition, for the very substance of the ambitious is merely the shadow of a dream.

*Ham.* A dream itself is but a shadow.

*Ros.* Truly, and I hold ambition of so airy and light a quality that it is but a shadow's shadow.

*Ham.* Then are our beggars bodies, and our monarchs and outstretched heroes the beggars' shadows. Shall we to the court? for, by my fay, I cannot reason.

*Ros.* } We'll wait upon you.
*Guil.* }

*Ham.* No such matter: I will not sort you with the rest of my servants, for, to speak to you like an honest man, I am most dreadfully attended. But, in the beaten way of friendship, what make you at Elsinore?

*Ros.* To visit you, my lord; no other occasion.

*Ham.* Beggar that I am, I am even poor in thanks; but I thank you: and sure, dear friends, my thanks are too dear a halfpenny. Were you not sent for? Is it your own inclining? Is it a free visitation? Come, deal justly with me: come, come; nay, speak.

*Guil.* What should we say, my lord?

*Ham.* Why, any thing, but to the purpose. You were sent for; and there is a kind of confession in your looks which your modesties have not craft enough to colour: I know the good king and queen have sent for you. 291

*Ros.* To what end, my lord?

*Ham.* That you must teach me.  But let me conjure you,
by the rights of our fellowship, by the consonancy of our
youth, by the obligation of our ever-preserved love, and by
what more dear a better proposer could charge you withal, be
even and direct with me, whether you were sent for, or no?

*Ros.* [*Aside to Guil.*] What say you?                     300

*Ham.* [*Aside*] Nay, then, I have an eye of you.—If you
love me, hold not off.

*Guil.* My lord, we were sent for.

*Ham.* I will tell you why ; so shall my anticipation prevent
your discovery, and your secrecy to the king and queen moult
no feather.  I have of late—but wherefore I know not—lost
all my mirth, forgone all custom of exercises ; and indeed it
goes so heavily with my disposition that this goodly frame,
the earth, seems to me a sterile promontory, this most excellent canopy, the air, look you, this brave o'erhanging firma-
ment, this majestical roof fretted with golden fire, why, it
appears no other thing to me than a foul and pestilent con-
gregation of vapours.  What a piece of work is a man!  how
noble in reason!  how infinite in faculty!  in form and moving
how express and admirable!  in action how like an angel!  in
apprehension how like a god!  the beauty of the world!  the
paragon of animals!  And yet, to me, what is this quintessence of dust?  man delights not me : no, nor woman neither,
though by your smiling you seem to say so.

*Ros.* My lord, there was no such stuff in my thoughts.

*Ham.* Why did you laugh then, when I said 'man delights
not me '?

*Ros.* To think, my lord, if you delight not in man, what
lenten entertainment the players shall receive from you : we
coted them on the way ; and hither are they coming, to offer
you service.

*Ham.* He that plays the king shall be welcome ; his
majesty shall have tribute of me ; the adventurous knight
shall use his foil and target ; the lover shall not sigh gratis ;
the humorous man shall end his part in peace ; the clown
shall make those laugh whose lungs are tickle o' the sere ;
and the lady shall say her mind freely, or the blank verse
shall halt for 't.  What players are they?                  340

*Ros.* Even those you were wont to take delight in, the
tragedians of the city.

*Ham.* How chances it they travel? their residence, both in
reputation and profit, was better both ways.

*Ros.* I think their inhibition comes by the means of the
late innovation.

*Ham.* Do they hold the same estimation they did when I was in the city? are they so followed? 350
*Ros.* No, indeed, are they not.
*Ham.* How comes it? do they grow rusty?
*Ros.* Nay, their endeavour keeps in the wontea pace: but there is, sir, an aery of children, little eyases, that cry out on the top of question, and are most tyrannically clapped for 't: these are now the fashion, and so berattle the common stages—so they call them—that many wearing rapiers are afraid of goose-quills and dare scarce come thither. 360
*Ham.* What, are they children? who maintains 'em? how are they escoted? Will they pursue the quality no longer than they can sing? will they not say afterwards, if they should grow themselves to common players—as it is most like, if their means are no better—their writers do them wrong, to make them exclaim against their own succession?
*Ros.* 'Faith, there has been much to do on both sides; and the nation holds it no sin to tarre them to controversy: there was, for a while, no money bid for argument, unless the poet and the player went to cuffs in the question.
*Ham.* Is 't possible?
*Guil.* O, there has been much throwing about of brains.
*Ham.* Do the boys carry it away?
*Ros.* Ay, that they do, my lord; Hercules and his load too. 379
*Ham.* It is not very strange; for mine uncle is king of Denmark, and those that would make mows at him while my father lived, give twenty, forty, fifty, an hundred ducats a-piece for his picture in little. 'Sblood, there is something in this more than natural, if philosophy could find it out.
[*Flourish of trumpets within.*
*Guil.* There are the players.
*Ham.* Gentlemen, you are welcome to Elsinore. Your hands, come then: the appurtenance of welcome is fashion and ceremony: let me comply with you in this garb, lest my extent to the players, which, I tell you, must show fairly outward, should more appear like entertainment than yours. You are welcome: but my uncle-father and aunt-mother are deceived.
*Guil.* In what, my dear lord?
*Ham.* I am but mad north-north-west: when the wind is southerly I know a hawk from a handsaw.
*Re-enter* POLONIUS.
*Pol.* Well be with you, gentlemen!
*Ham.* Hark you, Guildenstern; and you too: at each ear

a hearer: that great baby you see there is not yet out of his swaddling-clouts.

*Ros.* Happily he's the second time come to them; for they say an old man is twice a child.

*Ham.* I will prophesy he comes to tell me of the players; mark it. You say right, sir: o' Monday morning; 't was so indeed.

*Pol.* My lord, I have news to tell you.

*Ham.* My lord, I have news to tell you. When Roscius was an actor in Rome,—                                                410

*Pol.* The actors are come hither, my lord.

*Ham.* Buz, buz!

*Pol.* Upon mine honour,—

*Ham.* Then came each actor on his ass,—

*Pol.* The best actors in the world, either for tragedy, comedy, history, pastoral, pastoral-comical, historical-pastoral, tragical-historical, tragical-comical-historical-pastoral, scene individable, or poem unlimited: Seneca cannot be too heavy, nor Plautus too light. For the law of writ and the liberty, these are the only men.                                        421

*Ham.* O Jephthah, judge of Israel, what a treasure hadst thou!

*Pol.* What a treasure had he, my lord?

*Ham.* Why,
        'One fair daughter, and no more,
            The which he loved passing well'.

*Pol.* [*Aside*] Still on my daughter.

*Ham.* Am I not i' the right, old Jephthah?

*Pol.* If you call me Jephthah, my lord, I have a daughter that I love passing well.                                              431

*Ham.* Nay, that follows not.

*Pol.* What follows, then, my lord?

*Ham.* Why,
        'As by lot, God wot',
and then, you know,
        'It came to pass, as most like it was',—
the first row of the pious chanson will show you more; for look, where my abridgement comes.

### Enter four or five Players.

You are welcome, masters; welcome, all. I am glad to see thee well. Welcome, good friends. O, my old friend! thy face is valanced since I saw thee last: comest thou to beard me in Denmark? What, my young lady and mistress! By 'r lady, your ladyship is nearer to heaven than when I saw you

last, by the altitude of a chopine. Pray God, your voice,
like a piece of uncurrent gold, be not cracked within the
ring. Masters, you are all welcome. We'll e'en to't like
French falconers, fly at any thing we see: we'll have a speech
straight: come, give us a taste of your quality; come, a
passionate speech.

*First Player.* What speech, my lord?

*Ham.* I heard thee speak me a speech once, but it was
never acted; or, if it was, not above once; for the play, I
remember, pleased not the million; 't was caviare to the
general: but it was—as I received it, and others, whose
judgements in such matters cried in the top of mine—an excellent play, well digested in the scenes, set down with as
much modesty as cunning. I remember, one said there were
no sallets in the lines to make the matter savoury, nor no
matter in the phrase that might indict the author of affectation; but called it an honest method, as wholesome as sweet,
and by very much more handsome than fine. One speech in
it I chiefly loved: 't was Æneas' tale to Dido; and thereabout
of it especially, where he speaks of Priam's slaughter: if it
live in your memory, begin at this line: let me see, let me
see—                                                                      471
'The rugged Pyrrhus, like the Hyrcanian beast',—it is not so:
—it begins with Pyrrhus:—
  'The rugged Pyrrhus, he whose sable arms,
  Black as his purpose, did the night resemble
  When he lay couched in the ominous horse,
  Hath now this dread and black complexion smear'd
  With heraldry more dismal; head to foot
  Now is he total gules; horridly trick'd
  With blood of fathers, mothers, daughters, sons,
  Baked and impasted with the parching streets,
  That lend a tyrannous and damned light
  To their lord's murder: roasted in wrath and fire,
  And thus o'er-sized with coagulate gore,
  With eyes like carbuncles, the hellish Pyrrhus
  Old grandsire Priam seeks.'
So, proceed you.

*Pol.* 'Fore God, my lord, well spoken, with good accent and
good discretion.

*First Player.*                    'Anon he finds him
Striking too short at Greeks; his antique sword,
Rebellious to his arm, lies where it falls,
Repugnant to command: unequal match'd,
Pyrrhus at Priam drives; in rage strikes wide;

But with the whiff and wind of his fell sword
The unnerved father falls. Then senseless Ilium,
Seeming to feel this blow, with flaming top
Stoops to his base, and with a hideous crash
Takes prisoner Pyrrhus' ear: for, lo! his sword
Which was declining on the milky head          500
Of reverend Priam, seem'd i' the air to stick:
So, as a painted tyrant, Pyrrhus stood,
And like a neutral to his will and matter,
Did nothing.
But, as we often see, against some storm,
A silence in the heavens, the rack stand still,
The bold winds speechless and the orb below
As hush as death, anon the dreadful thunder
Doth rend the region, so, after Pyrrhus' pause,
Aroused vengeance sets him new a-work;          510
And never did the Cyclops' hammers fall
On Mars's armour forged for proof eterne
With less remorse than Pyrrhus' bleeding sword
Now falls on Priam.
Out, out, thou strumpet, Fortune! All you gods,
In general synod, take away her power:
Break all the spokes and fellies from her wheel,
And bowl the round nave down the hill of heaven,
As low as to the fiends!'
*Pol.* This is too long.          520
*Ham.* It shall to the barber's, with your beard. Prithee,
say on: he's for a jig or a tale of bawdry, or he sleeps: say
on: come to Hecuba.
*First Player.* 'But who, O, who had seen the mobled
queen—'
*Ham.* 'The mobled queen?'
*Pol.* That's good; 'mobled queen' is good.
*First Player.* 'Run barefoot up and down, threatening the
flames
With bisson rheum; a clout upon that head
Where late the diadem stood, and for a robe,          530
About her lank and all o'er-teemed loins,
A blanket, in the alarm of fear caught up;
Who this had seen, with tongue in venom steep'd,
'Gainst Fortune's state would treason have pronounced:
But if the gods themselves did see her then
When she saw Pyrrhus make malicious sport
In mincing with his sword her husband's limbs,
The instant burst of clamour that she made,

Unless things mortal move them not at all,
Would have made milch the burning eyes of heaven,   540
And passion in the gods.'
*Pol.* Look, whether he has not turned his colour and has
tears in 's eyes. Pray you, no more.
*Ham.* 'T is well; I 'll have thee speak out the rest soon.
Good my lord, will you see the players well bestowed? Do
you hear, let them be well used; for they are the abstract
and brief chronicles of the time: after your death you were
better have a bad epitaph than their ill report while you live.
*Pol.* My lord, I will use them according to their desert.
*Ham.* God's bodykins, man, much better: use every man
after his desert, and who should 'scape whipping? Use
them after your own honour and dignity: the less they
deserve, the more merit is in your bounty. Take them in.
*Pol.* Come, sirs.                                     559
*Ham.* Follow him, friends: we 'll hear a play to-morrow.
[*Exit Polonius with all the players but the First.*] Dost
thou hear me, old friend; can you play the Murder of Gon-
zago?
*First Player.* Ay, my lord.
*Ham.* We 'll ha 't to-morrow night. You could, for a need,
study a speech of some dozen or sixteen lines, which I would
set down and insert in 't, could you not?
*First Player.* Ay, my lord.                           569
*Ham.* Very well. Follow that lord; and look you mock
him not. [*Exit First Player.*] My good friends, I 'll leave
you till night: you are welcome to Elsinore.
*Ros.* Good my lord!
*Ham.* Ay, so, God be wi' ye; [*Exeunt Rosencrantz and
Guildenstern.*] Now I am alone.
O, what a rogue and peasant slave am I !
Is it not monstrous that this player here,
But in a fiction, in a dream of passion,
Could force his soul so to his own conceit
That from her working all his visage wann'd,      580
Tears in his eyes, distraction in 's aspect,
A broken voice, and his whole function suiting
With forms to his conceit? and all for nothing!
For Hecuba!
What 's Hecuba to him, or he to Hecuba,
That he should weep for her? What would he do,
Had he the motive and the cue for passion
That I have? He would drown the stage with tears
And cleave the general ear with horrid speech.

Make mad the guilty and appal the free,　　　　590
Confound the ignorant, and amaze indeed
The very faculties of eyes and ears.
Yet I,
A dull and muddy-mettled rascal, peak,
Like John-a-dreams, unpregnant of my cause,
And can say nothing; no, not for a king,
Upon whose property and most dear life
A damn'd defeat was made. Am I a coward?
Who calls me villain? breaks my pate across?
Plucks off my beard, and blows it in my face?　　　　600
Tweaks me by the nose? gives me the lie i' the throat,
As deep as to the lungs? who does me this?
Ha!
'Swounds, I should take it: for it cannot be
But I am pigeon-liver'd and lack gall
To make oppression bitter, or ere this
I should have fatted all the region kites
With this slave's offal: bloody, bawdy villain!
Remorseless, treacherous, lecherous, kindless villain!
O, vengeance!　　　　610
Why, what an ass am I! This is most brave,
That I, the son of a dear father murder'd,
Prompted to my revenge by heaven and hell,
Must, like a whore, unpack my heart with words,
And fall a-cursing, like a very drab,
A scullion!
Fie upon't! foh! About, my brain! I have heard
That guilty creatures sitting at a play
Have by the very cunning of the scene
Been struck so to the soul that presently　　　　620
They have proclaim'd their malefactions;
For murder, though it have no tongue, will speak
With most miraculous organ. I'll have these players
Play something like the murder of my father
Before mine uncle: I'll observe his looks;
I'll tent him to the quick: if he but blench,
I know my course. The spirit that I have seen
May be the devil: and the devil hath power
To assume a pleasing shape; yea, and perhaps
Out of my weakness and my melancholy,　　　　630
As he is very potent with such spirits,
Abuses me to damn me: I'll have grounds
More relative than this: the play's the thing
Wherein I'll catch the conscience of the king.　　　　*Exit.*

## ACT III.

### SCENE I. *A room in the castle.*

*Enter* KING, QUEEN, POLONIUS, OPHELIA, ROSENCRANTZ, *and* GUILDENSTERN.

  *King.* And can you, by no drift of circumstance,
Get from him why he puts on this confusion,
Grating so harshly all his days of quiet
With turbulent and dangerous lunacy?
  *Ros.* He does confess he feels himself distracted;
But from what cause he will by no means speak.
  *Guil.* Nor do we find him forward to be sounded,
But, with a crafty madness, keeps aloof,
When we would bring him on to some confession
Of his true state.
  *Queen.*          Did he receive you well?          10
  *Ros.* Most like a gentleman.
  *Guil.* But with much forcing of his disposition.
  *Ros.* Niggard of question; but, of our demands,
Most free in his reply.
  *Queen.*          Did you assay him
To any pastime?
  *Ros.* Madam, it so fell out, that certain players
We o'er-raught on the way: of these we told him;
And there did seem in him a kind of joy
To hear of it: they are about the court,
And, as I think, they have already order          20
This night to play before him.
  *Pol.*                    'T is most true:
And he beseech'd me to entreat your majesties
To hear and see the matter.
  *King.* With all my heart; and it doth much content me
To hear him so inclined.
Good gentlemen, give him a further edge,
And drive his purpose on to these delights.
  *Ros.* We shall, my lord.
                    [*Exeunt Rosencrantz and Guildenstern,*
  *King.*                    Sweet Gertrude, leave us too;
For we have closely sent for Hamlet hither,
That he, as 't were by accident, may here          30
Affront Ophelia:
Her father and myself, lawful espials,
Will so bestow ourselves that, seeing, unseen,

We may of their encounter frankly judge,
And gather by him, as he is behaved,
If 't be the affliction of his love or no
That thus he suffers for.
   *Queen.*           I shall obey you.
And for your part, Ophelia, I do wish
That your good beauties be the happy cause
Of Hamlet's wildness: so shall I hope your virtues          40
Will bring him to his wonted way again,
To both your honours.
   *Oph.*          Madam, I wish it may. [*Exit Queen.*
   *Pol.* Ophelia, walk you here.   Gracious, so please you,
We will bestow ourselves.   [*To Ophelia*] Read on this book;
That show of such an exercise may colour
Your loneliness.   We are oft to blame in this,—
'T is too much proved—that with devotion's visage
And pious action we do sugar o'er
The devil himself.
   *King.* [*Aside*]   O, 't is too true!
How smart a lash that speech doth give my conscience!   50
The harlot's cheek, beautied with plastering art,
Is not more ugly to the thing that helps it
Than is my deed to my most painted word:
O heavy burthen!
   *Pol.* I hear him coming: let's withdraw, my lord.
                 [*Exeunt King and Polonius.*

*Enter* HAMLET.

   *Ham.* To be, or not to be: that is the question:
Whether 't is nobler in the mind to suffer
The slings and arrows of outrageous fortune,
Or to take arms against a sea of troubles,
And by opposing end them?   To die: to sleep;          60
No more; and by a sleep to say we end
The heart-ache and the thousand natural shocks
That flesh is heir to, 't is a consummation
Devoutly to be wish'd.   To die, to sleep;
To sleep: perchance to dream: ay, there's the rub;
For in that sleep of death what dreams may come
When we have shuffled off this mortal coil,
Must give us pause: there's the respect
That makes calamity of so long life;
For who would bear the whips and scorns of time,          70
The oppressor's wrong, the proud man's contumely,
The pangs of despised love, the law's delay,

The insolence of office and the spurns
That patient merit of the unworthy takes,
When he himself might his quietus make
With a bare bodkin? who would fardels bear,
To grunt and sweat under a weary life,
But that the dread of something after death,
The undiscover'd country from whose bourn
No traveller returns, puzzles the will                    80
And makes us rather bear those ills we have
Than fly to others that we know not of?
Thus conscience does make cowards of us all;
'And thus the native hue of resolution
Is sicklied o'er with the pale cast of thought,
And enterprises of great pitch and moment
With this regard their currents turn awry,
And lose the name of action.—Soft you now!
The fair Ophelia!    Nymph, in thy orisons
Be all my sins remember'd.
    *Oph.*                    Good my lord,            90
How does your honour for this many a day?
    *Ham.* I humbly thank you; well, well, well.
    *Oph.* My lord, I have remembrances of yours,
That I have longed long to re-deliver;
I pray you, now receive them.
    *Ham.*                    No, not I;
I never gave you aught.
    *Oph.* My honour'd lord, you know right well you did;
And, with them, words of so sweet breath composed
As made the things more rich: their perfume lost,
Take these again; for to the noble mind            100
Rich gifts wax poor when givers prove unkind.
There, my lord.
    *Ham.* Ha, ha! are you honest?
    *Oph.* My lord?
    *Ham.* Are you fair?
    *Oph.* What means your lordship?
    *Ham.* That if you be honest and fair, your honesty should
admit no discourse to your beauty.
    *Oph.* Could beauty, my lord, have better commerce than
with honesty?                    110
    *Ham.* Ay, truly; for the power of beauty will sooner trans-
form honesty from what it is to a bawd than the force of
honesty can translate beauty into his likeness: this was sometime a paradox, but now the time gives it proof.    I did love
you once.

*Oph.* Indeed, my lord, you made me believe so.

*Ham.* You should not have believed me; for virtue cannot so inoculate our old stock but we shall relish of it: I loved you not.          120

*Oph.* I was the more deceived.

*Ham.* Get thee to a nunnery: why wouldst thou be a breeder of sinners? I am myself indifferent honest; but yet I could accuse me of such things that it were better my mother had not borne me: I am very proud, revengeful, ambitious, with more offences at my beck than I have thoughts to put them in, imagination to give them shape, or time to act them in. What should such fellows as I do crawling between earth and heaven? We are arrant knaves, all; believe none of us. Go thy ways to a nunnery. Where's your father?

*Oph.* At home, my lord.

*Ham.* Let the doors be shut upon him, that he may play the fool no where but in's own house. Farewell.

*Oph.* O, help him, you sweet heavens!

*Ham.* If thou dost marry, I'll give thee this plague for thy dowry: be thou as chaste as ice, as pure as snow, thou shalt not escape calumny. Get thee to a nunnery, go: farewell. Or, if thou wilt needs marry, marry a fool; for wise men know well enough what monsters you make of them. To a nunnery, go, and quickly too. Farewell.

*Oph.* O heavenly powers, restore him!

*Ham.* I have heard of your paintings too, well enough; God has given you one face, and you make yourselves another: you jig, you amble, and you lisp, and nick-name God's creatures, and make your wantonness your ignorance. Go to, I'll no more on't; it hath made me mad. I say, we will have no more marriages: those that are married already, all but one, shall live; the rest shall keep as they are. To a nunnery, go.          [*Exit.*

*Oph.* O, what a noble mind is here o'erthrown!
The courtier's, soldier's, scholar's, eye, tongue, sword;
The expectancy and rose of the fair state,          160
The glass of fashion and the mould of form,
The observed of all observers, quite, quite down!
And I, of ladies most deject and wretched,
That suck'd the honey of his music vows,
Now see that noble and most sovereign reason,
Like sweet bells jangled, out of tune and harsh;
That unmatch'd form and feature of blown youth
Blasted with ecstasy: O, woe is me,
To have seen what I have seen, see what I see!

*Re-enter* KING *and* POLONIUS.

*King.* Love! his affections do not that way tend;        170
Nor what he spake, though it lack'd form a little,
Was not like madness. There's something in his soul,
O'er which his melancholy sits on brood;
And I do doubt the hatch and the disclose
Will be some danger: which for to prevent,
I have in quick determination
Thus set it down: he shall with speed to England,
For the demand of our neglected tribute:
Haply the seas and countries different
With variable objects shall expel                         180
This something-settled matter in his heart,
Whereon his brains still beating puts him thus
From fashion of himself. What think you on 't?
*Pol.* It shall do well: but yet do I believe
The origin and commencement of his grief
Sprung from neglected love. How now, Ophelia!
You need not tell us what Lord Hamlet said;
We heard it all. My lord, do as you please;
But, if you hold it fit, after the play
Let his queen mother all alone entreat him                190
To show his grief: let her be round with him;
And I'll be placed, so please you, in the ear
Of all their conference. If she find him not,
To England send him, or confine him where
Your wisdom best shall think.
   *King.*                    It shall be so:
Madness in great ones must not unwatch'd go.    [*Exeunt.*

SCENE II. *A hall in the castle.*

*Enter* HAMLET *and* Players.

*Ham.* Speak the speech, I pray you, as I pronounced it to
you, trippingly on the tongue: but if you mouth it, as many
of your players do, I had as lief the town-crier spoke my lines.
Nor do not saw the air too much with your hand, thus, but
use all gently; for in the very torrent, tempest, and, as I may
say, the whirlwind of passion, you must acquire and beget a
temperance that may give it smoothness. O, it offends me to
the soul to hear a robustious periwig-pated fellow tear a passion to tatters, to very rags, to split the ears of the groundlings, who for the most part are capable of nothing but inex-
plicable dumb-shows and noise: I would have such a fellow

whipped for o'erdoing Termagant; it outherods Herod: pray
you, avoid it.

*First Player.* I warrant your honour.

*Ham.* Be not too tame neither, but let your own discretion
be your tutor: suit the action to the word, the word to the
action ; with this special observance, that you o'erstep not the
modesty of nature: for any thing so overdone is from the
purpose of playing, whose end, both at the first and now, was
and is, to hold, as 't were, the mirror up to nature ; to show
virtue her own feature, scorn her own image, and the very age
and body of the time his form and pressure.   Now this overdone, or come tardy off, though it make the unskilful laugh,
cannot but make the judicious grieve; the censure of the
which one must in your allowance o'erweigh a whole theatre
of others.   O, there be players that I have seen play, and
heard others praise, and that highly, not to speak it profanely,
that, neither having the accent of Christians nor the gait of
Christian, pagan, nor man, have so strutted and bellowed that I
have thought some of nature's journeymen had made men and
not made them well, they imitated humanity so abominably.

*First Player.* I hope we have reformed that indifferently
with us, sir.                                                                41

*Ham.* O, reform it altogether.   And let those that play
your clowns speak no more than is set down for them; for
there be of them that will themselves laugh, to set on some
quantity of barren spectators to laugh too; though, in the
mean time, some necessary question of the play be then to be
considered : that 's villanous, and shows a most pitiful ambition in the fool that uses it.   Go, make you ready.

                                              [*Exeunt Players.*

*Enter* POLONIUS, ROSENCRANTZ, *and* GUILDENSTERN.

How now, my lord ! will the king hear this piece of work?

*Pol.* And the queen too, and that presently.

*Ham.* Bid the players make haste. [*Exit Polonius.*] Will
      you two help to hasten them?

*Ros.*  }
*Guil.* }  We will, my lord.

                          [*Exeunt Rosencrantz and Guildenstern.*

*Ham.* What ho ! Horatio!

*Enter* HORATIO.

*Hor.* Here, sweet lord, at your service.

*Ham.* Horatio, thou art e'en as just a man
As e'er my conversation coped withal.                          60

*Hor.* O, my dear lord,—
*Ham.*                   Nay, do not think I flatter;
For what advancement may I hope from thee
That no revenue hast but thy good spirits,
To feed and clothe thee? Why should the poor be flatter'd?
No, let the candied tongue lick absurd pomp,
And crook the pregnant hinges of the knee
Where thrift may follow fawning. Dost thou hear?
Since my dear soul was mistress of her choice
And could of men distinguish, her election
Hath seal'd thee for herself; for thou hast been      70
As one, in suffering all, that suffers nothing,
A man that fortune's buffets and rewards
Hast ta'en with equal thanks: and blest are those
Whose blood and judgement are so well commingled,
That they are not a pipe for fortune's finger
To sound what stop she please. Give me that man
That is not passion's slave, and I will wear him
In my heart's core, ay, in my heart of heart,
As I do thee.—Something too much of this.—
There is a play to-night before the king;       80
One scene of it comes near the circumstance
Which I have told thee of my father's death:
I prithee, when thou seest that act afoot,
Even with the very comment of thy soul
Observe mine uncle: if his occulted guilt
Do not itself unkennel in one speech,
It is a damned ghost that we have seen,
And my imaginations are as foul
As Vulcan's stithy. Give him heedful note;
For I mine eyes will rivet to his face,        90
And after we will both our judgements join
In censure of his seeming.
*Hor.*                Well, my lord:
If he steal aught the whilst this play is playing,
And 'scape detecting, I will pay the theft.
   *Ham.* They are coming to the play; I must be idle:
Get you a place.

*Danish march. A flourish. Enter* KING, QUEEN, POLO-
   NIUS, OPHELIA, ROSENCRANTZ, GUILDENSTERN, *and
   others.*

   *King.* How fares our cousin Hamlet?
   *Ham.* Excellent, i' faith; of the chameleon's dish: I eat
the air, promise-crammed: you cannot feed capons so.   100

*King.* I have nothing with this answer, Hamlet; these words are not mine.

*Ham.* No, nor mine now. [*To Polonius*] My lord, you played once i' the university, you say?

*Pol.* That did I, my lord; and was accounted a good actor.

*Ham.* What did you enact?

*Pol.* I did enact Julius Cæsar: I was killed i' the Capitol; Brutus killed me.

*Ham.* It was a brute part of him to kill so capital a calf there.   Be the players ready?                              111

*Ros.* Ay, my lord; they stay upon your patience.

*Queen.* Come hither, my dear Hamlet, sit by me.

*Ham.* No, good mother, here's metal more attractive.

*Pol.* [*To the King*] O, ho! do you mark that?

*Oph.* You are merry, my lord.

*Ham.* Who, I?                                               130

*Oph.* Ay, my lord.

*Ham.* O God, your only jig-maker.  What should a man do but be merry? for, look you, how cheerfully my mother looks, and my father died within these two hours.

*Oph.* Nay, 't is twice two months, my lord.

*Ham.* So long?  Nay then, let the devil wear black, for I 'll have a suit of sables.   O heavens! die two months ago, and not forgotten yet?   Then there 's hope a great man's memory may outlive his life half a year: but, by 'r lady, he must build churches, then; or else shall he suffer not thinking on, with the hobby-horse, whose epitaph is 'For, O, for, O, the hobby-horse is forgot'.

*Hautboys play.   The dumb-show enters.*

*Enter a* King *and a* Queen *very lovingly; the* Queen *embracing him, and he her.   She kneels, and makes show of protestation unto him.   He takes her up, and declines his head upon her neck: lays him down upon a bank of flowers: she, seeing him asleep, leaves him.   Anon comes in a fellow, takes off his crown, kisses it, and pours poison in the* King's *ears, and exit.   The* Queen *returns; finds the* King *dead, and makes passionate action.   The* Poisoner, *with some two or three* Mutes, *comes in again, seeming to lament with her.   The dead body is carried away.   The* Poisoner *wooes the* Queen *with gifts: she seems loath and unwilling awhile, but in the end accepts his love.*                                              [*Exeunt.*

*Oph.* What means this, my lord?

*Ham.* Marry, this is miching mallecho; it means mischief.
*Oph.* Belike this show imports the argument of the play.

*Enter* Prologue.

*Ham.* We shall know by this fellow: the players cannot
keep counsel; they'll tell all.

*Pro.* For us, and for our tragedy,
　　Here stooping to your clemency,　　　　　　160
　　We beg your hearing patiently.　　　　　　·[*Exit.*

*Ham.* Is this a prologue, or the posy of a ring?
*Oph.* 'T is brief, my lord.
*Ham.* As woman's love.

*Enter two* Players, King *and* Queen.

*P. King.* Full thirty times hath Phœbus' cart gone round
Neptune's salt-wash and Tellus' orbed ground,
And thirty dozen moons with borrow'd sheen
About the world have times twelve thirties been
Since love our hearts and Hymen did our hands
Unite commutual in most sacred bands.　　　　　170
*P. Queen.* So many journeys may the sun and moon
Make us again count o'er ere love be done!
But, woe is me, you are so sick of late,
So far from cheer and from your former state,
That I distrust you.　Yet, though I distrust,
Discomfort you, my lord, it nothing must:
For women's fear and love holds quantity;
In neither aught, or in extremity.
Now, what my love is, proof hath made you know;
And as my love is sized, my fear is so:　　　　180
Where love is great, the littlest doubts are fear;
Where little fears grow great, great love grows there.
*P. King.* 'Faith, I must leave thee, love, and shortly too;
My operant powers their functions leave to do:
And thou shalt live in this fair world behind,
Honour'd, beloved; and haply one as kind
For husband shalt thou—
*P. Queen.*　　　　　　O, confound the rest!
Such love must needs be treason in my breast:
In second husband let me be accurst!
None wed the second but who kill'd the first.　　190

*Ham.* [*Aside*] Wormwood, wormwood.

*P. Queen.* The instances that second marriage move
Are base respects of thrift, but none of love:

A second time I kill my husband dead,
When second husband kisses me in bed.
   *P. King.* I do believe you think what now you speak;
But what we do determine oft we break.
Purpose is but the slave to memory, .
Of violent birth, but poor validity:
Which now, like fruit unripe, sticks on the tree;    200
But fall, unshaken, when they mellow be.
Most necessary 't is that we forget
To pay ourselves what to ourselves is debt:
What to ourselves in passion we propose,
The passion ending, doth the purpose lose.
The violence of either grief or joy
Their own enactures with themselves destroy:
Where joy most revels, grief doth most lament;
Grief joys, joy grieves, on slender accident.
This world is not for aye, nor 't is not strange
That even our loves should with our fortunes change;
For 't is a question left us yet to prove,
Whether love lead fortune, or else fortune love.
The great man down, you mark his favourite flies;
The poor advanced makes friends of enemies.
And hitherto doth love on fortune tend;
For who not needs shall never lack a friend,
And who in want a hollow friend doth try,
Directly seasons him his enemy.
But, orderly to end where I begun,      .    220
Our wills and fates do so contrary run
That our devices still are overthrown;
Our thoughts are ours, their ends none of our own:
So think thou wilt no second husband wed;
But die thy thoughts when thy first lord is dead.
   *P. Queen.* Nor earth to me give food, nor heaven light!
Sport and repose lock from me day and night!
To desperation turn my trust and hope!
An anchor's cheer in prison be my scope!
Each opposite that blanks the face of joy    230
Meet what I would have well and it destroy!
Both here and hence pursue me lasting strife,
If, once a widow, ever I be wife!
  *Ham.* If she should break it now!
   *P. King.* 'T is deeply sworn. Sweet, leave me here
    awhile;
My spirits grow dull, and fain I would beguile
The tedious day with sleep.        [Slee†

*P. Queen.*                    Sleep rock thy brain ;
And never come mischance between us twain !          [*Exit.*
*Ham.* Madam, how like you this play?
*Queen.* The lady doth protest too much, methinks.          240
*Ham.* O, but she 'll keep her word.
*King.* Have you heard the argument? Is there no offence
in 't?
*Ham.* No, no, they do but jest, poison in jest; no offence
i' the world.
*King.* What do you call the play?
*Ham.* The mouse-trap. Marry, how? Tropically. This
play is the image of a murder done in Vienna: Gonzago is
the duke's name; his wife, Baptista: you shall see anon; 't is
a knavish piece of work: but what o' that? your majesty
and we that have free souls, it touches us not: let the galled
jade wince, our withers are unwrung.

*Enter* LUCIANUS.

This is one Lucianus, nephew to the king.
*Oph.* You are as good as a chorus, my lord.
*Ham.* I could interpret between you and your love, if I
could see the puppets dallying.
*Oph.* Still better, and worse.          261
*Ham.* So you mistake your husbands. Begin, murderer;
pox, leave thy damnable faces, and begin. Come: 'the
croaking raven doth bellow for revenge'.
     *Luc.* Thoughts black, hands apt, drugs fit, and time
          agreeing ;
     Confederate season, else no creature seeing;
     Thou mixture rank, of midnight weeds collected,
     With Hecate's ban thrice blasted, thrice infected,
     Thy natural magic and dire property,          270
     On wholesome life usurp immediately.
               [*Pours the poison into the sleeper's ears.*
*Ham.* He poisons him i' the garden for's estate. His
name's Gonzago: the story is extant, and writ in choice
Italian: you shall see anon how the murderer gets the love
of Gonzago's wife.
*Oph.* The king rises.
*Ham.* What, frighted with false fire !
*Queen.* How fares my lord?
*Pol.* Give o'er the play.
*King.* Give me some light: away !          280
*All.* Lights, lights, lights !
               [*Exeunt all but Hamlet and Horatio.*

*Ham.* Why, let the stricken deer go weep,
    The hart ungalled play;
    For some must watch, while some must sleep:
    So runs the world away.
Would not this, sir, and a forest of feathers—if the rest of
my fortunes turn Turk with me—with two Provincial roses
on my razed shoes, get me a fellowship in a cry of players,
sir?

*Hor.* Half a share.                                        290

*Ham.* A whole one, I.
    For thou dost know, O Damon dear,
      This realm dismantled was
    Of Jove himself; and now reigns here
      A very, very—pajock.

*Hor.* You might have rhymed.

*Ham.* O good Horatio, I'll take the ghost's word for a
thousand pound. Didst perceive?

*Hor.* Very well, my lord.

*Ham.* Upon the talk of the poisoning?                      300

*Hor.* I did very well note him.

*Ham.* Ah, ha! Come, some music! come, the recorders!
    For if the king like not the comedy,
    Why then, belike, he likes it not, perdy.
. Come, some music!

*Re-enter* ROSENCRANTZ *and* GUILDENSTERN.

*Guil.* Good my lord, vouchsafe me a word with you.

*Ham.* Sir, a whole history.

*Guil.* The king, sir,—                                     310

*Ham.* Ay, sir, what of him?

*Guil.* Is in his retirement marvellous distempered.

*Ham.* With drink, sir?

*Guil.* No, my lord, rather with choler.

*Ham.* Your wisdom should show itself more richer to
signify this to his doctor; for, for me to put him to his purga-
tion would perhaps plunge him into far more choler.        319

*Guil.* Good my lord, put your discourse into some frame,
and start not so wildly from my affair.

*Ham.* I am tame, sir: pronounce.

*Guil.* The queen, your mother, in most great affliction of
spirit, hath sent me to you.

*Ham.* You are welcome.

*Guil.* Nay, good my lord, this courtesy is not of the right
breed. If it shall please you to make me a wholesom

answer, I will do your mother's commandment: if not, your pardon and my return shall be the end of my business.

*Ham.* Sir, I cannot.                                    331

*Guil.* What, my lord?

*Ham.* Make you a wholesome answer; my wit's diseased: but, sir, such answer as I can make, you shall command; or, rather, as you say, my mother: therefore no more, but to the matter: my mother, you say,—

*Ros.* Then thus she says; your behaviour hath struck her into amazement and admiration.                        339

*Ham.* O wonderful son, that can so astonish a mother! But is there no sequel at the heels of this mother's admiration? Impart.

*Ros.* She desires to speak with you in her closet, ere you go to bed.

*Ham.* We shall obey, were she ten times our mother. Have you any further trade with us?

*Ros.* My lord, you once did love me.

*Ham.* So I do still, by these pickers and stealers.    349

*Ros.* Good my lord, what is your cause of distemper? you do, surely, bar the door upon your own liberty, if you deny your griefs to your friend.

*Ham.* Sir, I lack advancement.

*Ros.* How can that be, when you have the voice of the king himself for your succession in Denmark?

*Ham.* Ay, sir, but, 'While the grass grows',—the proverb is something musty.                                    359

*Re-enter* Players *with recorders.*

O, the recorders! let me see one.   To withdraw with you:— why do you go about to recover the wind of me, as if you would drive me into a toil?

*Guil.* O, my lord, if my duty be too bold, my love is too unmannerly.

*Ham.* I do not well understand that.   Will you play upon this pipe?

*Guil.* My lord, I cannot.

*Ham.* I pray you.

*Guil.* Believe me, I cannot.

*Ham.* I do beseech you.                                370

*Guil.* I know no touch of it, my lord.

*Ham.* 'T is as easy as lying: govern these ventages with your fingers and thumb, give it breath with your mouth, and it will discourse most eloquent music.   Look you, these are the stops.

*Guil.* But these cannot I command to any utterance of harmony; I have not the skill.

*Ham.* Why, look you now, how unworthy a thing you make of me! You would play upon me; you would seem to know my stops; you would pluck out the heart of my mystery; you would sound me from my lowest note to the top of my compass: and there is much music, excellent voice, in this little organ; yet cannot you make it speak. 'Sblood, do you think I am easier to be played on than a pipe? Call me what instrument you will, though you can fret me, yet you cannot play upon me.

*Enter* POLONIUS.

God bless you, sir!                                            390

*Pol.* My lord, the queen would speak with you, and presently.

*Ham.* Do you see yonder cloud that's almost in shape of a camel?

*Pol.* By the mass, and 't is like a camel, indeed.

*Ham.* Methinks it is like a weasel.

*Pol.* It is backed like a weasel.

*Ham.* Or like a whale?

*Pol.* Very like a whale.                                      399

*Ham.* Then I will come to my mother by and by. They fool me to the top of my bent. I will come by and by.

*Pol.* I will say so.

*Ham.* By and by is easily said. [*Exit Polonius.*] Leave me, friends.                          [*Exeunt all but Hamlet.*

'T is now the very witching time of night,
When churchyards yawn and hell itself breathes out
Contagion to this world: now could I drink hot blood,
And do such bitter business as the day
Would quake to look on. Soft! now to my mother.     410
O heart, lose not thy nature; let not ever
The soul of Nero enter this firm bosom:
Let me be cruel, not unnatural:
I will speak daggers to her, but use none;
My tongue and soul in this be hypocrites;
How in my words soever she be shent,
To give them seals never, my soul, consent!              [*Exit.*

## SCENE III. *A room in the castle.*

*Enter* KING, ROSENCRANTZ, *and* GUILDENSTERN.

*King.* I like him not, nor stands it safe with us
To let his madness range. Therefore prepare you;

I your commission will forthwith dispatch,
And he to England shall along with you:
The terms of our estate may not endure
Hazard so near us as doth hourly grow
Out of his lunacies.
  *Guil.*    We will ourselves provide:
Most holy and religious fear it is
To keep those many many bodies safe
That live and feed upon your majesty.    10
  *Ros.* The single and peculiar life is bound,
With all the strength and armour of the mind,
To keep itself from noyance; but much more
That spirit upon whose weal depend and rest
The lives of many. The cease of majesty
Dies not alone; but, like a gulf, doth draw
What's near it with it: it is a massy wheel,
Fix'd on the summit of the highest mount,
To whose huge spokes ten thousand lesser things
Are mortised and adjoin'd; which, when it falls,  20
Each small annexment, petty consequence,
Attends the boisterous ruin. Never alone
Did the king sigh, but with a general groan.
  *King.* Arm you, I pray you, to this speedy voyage;
For we will fetters put upon this fear,
Which now goes too free-footed.
  *Ros.*  &#125;
  *Guil.* &#125;    We will haste us.

    *[Exeunt Rosencrantz and Guildenstern.*

    *Enter* POLONIUS.

  *Pol.* My lord, he's going to his mother's closet:
Behind the arras I'll convey myself,
To hear the process; I'll warrant she'll tax him home:
And, as you said, and wisely was it said,    30
'T is meet that some more audience than a mother,
Since nature makes them partial, should o'erhear
The speech, of vantage. Fare you well, my liege:
I'll call upon you ere you go to bed,
And tell you what I know.
  *King.*    Thanks, dear my lord.  *[Exit Polonius.*
O, my offence is rank, it smells to heaven;
It hath the primal eldest curse upon't,
A brother's murder. Pray can I not,
Though inclination be as sharp as will:
My stronger guilt defeats my strong intent;  40

And, like a man to double business bound,
I stand in pause where I shall first begin,
And both neglect.   What if this cursed hand
Were thicker than itself with brother's blood,
Is there not rain enough in the sweet heavens
To wash it white as snow?   Whereto serves mercy
But to confront the visage of offence?
And what 's in prayer but this two-fold force,
To be forestalled ere we come to fall,
Or pardon'd being down?   Then I 'll look up;               50
My fault is past.   But, O, what form of prayer
Can serve my turn?   ' Forgive me my foul murder'?
That cannot be; since I am still possess'd
Of those effects for which I did the murder,
My crown, mine own ambition and my queen.
May one be pardon'd and retain the offence?
In the corrupted currents of this world
Offence's gilded hand may shove by justice,
And oft 't is seen the wicked prize itself
Buys out the law: but 't is not so above;                  60
There is no shuffling, there the action lies
In his true nature; and we ourselves compell'd,
Even to the teeth and forehead of our faults,
To give in evidence.   What then?   what rests?
Try what repentance can: what can it not?
Yet what can it when one can not repent?
O wretched state!   O bosom black as death!
O limed soul, that, struggling to be free,
Art more engaged!   Help, angels!   Make assay!
Bow, stubborn knees; and, heart with strings of steel,      70
Be soft as sinews of the new-born babe!
All may be well.                          [*Retires and kneels.*

*Enter* HAMLET.

*Ham.* Now might I do it pat, now he is praying;
And now I 'll do 't.   And so he goes to heaven;
And so am I revenged.   That would be scann'd:
A villain kills my father; and for that,
I, his sole son, do this same villain send
To heaven.
O, this is hire and salary, not revenge.
He took my father grossly, full of bread,
With all his crimes broad blown, as flush as May;
And how his audit stands who knows save heaven?
But in our circumstance and course of thought,

'T is heavy with him: and am I then revenged,
To take him in the purging of his soul,
When he is fit and season'd for his passage?
No!
Up, sword; and know thou a more horrid hent:
When he is drunk asleep, or in his rage,
Or in the incestuous pleasure of his bed;         90
At gaming, swearing, or about some act
That has no relish of salvation in 't;
Then trip him, that his heels may kick at heaven,
And that his soul may be as damn'd and black
As hell, whereto it goes.  My mother stays:
This physic but prolongs thy sickly days.    *[Exit.*
  *King. [Rising]* My words fly up, my thoughts remain
    below:
Words without thoughts never to heaven go.    *[Exit.*

### Scene IV. *The Queen's closet.*

### *Enter* Queen *and* Polonius.

  *Pol.* He will come straight.  Look you lay home to him:
Tell him his pranks have been too broad to bear with,
And that your grace hath screen'd and stood between
Much heat and him.  I 'll silence me even here.
Pray you, be round with him.
  *Ham.* [*Within*] Mother, mother, mother!
  *Queen.*                       I 'll warrant you,
Fear me not: withdraw, I hear him coming.
        *[Polonius hides behind the arras.*

### *Enter* Hamlet.

  *Ham.* Now, mother, what 's the matter?
  *Queen.* Hamlet, thou hast thy father much offended.
  *Ham.* Mother, you have my father much offended.    10
  *Queen.* Come, come, you answer with an idle tongue.
  *Ham.* Go, go, you question with a wicked tongue.
  *Queen.* Why, how now, Hamlet!
  *Ham.* -                  What 's the matter now?
  *Queen.* Have you forgot me?
  *Ham.*             No, by the rood, not so:
You are the queen, your husband's brother's wife;
And—would it were not so!—you are my mother.
  *Queen.* Nay, then, I 'll set those to you that can

*Ham.* Come, come, and sit you down ; you shall not budge;
You go not till I set you up a glass
Where you may see the inmost part of you. 20
    *Queen.* What wilt thou do? thou wilt not murder me?
Help, help, ho!
    *Pol.* [*Behind*] What, ho! help, help, help!
    *Ham.* [*Drawing*] How now! a rat? Dead, for a ducat,
        dead!        [*Makes a pass through the arras.*
    *Pol.* [*Behind*] O, I am slain!        [*Falls and dies.*
    *Queen.* O me, what hast thou done?
    *Ham.*                Nay, I know not:
Is it the king?
    *Queen.* O, what a rash and bloody deed is this!
    *Ham.* A bloody deed! almost as bad, good mother,
As kill a king, and marry with his brother.
    *Queen.* As kill a king!
    *Ham.*                Ay, lady, 't was my word. 30
        [*Lifts up the arras and discovers Polonius.*
Thou wretched, rash, intruding fool, farewell!
I took thee for thy better: take thy fortune;
Thou find'st to be too busy is some danger.
Leave wringing of your hands: peace! sit you down,
And let me wring your heart; for so I shall,
If it be made of penetrable stuff,
If damned custom have not brass'd it so
That it be proof and bulwark against sense.
    *Queen.* What have I done, that thou darest wag thy tongue
In noise so rude against me?
    *Ham.*                Such an act 40
That blurs the grace and blush of modesty,
Calls virtue hypocrite, takes off the rose
From the fair forehead of an innocent love
And sets a blister there, makes marriage-vows
As false as dicers' oaths: O, such a deed
As from the body of contraction plucks
The very soul, and sweet religion makes
A rhapsody of words: heaven's face doth glow;
Yea, this solidity and compound mass,
With tristful visage, as against the doom, 50
Is thought-sick at the act.
    *Queen.*                Ay me, what act,
That roars so loud, and thunders in the index?
    *Ham.* Look here       picture, and on this,
  The                        brothers.
                        brow ;

Hyperion's curls; the front of Jove himself;
An eye like Mars, to threaten and command;
A station like the herald Mercury
New-lighted on a heaven-kissing hill;
A combination and a form indeed, 60
Where every god did seem to set his seal,
To give the world assurance of a man:
This was your husband. Look you now, what follows:
Here is your husband; like a mildew'd ear,
Blasting his wholesome brother. Have you eyes?
Could you on this fair mountain leave to feed,
And batten on this moor? Ha! have you eyes?
You cannot call it love; for at your age
The hey-day in the blood is tame, it's humble,
And waits upon the judgement: and what judgement 70
Would step from this to this? Sense, sure, you have,
Else could you not have motion; but sure, that sense
Is apoplex'd; for madness would not err,
Nor sense to ecstasy was ne'er so thrall'd
But it reserved some quantity of choice,
To serve in such a difference. What devil was 't
That thus hath cozen'd you at hoodman-blind?
Eyes without feeling, feeling without sight,
Ears without hands or eyes, smelling sans all,
Or but a sickly part of one true sense 80
Could not so mope.
O shame! where is thy blush? Rebellious hell,
If thou canst mutine in a matron's bones,
To flaming youth let virtue be as wax,
And melt in her own fire: proclaim no shame
When the compulsive ardour gives the charge,
Since frost itself as actively doth burn
And reason pandars will.
    *Queen.*            O Hamlet, speak no more:
Thou turn'st mine eyes into my very soul;
And there I see such black and grained spots 90
As will not leave their tinct. O, speak to me no more;
These words, like daggers, enter in mine ears;
No more, sweet Hamlet!
    *Ham.*            A murderer and a villain;
A slave that is not twentieth part the tithe
Of your precedent lord; a vice of kings;
A cutpurse of the empire and the rule,
That from a shelf the precious diadem stole, 100
And put it in his pocket!

*Queen.*　　　　　　No more!
*Ham.* A king of shreds and patches,—

*Enter* Ghost.

Save me, and hover o'er me with your wings,
You heavenly guards! What would your gracious figure
*Queen.* Alas, he's mad!
*Ham.* Do you not come your tardy son to chide,
That, lapsed in time and passion, lets go by
The important acting of your dread command?
O, say!
　　*Ghost.* Do not forget: this visitation　　　　110
Is but to whet thy almost blunted purpose.
But, look, amazement on thy mother sits:
O, step between her and her fighting soul:
Conceit in weakest bodies strongest works:
Speak to her, Hamlet.
　　*Ham.*　　　　　How is it with you, lady?
　　*Queen.* Alas, how is't with you,
That you do bend your eye on vacancy
And with the incorporal air do hold discourse?
Forth at your eyes your spirits wildly peep;
And, as the sleeping soldiers in the alarm,　　　120
Your bedded hair, like life in excrements,
Start up, and stand an end. O gentle son,
Upon the heat and flame of thy distemper
Sprinkle cool patience. Whereon do you look?
　　*Ham.* On him, on him! Look you, how pale he glares!
His form and cause conjoin'd, preaching to stones,
Would make them capable. Do not look upon me;
Lest with this piteous action you convert
My stern effects: then what I have to do
Will want true colour; tears perchance for blood.　　130
　　*Queen.* To whom do you speak this?
　　*Ham.*　　　　　　　Do you see nothing there?
　　*Queen.* Nothing at all; yet all that is I see.
　　*Ham.* Nor did you nothing hear?
　　*Queen.*　　　　　　No, nothing but ourselves
　　*Ham.* Why, look you there! look, how it steals away!
My father, in his habit as he lived!
Look, where he goes, even now, out at the portal!
　　　　　　　　　　　　　　　　　[*Exit Ghost*
　　*Queen.* This is the very coinage of your brain:
This bodiless creation ecstasy
Is very cunning in.

*Ham.*                Ecstasy!
My pulse, as yours, doth temperately keep time,          140
And makes as healthful music: it is not madness
That I have utter'd: bring me to the test,
And I the matter will re-word; which madness
Would gambol from.    Mother, for love of grace,
Lay not that flattering unction to your soul,
That not your trespass, but my madness speaks:
It will but skin and film the ulcerous place,
Whiles rank corruption, mining all within,
Infects unseen.    Confess yourself to heaven;
Repent what's past; avoid what is to come;          150
And do not spread the compost on the weeds,
To make them ranker.    Forgive me this my virtue;
For in the fatness of these pursy times
Virtue itself of vice must pardon beg,
Yea, curb and woo for leave to do him good.
    *Queen.* O Hamlet, thou hast cleft my heart in twain.
    *Ham.* O, throw away the worser part of it,
And live the purer with the other half.
Good night: but go not to mine uncle's bed;
Assume a virtue, if you have it not.                    160
That monster, custom, who all sense doth eat,
Of habits devil, is angel yet in this,
That to the use of actions fair and good
He likewise gives a frock or livery,
That aptly is put on.    Refrain to-night,
And that shall lend a kind of easiness
To the next abstinence: the next more easy;
For use almost can change the stamp of nature,
And either......the devil, or throw him out
With wondrous potency.    Once more, good night:          170
And when you are desirous to be bless'd,
I'll blessing beg of you.    For this same lord,
                                        [*Pointing to Polonius.*
I do repent: but heaven hath pleased it so,
To punish me with this and this with me,
That I must be their scourge and minister.
I will bestow him, and will answer well
The death I gave him.    So, again, good night.
I must be cruel, only to be kind:
Thus bad begins and worse remains behind.
One word more, good lady.
    *Queen.*                What shall I do?          180
    *Ham.* Not this, by no means, that I bid you do:

Let the bloat king tempt you again to bed;
Pinch wanton on your cheek; call you his mouse;
And let him, for a pair of reechy kisses,
Or paddling in your neck with his damn'd fingers,
Make you to ravel all this matter out,
That I essentially am not in madness,
But mad in craft. 'T were good you let him know
For who, that's but a queen, fair, sober, wise,
Would from a paddock, from a bat, a gib,　　　　190
Such dear concernings hide? who would do so?
No, in despite of sense and secrecy,
Unpeg the basket on the house's top,
Let the birds fly, and, like the famous ape,
To try conclusions, in the basket creep,
And break your own neck down.
　　*Queen.* Be thou assured, if words be made of breath,
And breath of life, I have no life to breathe
What thou hast said to me.
　　*Ham.* I must to England; you know that?
　　*Queen.*　　　　　　　　　　　　　Alack,　　200
I had forgot: 't is so concluded on.
　　*Ham.* There's letters seal'd: and my two schoolfellows,
Whom I will trust as I will adders fang'd,
They bear the mandate; they must sweep my way,
And marshal me to knavery. Let it work;
For 't is the sport to have the enginer
Hoist with his own petar: and 't shall go hard
But I will delve one yard below their mines,
And blow them at the moon: O, 't is most sweet,
When in one line two crafts directly meet.　　　　210
This man shall set me packing:
I 'll lug the guts into the neighbour room.
Mother, good night. Indeed this counsellor
Is now most still, most secret and most grave,
Who was in life a foolish prating knave.
Come, sir, to draw toward an end with you.
Good night, mother.
　　　　　*[Exeunt severally; Hamlet dragging in Polonius.*

## ACT IV..

### SCENE I.   *A room in the castle.*

*Enter* KING, QUEEN, ROSENCRANTZ, *and* GUILDENSTERN.

   *King.* There's matter in these sighs, these profound
    heaves:
You must translate: 'tis fit we understand them.
Where is your son?
   *Queen.* Bestow this place on us a little while.
           [*Exeunt Rosencrantz and Guildenstern.*
Ah, mine own lord, what have I seen to-night!
   *King.* What, Gertrude? How does Hamlet?
   *Queen.* Mad as the sea and wind, when both contend
Which is the mightier: in his lawless fit,
Behind the arras hearing something stir,
Whips out his rapier, cries, 'A rat, a rat!'                10
And, in this brainish apprehension, kills
The unseen good old man.
   *King.*         O heavy deed!
It had been so with us, had we been there:
His liberty is full of threats to all;
To you yourself, to us, to every one.
Alas, how shall this bloody deed be answer'd?
It will be laid to us, whose providence
Should have kept short, restrain'd and out of haunt,
This mad young man: but so much was our love,
We would not understand what was most fit;                20
But, like the owner of a foul disease,
To keep it from divulging, let it feed
Even on the pith of life.   Where is he gone?
   *Queen.* To draw apart the body he hath kill'd:
O'er whom his very madness, like some ore
Among a mineral of metals base,
Shows itself pure; he weeps for what is done.
   *King.* O Gertrude, come away!
The sun no sooner shall the mountains touch,
But we will ship him hence: and this vile deed                30
We must, with all our majesty and skill,
Both countenance and excuse.   Ho, Guildenstern!

    *Re-enter* ROSENCRANTZ *and* GUILDENSTERN.

Friends both, go join you with some further aid:
Hamlet in madness hath Polonius slain,

And from his mother's closet hath he dragg'd him:
Go seek him out; speak fair, and bring the body
Into the chapel. I pray you, haste in this.
                    [*Exeunt Rosencrantz and Guildenstern.*
Come, Gertrude, we 'll call up our wisest friends;
And let them know, both what we mean to do,
And what's untimely done............                    40
Whose whisper o'er the world's diameter,
As level as the cannon to his blank,
Transports his poison'd shot, may miss our name,
And hit the woundless air. O, come away!
My soul is full of discord and dismay.                    [*Exeunt.*

SCENE II.    *Another room in the castle.*

*Enter* HAMLET.

*Ham.* Safely stowed.
*Ros.* }
*Guil.* } [*Within*] Hamlet! Lord Hamlet!
*Ham.* But soft, what noise? who calls on Hamlet? O,
here they come.

*Enter* ROSENCRANTZ *and* GUILDENSTERN.

*Ros.* What have you done, my lord, with the dead body?
*Ham.* Compounded it with dust, whereto 't is kin.
*Ros.* Tell us where 't is, that we may take it thence
And bear it to the chapel.
*Ham.* Do not believe it.
*Ros.* Believe what?                    10
*Ham.* That I can keep your counsel and not mine own.
Besides, to be demanded of a sponge! what replication should
be made by the son of a king?
*Ros.* Take you me for a sponge, my lord?
*Ham.* Ay, sir, that soaks up the king's countenance, his
rewards, his authorities. But such officers do the king best
service in the end: he keeps them, like an ape, in the corner
of his jaw; first mouthed, to be last swallowed: when he
needs what you have gleaned, it is but squeezing you, and,
sponge, you shall be dry again.
*Ros.* I understand you not, my lord.
*Ham.* I am glad of it: a knavish speech sleeps in a foolish
ear.
*Ros.* My lord, you must tell us where the body is, and go
with us to the king.

*Ham.* The body is with the king, but the king is not with
the body.  The king is a thing—   .                          30
   *Guil.* A thing, my lord!
   *Ham.* Of nothing: bring me to him.  Hide fox, and all
after.                                                  [*Exeunt.*

SCENE III.   Another room in the castle.

Enter KING, attended.

   *King.* I have sent to seek him, and to find the body.
How dangerous is it that this man goes loose!
Yet must not we put the strong law on him:
He's loved of the distracted multitude,
Who like not in their judgement, but their eyes;
And where 't is so, the offender's scourge is weigh'd,
But never the offence.  To bear all smooth and even,
This sudden sending him away must seem
Deliberate pause: diseases desperate grown
By desperate appliance are relieved,                        ·   10
Or not at all.

Enter ROSENCRANTZ.

         How now! what hath befall'n?
   *Ros.* Where the dead body is bestow'd, my lord,
We cannot get from him.
   *King.*           But where is he?
   *Ros.* Without, my lord; guarded, to know your pleasure.
   *King.* Bring him before us.
   *Ros.* Ho, Guildenstern! bring in my lord.

Enter HAMLET and GUILDENSTERN.

   *King.* Now, Hamlet, where's Polonius?
   *Ham.* At supper.
   *King.* At supper! where?                               19
   *Ham.* Not where he eats, but where he is eaten: a certain
convocation of politic worms are e'en at him.  Your worm is
your only emperor for diet: we fat all creatures else to fat us,
and we fat ourselves for maggots: your fat king and your
lean beggar is but variable service, two dishes, but to one
table: that's the end.
   *King.* Alas, alas!
   *Ham.* A man may fish with the worm that hath eat of a
king, and eat of the fish that hath fed of that worm.        30

*King*. What dost thou mean by this?

*Ham*. Nothing but to show you how a king may go a pro
gress through the guts of a beggar.

*King*. Where is Polonius?

*Ham*. In heaven; send thither to see: if your messenger
find him not there, seek him i' the other place yourself.   But
indeed, if you find him not within this month, you shall nose
him as you go up the stairs into the lobby.                    39

*King*. Go seek him there.            [*To some Attendants.*

*Ham*. He will stay till you come.   [*Exeunt Attendants.*

*King*. Hamlet, this deed, for thine especial safety,—
Which we do tender, as we dearly grieve
For that which thou hast done,—must send thee hence
With fiery quickness: therefore prepare thyself;
The bark is ready, and the wind at help,
The associates tend, and every thing is bent
For England.

*Ham*.          For England!

*King*.                          Ay, Hamlet.

*Ham*.                                    Good.

*King*. So is it, if thou knew'st our purposes.

*Ham*. I see a cherub that sees them.   But, come; for England!   Farewell, dear mother.                                51

*King*. Thy loving father, Hamlet.

*Ham*. My mother: father and mother is man and wife;
man and wife is one flesh; and so, my mother.   Come, for
England!                                                  [*Exit.*

*King*. Follow him at foot; tempt him with speed aboard;
Delay it not; I 'll have him hence to-night:
Away! for every thing is seal'd and done
That else leans on the affair: pray you, make haste.

          [*Exeunt Rosencrantz and Guildenstern.*

And, England, if my love thou hold'st at aught—
As my great power thereof may give thee sense,
Since yet thy cicatrice looks raw and red
After the Danish sword, and thy free awe
Pays homage to us—thou mayst not coldly set
Our sovereign process; which imports at full,
By letters congruing to that effect,
The present death of Hamlet.   Do it, England;
For like the hectic in my blood he rages,
And thou must cure me: till I know 't is done,                69
Howe'er my haps, my joys were ne'er begun.           [*Exit.*

SCENE IV. *A plain in Denmark.*

*Enter* FORTINBRAS, *a* Captain, *and* Soldiers, *marching.*

*For.* Go, captain, from me greet the Danish king;
Tell him that, by his license, Fortinbras
Craves the conveyance of a promised march
Over his kingdom. You know the rendezvous.
If that his majesty would aught with us,
We shall express our duty in his eye;
And let him know so.
   *Cap.*        I will do 't, my lord.
   *For.* Go softly on.   · [*Exeunt Fortinbras and Soldiers.*

*Enter* HAMLET, ROSENCRANTZ, GUILDENSTERN, *and
others.*

   *Ham.* Good sir, whose powers are these?
   *Cap.* They are of Norway, sir.             10
   *Ham.* How purposed, sir, I pray you?
   *Cap.* Against some part of Poland.
   *Ham.* Who commands them, sir?
   *Cap.* The nephew to old Norway, Fortinbras.
   *Ham.* Goes it against the main of Poland, sir,
Or for some frontier?
   *Cap.* Truly to speak, and with no addition,
We go to gain a little patch of ground
That hath in it no profit but the name.
To pay five ducats, five, I would not farm it:    20
Nor will it yield to Norway or the Pole
A ranker rate, should it be sold in fee.
   *Ham.* Why, then the Polack never will defend it.
   *Cap.* Yes, it is already garrison'd.
   *Ham.* Two thousand souls and twenty thousand ducats
Will not debate the question of this straw:
This is the imposthume of much wealth and peace,
That inward breaks, and shows no cause without
Why the man dies. I humbly thank you, sir.
   *Cap.* God be wi' you, sir.             [*Exit.*
   *Ros.*            Will 't please you go, my lord?
   *Ham.* I 'll be with you straight. Go a little before.   31
            [*Exeunt all except Hamlet.*
How all occasions do inform against me,
And spur my dull revenge! What is a man,
If his chief good and market of his time
Be but to sleep and feed? a beast, no more.

Sure, he that made us with such large discourse,
Looking before and after, gave us not
That capability and god-like reason
To fust in us unused.  Now, whether it be
Bestial oblivion, or some craven scruple          40
Of thinking too precisely on the event,
A thought which, quarter'd, hath but one part wisdom
And ever three parts coward, I do not know
Why yet I live to say 'This thing's to do';
Sith I have cause and will and strength and means
To do 't.  Examples gross as earth exhort me:
Witness this army of such mass and charge
Led by a delicate and tender prince,
Whose spirit with divine ambition puff'd
Makes mouths at the invisible event,          50
Exposing what is mortal and unsure
To all that fortune, death and danger dare,
Even for an egg-shell.  Rightly to be great
Is not to stir without great argument,
But greatly to find quarrel in a straw
When honour's at the stake.  How stand I then,
That have a father kill'd, a mother stain'd,
Excitements of my reason and my blood,
And let all sleep? while, to my shame, I see
The imminent death of twenty thousand men,          60
That, for a fantasy and trick of fame,
Go to their graves like beds, fight for a plot
Whereon the numbers cannot try the cause,
Which is not tomb enough and continent
To hide the slain?  O, from this time forth,
My thoughts be bloody, or be nothing worth!          [*Exit.*

SCENE V.  *Elsinore.  A room in the castle.*

*Enter* QUEEN, HORATIO, *and a* Gentleman.

*Queen.*  I will not speak with her.
   *Gent.*  She is importunate, indeed distract:
Her mood will needs be pitied.
   *Queen.*                                What would she have?
   *Gent.*  She speaks much of her father; says she hears
There's tricks i' the world; and hems, and beats her heart;
Spurns enviously at straws; speaks things in doubt,
That carry but half sense: her speech is nothing,
Yet the unshaped use of it doth move

The hearers to collection; they aim at it,
And botch the words up fit to their own thoughts;          10
Which, as her winks, and nods, and gestures yield them,
Indeed would make one think there might be thought,
Though nothing sure, yet much unhappily.
 *Hor.* 'T were good she were spoken with; for she may
  strew
Dangerous conjectures in ill-breeding minds.
 *Queen.* Let her come in.     [*Exit Horatio.*
To my sick soul, as sin's true nature is,
Each toy seems prologue to some great amiss:
So full of artless jealousy is guilt,
It spills itself in fearing to be spilt.                    20

   *Re-enter* HORATIO, *with* OPHELIA.

 *Oph.* Where is the beauteous majesty of Denmark?
 *Queen.* How now, Ophelia!
 *Oph.* [*Sings*] How should I your true love know
    From another one?
   By his cockle hat and staff,
    And his sandal shoon.
 *Queen.* Alas, sweet lady, what imports this song?
 *Oph.* Say you? nay, pray you, mark.
 [*Sings*] He is dead and gone, lady,
    He is dead and gone;                    30
   At his head a grass-green turf,
    At his heels a stone.
 *Queen.* Nay, but, Ophelia,—
 *Oph.* Pray you, mark.
 [*Sings*] White his shroud as the mountain snow,—

    *Enter* KING.

 *Queen.* Alas, look here, my lord.
 *Oph.* [*Sings.*] Larded with sweet flowers;
   Which bewept to the grave did go
    With true-love showers.
 *King.* How do you, pretty lady?                    40
 *Oph.* Well, God dild you! They say the owl was a baker's
daughter. Lord, we know what we are, but know not what
we may be. God be at your table!
 *King.* Conceit upon her father.
 *Oph.* Pray you, let's have no words of this; but when they
ask you what it means, say you this:

[*Sings*] To-morrow is Saint Valentine's day,
    All in the morning betime,
    And I a maid at your window,        50
    To be your Valentine.
  *King.* How long hath she been thus?
  *Oph.* I hope all will be well. We must be patient: but I
cannot choose but weep, to think they should lay him i' the
cold ground. My brother shall know of it: and so I thank
you for your good counsel. Come, my coach! Good night,
ladies; good night, sweet ladies; good night, good night.
                                     [*Exit.*
  *King.* Follow her close; give her good watch, I pray you.
                            [*Exit Horatio.*
O, this is the poison of deep grief; it springs
All from her father's death. O Gertrude, Gertrude,
When sorrows come, they come not single spies,
But in battalions. First, her father slain:
Next, your son gone; and he most violent author      80
Of his own just remove: the people muddied,
Thick and unwholesome in their thoughts and whispers,
For good Polonius' death; and we have done but greenly,
In hugger-mugger to inter him: poor Ophelia
Divided from herself and her fair judgement,
Without the which we are pictures, or mere beasts:
Last, and as much containing as all these,
Her brother is in secret come from France;
Feeds on his wonder, keeps himself in clouds,
And wants not buzzers to infect his ear        90
With pestilent speeches of his father's death;
Wherein necessity, of matter beggar'd,
Will nothing stick our person to arraign
In ear and ear. O my dear Gertrude, this,
Like to a murdering-piece, in many places
Gives me superfluous death.        [*A noise within.*
  *Queen.*               Alack, what noise is this?
  *King.* Where are my Switzers? Let them guard the door.

           *Enter another* Gentleman.

What is the matter?
  *Gent.*            Save yourself, my lord:
The ocean, overpeering of his list,
Eats not the flats with more impetuous haste      100
Than young Laertes, in a riotous head,
O'erbears your officers. The rabble call him lord;
And, as the world were now but to begin,

Antiquity forgot, custom not known,
The ratifiers and props of every word,
They cry 'Choose we: Laertes shall be king':
Caps, hands, and tongues, applaud it to the clouds:
'Laertes shall be king, Laertes king!'
 *Queen.* How cheerfully on the false trail they cry!
O, this is counter, you false Danish dogs!   110
 *King.* The doors are broke.    [*Noise within.*

   *Enter* LAERTES, *armed;* Danes *following.*

 *Laer.* Where is this king? Sirs, stand you all without.
 *Danes.* No, let's come in.
 *Laer.*     I pray you, give me leave.
 *Danes.* We will, we will.  [*They retire without the door.*
 *Laer.* I thank you: keep the door. O thou vile king,
Give me my father!
 *Queen.*    Calmly, good Laertes.
 *Laer.* That drop of blood that's calm proclaims me bas-
  tard,
Cries cuckold to my father, brands the harlot
Even here, between the chaste unsmirched brows
Of my true mother.
 *King.*    What is the cause, Laertes,  120
That thy rebellion looks so giant-like?
Let him go, Gertrude; do not fear our person:
There's such divinity doth hedge a king,
That treason can but peep to what it would,
Acts little of his will. Tell me, Laertes,
Why thou art thus incensed. Let him go, Gertrude.
Speak, man.
 *Laer.* Where is my father?
 *King.*    Dead.
 *Queen.*      But not by him.
 *King.* Let him demand his fill.
 *Laer.* How came he dead? I'll not be juggled with: 130
To hell, allegiance! vows, to the blackest devil!
Conscience and grace, to the profoundest pit!
I dare damnation. To this point I stand,
That both the worlds I give to negligence,
Let come what comes; only I'll be revenged
Most throughly for my father.
 *King.*     Who shall stay you?
 *Laer.* My will, not all the world:
And for my means, I'll husband them so well,
They shall go far with little.

*King.*　　　　　　　　　　Good Laertes,
If you desire to know the certainty　　　　　　　140
Of your dear father's death, is 't writ in your revenge,
That, swoopstake, you will draw both friend and foe,
Winner and loser?
　　*Laer.* None but his enemies.
　　*King.*　　　　　　　　Will you know them then?
　　*Laer.* To his good friends thus wide I 'll ope my arms;
And like the kind life-rendering pelican,
Repast them with my blood.
　　*King.*　　　　　　　Why, now you speak
Like a good child and a true gentleman.
That I am guiltless of your father's death,
And am most sensibly in grief for it,　　　　　　150
It shall as level to your judgement pierce
As day does to your eye.
　　*Danes.* [*Within*] Let her come in.
　　*Laer.* How now! what noise is that?

### Re-enter OPHELIA.

O heat, dry up my brains! tears seven times salt,
Burn out the sense and virtue of mine eye!
By heaven, thy madness shall be paid with weight,
Till our scale turn the beam. O rose of May!
Dear maid, kind sister, sweet Ophelia!
O heavens! is 't possible, a young maid's wits
Should be as mortal as an old man's life?　　　　160
Nature is fine in love, and where 't is fine,
It sends some precious instance of itself
After the thing it loves.
　　*Oph.* [*Sings*]
　　　　　They bore him barefaced on the bier;
　　　　　　Hey non nonny, nonny, hey nonny;
　　　　　And in his grave rain'd many a tear:—
Fare you well, my dove!
　　*Laer.* Hadst thou thy wits, and didst persuade revenge,
It could not move thus.
　　*Oph.* [*Sings*] You must sing a-down a-down,
　　　　　An you call him a-down-a.　　　　　171
O, how the wheel becomes it! It is the false steward, that
stole his master's daughter.
　　*Laer.* This nothing 's more than matter.
　　*Oph.* There 's rosemary, that 's for remembrance; pray,
love, remember: and there is pansies, that 's for thoughts.

*Laer.* A document in madness, thoughts and remembrance
fitted.                                                  179
*Oph.* There's fennel for you, and columbines: there's rue
for you; and here's some for me: we may call it herb-grace
o' Sundays: O, you must wear your rue with a difference.
There's a daisy: I would give you some violets, but they
withered all when my father died: they say he made a good
end,—
    [*Sings*] For bonny sweet Robin is all my joy.
*Laer.* Thought and affliction, passion, hell itself,
She turns to favour and to prettiness.
    *Oph.* [*Sings*] And will he not come again?          190
            And will he not come again?
                No, no, he is dead:
                Go to thy death-bed:
            He never will come again.

            His beard was as white as snow,
            All flaxen was his poll:
                He is gone, he is gone,
                And we cast away moan:
            God ha' mercy on his soul!
And of all Christian souls, I pray God.   God be wi' ye.
                                                   [*Exit.*
    *Laer.* Do you see this, O God?                       201
    *King.* Laertes, I must commune with your grief,
Or you deny me right.   Go but apart,
Make choice of whom your wisest friends you will,
And they shall hear and judge 'twixt you and me:
If by direct or by collateral hand
They find us touch'd, we will our kingdom give,
Our crown, our life, and all that we call ours,
To you in satisfaction; but if not,
Be you content to lend your patience to us,               210
And we shall jointly labour with your soul
To give it due content.
    *Laer.*                Let this be so;
His means of death, his obscure burial—
No trophy, sword, nor hatchment o'er his bones,
No noble rite nor formal ostentation—
Cry to be heard, as 't were from heaven to earth,
That I must call 't in question.
    *King.*                    So you shall;
And where the offence is let the great axe fall.
I pray you, go with me.                         [*Exeunt.*

SCENE VI. *Another room in the castle.*

*Enter* HORATIO *and a* Servant.

*Hor.* What are they that would speak with me?

*Serv.* Sea-faring men, sir: they say they have letters for you.

*Hor.* Let them come in.                    [*Exit servant.*
I do not know from what part of the world
I should be greeted, if not from lord Hamlet.

*Enter* Sailors.

*First Sailor.* God bless you, sir.

*Hor.* Let him bless thee too.

*First Sailor.* He shall, sir, an 't please him. There's a letter for you, sir; it comes from the ambassador that was bound for England; if your name be Horatio, as I am let to know it is.                    11

*Hor.* [*Reads*] 'Horatio, when thou shalt have overlooked this, give these fellows some means to the king: they have letters for him. Ere we were two days old at sea, a pirate of very warlike appointment gave us chase. Finding ourselves too slow of sail, we put on a compelled valour, and in the grapple I boarded them: on the instant they got clear of our ship; so I alone became their prisoner. They have dealt with me like thieves of mercy: but they knew what they did; I am to do a good turn for them. Let the king have the letters I have sent; and repair thou to me with as much speed as thou wouldst fly death. I have words to speak in thine ear will make thee dumb; yet are they much too light for the bore of the matter. These good fellows will bring thee where I am. Rosencrantz and Guildenstern hold their course for England: of them I have much to tell thee. Farewell.                    30

'He that thou knowest thine, HAMLET.'
Come, I will make you way for these your letters;
And do 't the speedier, that you may direct me
To him from whom you brought them.          [*Exeunt.*

SCENE VII. *Another room in the castle.*

*Enter* KING *and* LAERTES.

*King.* Now must your conscience my acquittance seal,
And you must put me in your heart for friend,
Sith you have heard, and with a knowing ear,
That he which hath your noble father slain
Pursued my life.

   *Laer.*        It well appears: but tell me
Why you proceeded not against these feats,
So crimeful and so capital in nature,
As by your safety, wisdom, all things else,
You mainly were stirr'd up.
   *King.*        O, for two special reasons;
Which may to you, perhaps, seem much unsinew'd,    10
But yet to me they are strong.  The queen his mother
Lives almost by his looks; and for myself—
My virtue or my plague, be it either which—
She's so conjunctive to my life and soul,
That, as the star moves not but in his sphere,
I could not but by her.  The other motive,
Why to a public count I might not go,
Is the great love the general gender bear him;
Who, dipping all his faults in their affection,
Would, like the spring that turneth wood to stone,    20
Convert his gyves to graces; so that my arrows,
Too slightly timber'd for so loud a wind,
Would have reverted to my bow again,
And not where I had aim'd them.
   *Laer.* And so have I a noble father lost;
A sister driven into desperate terms,
Whose worth, if praises may go back again,
Stood challenger on mount of all the age
For her perfections: but my revenge will come.
   *King.* Break not your sleeps for that: you must not think
That we are made of stuff so flat and dull    31
That we can let our beard be shook with danger
And think it pastime.  You shortly shall hear more:
I loved your father, and we love ourself;
And that, I hope, will teach you to imagine—

               *Enter a* Messenger.

How now! what news?
   *Mess.*        Letters, my lord, from Hamlet:
This to your majesty; this to the queen.
   *King.* From Hamlet! who brought them?
   *Mess.* Sailors, my lord, they say; I saw them not:
They were given me by Claudio; he received them    40
Of him that brought them.
   *King.*        Laertes, you shall hear them.
Leave us.                      *[Exit Messenger.*
   [*Reads*] 'High and mighty, You shall know I am set
naked on your kingdom.  To-morrow shall I beg leave to

see your kingly eyes: when I shall, first asking your pardon
thereunto, recount the occasion of my sudden and more
strange return.                         'HAMLET.'
What should this mean?   Are all the rest come back?      50
Or is it some abuse, and no such thing?
    *Laer.* Know you the hand?
    *King.*                    'T is Hamlet's character.   'Naked!'
And in a postscript here, he says 'alone'.
Can you advise me?
    *Laer.* I 'm lost in it, my lord.   But let him come;
It warms the very sickness in my heart,
That I shall live and tell him to his teeth,
'Thus didest thou'.
    *King.*               If it be so, Laertes—
As how should it be so? how otherwise?—
Will you be ruled by me?
    *Laer.*                 Ay, my lord;             60
So you will not o'errule me to a peace.
    *King.* To thine own peace.   If he be now return'd,
As checking at his voyage, and that he means
No more to undertake it, I will work him
To an exploit, now ripe in my device,
Under the which he shall not choose but fall:
And for his death no wind of blame shall breathe,
But even his mother shall uncharge the practice
And call it accident.
    *Laer.*               My lord, I will be ruled;
The rather, if you could devise it so             70
That I might be the organ.
    *King.*                  It falls right.
You have been talk'd of since your travel much,
And that in Hamlet's hearing, for a quality
Wherein, they say, you shine: your sum of parts
Did not together pluck such envy from him
As did that one, and that, in my regard,
Of the unworthiest siege.
    *Laer.*               What part is that, my lord?
    *King.* A very riband in the cap of youth,
Yet needful too; for youth no less becomes
The light and careless livery that it wears             80
Than settled age his sables and his weeds,
Importing health and graveness.   Two months since,
Here was a gentleman of Normandy:—
I 've seen myself, and served against, the French,
And they can well on horseback: but this gallant

Had witchcraft in't; he grew unto his seat;
And to such wondrous doing brought his horse,
As had he been incorpsed and demi-natured
With the brave beast: so far he topp'd my thought,
That I, in forgery of shapes and tricks,     90
Come short of what he did.
    *Laer.*            A Norman was't?
    *King.* A Norman.
    *Laer.* Upon my life, Lamond.
    *King.*           The very same.
    *Laer.* I know him well: he is the brooch indeed
And gem of all the nation.
    *King.* He made confession of you,
And gave you such a masterly report
For art and exercise in your defence
And for your rapier most especial,
That he cried out, 't would be a sight indeed,     100
If one could match you: the scrimers of their nation,
He swore, had neither motion, guard, nor eye
If you opposed them. Sir, this report of his
Did Hamlet so envenom with his envy
That he could nothing do but wish and beg
Your sudden coming o'er, to play with him.
Now, out of this,—
    *Laer.* What out of this, my lord?
    *King.* Laertes, was your father dear to you?
Or are you like the painting of a sorrow,
A face without a heart?
    *Laer.*          Why ask you this?     110
    *King.* Not that I think you did not love your father;
But that I know love is begun by time;
And that I see, in passages of proof,
Time qualifies the spark and fire of it.
There lives within the very flame of love
A kind of wick or snuff that will abate it;
And nothing is at a like goodness still;
For goodness, growing to a plurisy,
Dies in his own too much: that we would do,
We should do when we would; for this 'would' changes 120
And hath abatements and delays as many
As there are tongues, are hands, are accidents;
And then this 'should' is like a spendthrift's sigh,
That hurts by easing. But, to the quick o' the ulcer:—
*Hamlet comes back:* what would you undertake,
*To show yourself* your father's son in deed

More than in words?
    *Laer.*             To cut his throat i' the church.
    *King.* No place, indeed, should murder sanctuarize;
Revenge should have no bounds.   But, good Laertes,
Will you do this, keep close within your chamber.        130
Hamlet return'd shall know you are come home:
We'll put on those shall praise your excellence
And set a double varnish on the fame
The Frenchman gave you, bring you in fine together
And wager on your heads: he, being remiss,
Most generous and free from all contriving,
Will not peruse the foils; so that, with ease,
Or with a little shuffling, you may choose
A sword unbated, and in a pass of practice
Requite him for your father.
    *Laer.*          I will do't:        140
And, for that purpose, I'll anoint my sword.
I bought an unction of a mountebank,
So mortal that, but dip a knife in it,
Where it draws blood no cataplasm so rare,
Collected from all simples that have virtue
Under the moon, can save the thing from death
That is but scratch'd withal: I'll touch my point
With this contagion, that, if I gall him slightly,
It may be death.
    *King.*      Let's further think of this;
Weigh what convenience both of time and means        150
May fit us to our shape: if this should fail,
And that our drift look through our bad performance,
'T were better not assay'd: therefore this project
Should have a back or second, that might hold,
If this should blast in proof.   Soft! let me see:
We'll make a solemn wager on your cunnings:
I ha't:
When in your motion you are hot and dry—
As make your bouts more violent to that end—
And that he calls for drink, I'll have prepared him        160
A chalice for the nonce, whereon but sipping,
If he by chance escape your venom'd stuck,
Our purpose may hold there.

            *Enter* QUEEN.

               How now, sweet queen!
    *Queen.* One woe doth tread upon another's heel,
So fast they follow: your sister's drown'd, Laertes.

*Laer.* Drown'd! O, where?

. *Queen.* There is a willow grows aslant a brook,
That shows his hoar leaves in the glassy stream;
There with fantastic garlands did she come
Of crow-flowers, nettles, daisies, and long purples       170
That liberal shepherds give a grosser name,                    .
But our cold maids do dead men's fingers call them:
There, on the pendent boughs her coronet weeds
Clambering to hang, an envious sliver broke;
When down her weedy trophies and herself
Fell in the weeping brook.  Her clothes spread wide;
And, mermaid-like, awhile they bore her up:
Which time she chanted snatches of old tunes;
As one incapable of her own distress,
Or like a creature native and indued                       180
Unto that element: but long it could not be
Till that her garments, heavy with their drink,
Pull'd the poor wretch from her melodious lay
To muddy death.
    *Laer.*              Alas, then, she is drown'd?
    *Queen.* Drown'd, drown'd.
    *Laer.* Too much of water hast thou, poor Ophelia,
And therefore I forbid my tears: but yet
It is our trick; nature her custom holds,
Let shame say what it will: when these are gone,
The woman will be out.  Adieu, my lord:                    190
I have a speech of fire, that fain would blaze,
But that this folly douts it.                       [*Exit.*
    *King.*                    Let's follow, Gertrude:
How much I had to do to calm his rage!
Now fear I this will give it start again;
Therefore let's follow.                       [*Exeunt.*

----

## ACT V.

### Scene I.  *A churchyard.*

#### Enter *two* Clowns, *with spades, &c.*

*First Clo.* Is she to be buried in Christian burial that wil-
fully seeks her own salvation?

*Sec. Clo.* I tell thee she is: and therefore make her grave
*straight:* the crowner hath sat on her, and finds it Christian
*burial.*

*First Clo.* How can that be, unless she drowned herself in her own defence?

*Sec. Clo.* Why, 't is found so.

*First Clo.* It must be 'se offendendo'; it cannot be else. For here lies the point: if I drown myself wittingly, it argues an act: and an act hath three branches; it is, to act, to do, and to perform: argal, she drowned herself wittingly.

*Sec. Clo.* Nay, but hear you, goodman delver,—

*First Clo.* Give me leave. Here lies the water; good: here stands the man; good: if the man go to this water, and drown himself, it is, will he, nill he, he goes,—mark you that; but if the water come to him and drown him, he drowns not himself: argal, he that is not guilty of his own death shortens not his own life.

*Sec. Clo.* But is this law?

*First Clo.* Ay, marry, is 't; crowner's quest law.

*Sec. Clo.* Will you ha' the truth on 't? If this had not been a gentlewoman, she should have been buried out o' Christian burial.

*First Clo.* Why, there thou say'st: and the more pity that great folk should have countenance in this world to drown or hang themselves, more than their even Christian. Come, my spade. There is no ancient gentlemen but gardeners, ditchers, and grave-makers: they hold up Adam's profession.

*Sec. Clo.* Was he a gentleman?

*First Clo.* 'A was the first that ever bore arms.

*Sec. Clo.* Why, he had none.                                    39

*First Clo.* What, art a heathen? How dost thou understand the Scripture? The Scripture says 'Adam digged': could he dig without arms? I 'll put another question to thee: if thou answerest me not to the purpose, confess thyself—

*Sec. Clo.* Go to.

*First Clo.* What is he that builds stronger than either the mason, the shipwright, or the carpenter?

*Sec. Clo.* The gallows-maker; for that frame outlives a thousand tenants.                                              50

*First Clo.* I like thy wit well, in good faith: the gallows does well; but how does it well? it does well to those who do ill: now thou dost ill to say the gallows is built stronger than the church: argal, the gallows may do well to thee. To 't again, come.

*Sec. Clo.* 'Who builds stronger than a mason, a shipwright, or a carpenter?'

*First Clo.* Ay, tell me that, and unyoke.

*Sec. Clo.* Marry, now I can tell.                    60
*First Clo.* To 't.
*Sec. Clo.* Mass, I cannot tell.


*Enter* HAMLET *and* HORATIO, *at a distance.*

*First Clo.* Cudgel thy brains no more about it, for your
dull ass will not mend his pace with beating; and, when you
are asked this question next, say 'a grave-maker': the houses
that he makes last till doomsday. Go, get thee to Yaughan:
fetch me a stoup of liquor.          .          [*Exit Sec. Clown.*
                                        [*He digs, and sings.*
>    In youth, when I did love, did love,
>        Methought it was very sweet,                    70
>    To contract, O, the time, for, ah, my behove,
>        O, methought, there was nothing meet.

*Ham.* Has this fellow no feeling of his business, that he
sings at grave-making?
*Hor.* Custom hath made it in him a property of easiness.
*Ham.* 'T is e'en so: the hand of little employment hath the
daintier sense.
*First Clo.*     [*Sings*]
>    But age, with his stealing steps
>        Hath claw'd me in his clutch,                    80
>    And hath shipped me intil the land,
>        As if I had never been such.

                                        [*Throws up a skull.*
*Ham.* That skull had a tongue in it, and could sing once:
how the knave jowls it to the ground, as if it were Cain's jaw-
bone, that did the first murder! It might be the pate of a
politician, which this ass now o'er-reaches; one that would
circumvent God, might it not?
*Hor.* It might, my lord.                    89
*Ham.* Or of a courtier: which could say 'Good morrow,
sweet lord! How dost thou, good lord?' This might be my
lord such-a-one,that praised my lord such-a-one's horse, when
he meant to beg it; might it not?
*Hor.* Ay, my lord.
*Ham.* Why, e'en so: and now my Lady Worm's; chapless,
and knocked about the mazzard with a sexton's spade: here's
fine revolution, an we had the trick to see 't. Did these bones
cost no more the breeding, but to play at loggats with 'em?
mine ache to think on 't.                    101

*First Clo.* [*Sings*]
    A pick-axe, and a spade, a spade,
      For and a shrouding sheet:
    O, a pit of clay for to be made
      For such a guest is meet.
                        [*Throws up another skull.*

*Ham.* There's another: why may not that be the skull of a lawyer? Where be his quiddities now, his quillets, his cases, his tenures, and his tricks? why does he suffer this rude knave now to knock him about the sconce with a dirty shovel, and will not tell him of his action of battery? Hum! This fellow might be in's time a great buyer of land, with his statutes, his recognizances, his fines, his double vouchers, his recoveries: is this the fine of his fines, and the recovery of his recoveries, to have his fine pate full of fine dirt? will his vouchers vouch him no more of his purchases, and double ones too, than the length and breadth of a pair of indentures? The very conveyances of his lands will hardly lie in this box; and must the inheritor himself have no more, ha?

*Hor.* Not a jot more, my lord.

*Ham.* Is not parchment made of sheep-skins?

*Hor.* Ay, my lord, and of calf-skins too.

*Ham.* They are sheep and calves which seek out assurance in that. I will speak to this fellow. Whose grave's this, sirrah?

*First Clo.* Mine, sir.
[*Sings*] O, a pit of clay for to be made
     For such a guest is meet.           130

*Ham.* I think it be thine, indeed; for thou liest in't.

*First Clo.* You lie out on't, sir, and therefore it is not yours: for my part, I do not lie in't, and yet it is mine.

*Ham.* Thou dost lie in't, to be in't and say it is thine: 'tis for the dead, not for the quick; therefore thou liest.

*First Clo.* 'Tis a quick lie, sir; 'twill away again, from me to you.          140

*Ham.* What man dost thou dig it for?

*First Clo.* For no man, sir.

*Ham.* What woman, then?

*First Clo.* For none, neither.

*Ham.* Who is to be buried in't?

*First Clo.* One that was a woman, sir; but, rest her soul, she's dead.

*Ham.* How absolute the knave is! we must speak by the card, or equivocation will undo us. By the Lord, Horatio, these three years I have taken note of it; the age is grown

so picked that the toe of the peasant comes so near the heel
of the courtier, he galls his kibe.   How long hast thou been
a grave-maker?

*First Clo.* Of all the days i' the year, I came to 't that day
that our last king Hamlet overcame Fortinbras.

*Ham.* How long is that since?

*First Clo.* Cannot you tell that? every fool can tell that:
it was the very day that young Hamlet was born; he that is
mad, and sent into England.

*Ham.* Ay, marry, why was he sent into England?

*First Clo.* Why, because he was mad: he shall recover his
wits there; or, if he do not, it's no great matter there.

*Ham.* Why?

*First Clo.* 'T will not be seen in him there; there the men
are as mad as he.                                        170

*Ham.* How came he mad?

*First Clo.* Very strangely, they say.

*Ham.* How strangely?

*First Clo.* Faith, e'en with losing his wits.

*Ham.* Upon what ground?

*First Clo.* Why, here in Denmark: I have been sexton
here, man and boy, thirty years.

*Ham.* How long will a man lie i' the earth ere he rot?  179

*First Clo.* I' faith, if he be not rotten before he die, he
will last you some eight year or nine year: a tanner will last
you nine year.

*Ham.* Why he more than another?

*First Clo.* Why, sir, his hide is so tanned with his trade,
that he will keep out water a great while; and your water is
a sore decayer of your dead body.   Here's a skull now; this
skull has lain in the earth three and twenty years.      191

*Ham.* Whose was it?

*First Clo.* A mad fellow's it was: whose do you think it
was?

*Ham.* Nay, I know not.

*First Clo.* A pestilence on him for a mad rogue! a' poured
a flagon of Rhenish on my head once.   This same skull, sir,
was Yorick's skull, the king's jester.

*Ham.* This?                                             200

*First Clo.* E'en that.

*Ham.* Let me see.                          [*Takes the skull.*]
Alas, poor Yorick!   I knew him, Horatio: a fellow of infinite
jest, of most excellent fancy: he hath borne me on his back
*a thousand times;* and now, how abhorred in my imagina-
*tion it is! my gorge* rises at it.   Here hung those lips that 1

have kissed I know not how oft. Where be your gibes now?
your gambols? your songs? your flashes of merriment, that
were wont to set the table on a roar? Not one now, to mock
your own grinning? quite chap-fallen? Now get you to my
lady's chamber, and tell her, let her paint an inch thick, to
this favour she must come; make her laugh at that. Prithee,
Horatio, tell me one thing.

*Hor.* What's that, my lord?

*Ham.* Dost thou think Alexander looked o' this fashion
i' the earth?

*Hor.* E'en so. 220

*Ham.* And smelt so? pah!  *[Puts down the skull.*

*Hor.* E'en so, my lord.

*Ham.* To what base uses we may return, Horatio! Why
may not imagination trace the noble dust of Alexander, till
he find it stopping a bung-hole?

*Hor.* 'T were to consider too curiously, to consider so.

*Ham.* No, faith, not a jot; but to follow him thither with
modesty enough, and likelihood to lead it: as thus: Alexander died, Alexander was buried, Alexander returneth into
dust; the dust is earth; of earth we make loam; and why of
that loam, whereto he was converted, might they not stop a
beer-barrel?

> Imperious Cæsar, dead and turn'd to clay,
> Might stop a hole to keep the wind away:
> O, that that earth, which kept the world in awe,
> Should patch a wall to expel the winter's flaw!

But soft! but soft! aside: here comes the king,

*Enter* Priests, &*c. in procession; the Corpse of* OPHELIA,
LAERTES *and* Mourners *following;* KING, QUEEN, *their
trains,* &*c.*

The queen, the courtiers: who is this they follow?
And with such maimed rites? This doth betoken
The corse they follow did with desperate hand
Fordo it own life: 't was of some estate.
Couch we awhile, and mark.  *[Retiring with Horatio.*

*Laer.* What ceremony else?

*Ham.*  That is Laertes,
A very noble youth: mark.

*Laer.* What ceremony else?

*First Priest.* Her obsequies have been as far enlarged
As we have warranty: her death was doubtful; 250
And, but that great command o'ersways the order,
She should in ground unsanctified have lodged

Till the last trumpet; for charitable prayers,
Shards, flints and pebbles should be thrown on her:
Yet here she is allow'd her virgin crants,
Her maiden strewments and the bringing home
Of bell and burial.
   *Laer.* Must there no more be done?
   *First Priest.*              No more be done:
We should profane the service of the dead
To sing a requiem and such rest to her         260
As to peace-parted souls.
   *Laer.*           Lay her i' the earth:
And from her fair and unpolluted flesh
May violets spring! I tell thee, churlish priest,
A ministering angel shall my sister be,
When thou liest howling.
   *Ham.*          What, the fair Ophelia!
   *Queen.* Sweets to the sweet: farewell! [*Scattering flowers.*
I hoped thou shouldst have been my Hamlet's wife;
I thought thy bride-bed to have deck'd, sweet maid,
And not have strew'd thy grave.
   *Laer.*          O, treble woe
Fall ten times treble on that cursed head,     270
Whose wicked deed thy most ingenious sense
Deprived thee of! Hold off the earth awhile,
Till I have caught her once more in mine arms:
                      [*Leaps into the grave.*
Now pile your dust upon the quick and dead,
Till of this flat a mountain you have made,
To o'ertop old Pelion, or the skyish head
Of blue Olympus.
   *Ham.* [*Advancing*] What is he whose grief
Bears such an emphasis? whose phrase of sorrow
Conjures the wandering stars, and makes them stand
Like wonder-wounded heroes? This is I,     280
Hamlet the Dane.         [*Leaps into the grave.*
   *Laer.*       The devil take thy soul!
                      [*Grappling with him.*
   *Ham.* Thou pray'st not well.
I prithee, take thy fingers from my throat;
For, though I am not splenitive and rash,
Yet have I something in me dangerous,
Which let thy wiseness fear: hold off thy hand.
   *King.* Pluck them asunder.
   *Queen.*         Hamlet, Hamlet!
   *All.* Gentlemen,—

*Hor.*          Good my lord, be quiet.
      [*The Attendants part them, and they come out of the*
                                                      *grave.*
*Ham.* Why, I will fight with him upon this theme
Until my eyelids will no longer wag.                    290
      *Queen.* O my son, what theme?
      *Ham.* I loved Ophelia: forty thousand brothers
Could not, with all their quantity of love,
Make up my sum.   What wilt thou do for her?
      *King.* O, he is mad, Laertes.
      *Queen.* For love of God, forbear him.
      *Ham.* 'S wounds, show me what thou'lt do:
Woo't weep? woo't fight? woo't fast? woo't tear thyself?
Woo't drink up eisel? eat a crocodile?
I'll do't.   Dost thou come here to whine?            300
To outface me with leaping in her grave?
Be buried quick with her, and so will I:
And, if thou prate of mountains, let them throw
Millions of acres on us, till our ground,
Singeing his pate against the burning zone,
Make Ossa like a wart!   Nay, an thou'lt mouth,
I'll rant as well as thou.
      *Queen.*          This is mere madness:
And thus awhile the fit will work on him;
Anon, as patient as the female dove,
When that her golden couplets are disclosed,           310
His silence will sit drooping.
      *Ham.*          Hear you, sir;
What is the reason that you use me thus?
I loved you ever: but it is no matter;
Let Hercules himself do what he may,
The cat will mew and dog will have his day.          [*Exit.*
      *King.* I pray you, good Horatio, wait upon him.
                                        [*Exit Horatio.*
[*To Laertes*] Strengthen your patience in our last night's
      speech;
We'll put the matter to the present push.
Good Gertrude, set some watch over your son.
This grave shall have a living monument:               320
An hour of quiet shortly shall we see;
Till then, in patience our proceeding be.          [*Exeunt.*

### SCENE II.  *A hall in the castle.*

*Enter* HAMLET *and* HORATIO.

*Ham.*  So much for this, sir: now shall you see the other;
You do remember all the circumstance?
   *Hor.*  Remember it, my lord!
   *Ham.*  Sir, in my heart there was a kind of fighting,
That would not let me sleep: methought I lay
Worse than the mutines in the bilboes.  Rashly—
And praised be rashness for it, let us know,
Our indiscretion sometimes serves us well,
When our deep plots do pall: and that should teach us
There's a divinity that shapes our ends,                          10
Rough-hew them how we will,—
   *Hor.*                              That is most certain.
   *Ham.*  —Up from my cabin,
My sea-gown scarf'd about me, in the dark
Groped I to find out them; had my desire,
Finger'd their packet, and in fine withdrew
To mine own room again; making so bold,
My fears forgetting manners, to unseal
Their grand commission; where I found, Horatio,—
O royal knavery!—an exact command,
Larded with many several sorts of reasons                         20
Importing Denmark's health and England's too,
With, ho! such bugs and goblins in my life,
That, on the supervise, no leisure bated,
No, not to stay the grinding of the axe,
My head should be struck off.
   *Hor.*                              Is't possible?
   *Ham.*  Here's the commission: read it at more leisure.
But wilt thou hear me how I did proceed?
   *Hor.*  I beseech you.
   *Ham.*  Being thus be-netted round with villanies,—
Ere I could make a prologue to my brains,                         30
They had begun the play—I sat me down,
Devised a new commission, wrote it fair:
I once did hold it, as our statists do,
A baseness to write fair and labour'd much
How to forget that learning, but, sir, now
It did me yeoman's service: wilt thou know
The effect of what I wrote?
   *Hor.*                              Ay, good my lord.
   *Ham.*  An earnest conjuration from the king,

As England was his faithful tributary,
As love between them like the palm might flourish,     40
As peace should still her wheaten garland wear
And stand a comma 'tween their amities,
And many such-like 'As 'es of great charge,
That, on the view and knowing of these contents,
Without debatement further, more or less,
He should the bearers put to sudden death,
Not shriving-time allow'd.
    *Hor.*            How was this seal'd?
    *Ham.* Why, even in that was heaven ordinant.
I had my father's signet in my purse,
Which was the model of that Danish seal;      50
Folded the writ up in form of the other,
Subscribed it, gave't the impression, placed it safely,
The changeling never known. Now, the next day
Was our sea-fight; and what to this was sequent
Thou know'st already.
    *Hor.* So Guildenstern and Rosencrantz go to't.
    *Ham.* Why, man, they did make love to this employment;
They are not near my conscience; their defeat
Does by their own insinuation grow:
'T is dangerous when the baser nature comes      60
Between the pass and fell incensed points
Of mighty opposites.
    *Hor.*           Why, what a king is this!
    *Ham.* Does it not, think'st thee, stand me now upon—
He that hath kill'd my king and whored my mother,
Popp'd in between the election and my hopes,
Thrown out his angle for my proper life,
And with such cozenage—is't not perfect conscience,.
To quit him with this arm? and is't not to be damn'd,
To let this canker of our nature come
In further evil?      70
    *Hor.* It must be shortly known to him from England
What is the issue of the business there.
    *Ham.* It will be short: the interim is mine;
And a man's life's no more than to say 'One'.
But I am very sorry, good Horatio,
That to Laertes I forgot myself;
For, by the image of my cause, I see
The portraiture of his: I 'll court his favour:
But, sure, the bravery of his grief did put me
Into a towering passion.
    *Hor.*           Peace! who comes here?     80

*Enter* OSRIC.

*Osr.* Your lordship is right welcome back to Denmark.

*Ham.* I humbly thank you, sir.   Dost know this water-fly?

*Hor.* No, my good lord.

*Ham.* Thy state is the more gracious; for 't is a vice to know him.   He hath much land, and fertile: let a beast be lord of beasts, and his crib shall stand at the king's mess: 't is a chough; but, as I say, spacious in the possession of dirt.                                                                      90

*Osr.* Sweet lord, if your lordship were at leisure, I should impart a thing to you from his majesty.

*Ham.* I will receive it, sir, with all diligence of spirit.   Put your bonnet to his right use; 't is for the head.

*Osr.* I thank your lordship, it is very hot.

*Ham.* No, believe me, 't is very cold; the wind is northerly.

*Osr.* It is indifferent cold, my lord, indeed.              100

*Ham.* But yet methinks it is very sultry and hot for my complexion.

*Osr.* Exceedingly, my lord; it is very sultry,—as 't were,—I cannot tell how.   But, my lord, his majesty bade me signify to you that he has laid a great wager on your head: sir, this is the matter,—

*Ham.* I beseech you, remember—

                              [*Hamlet moves him to put on his hat.*

*Osr.* Nay, good my lord; for mine ease, in good faith. Sir, here is newly come to court Laertes; believe me, an absolute gentleman, full of most excellent differences, of very soft society and great showing: indeed, to speak feelingly of him, he is the card or calendar of gentry, for you shall find in him the continent of what part a gentleman would see.

*Ham.* Sir, his definement suffers no perdition in you; though, I know, to divide him inventorially would dizzy the arithmetic of memory, and yet but yaw neither, in respect of his quick sail.   But, in the verity of extolment, I take him to be a soul of great article; and his infusion of such dearth and rareness, as, to make true diction of him, his semblable is his mirror; and who else would trace him, his umbrage, nothing more.

*Osr.* Your lordship speaks most infallibly of him.

*Ham.* The concernancy, sir? why do we wrap the gentle man in our more rawer breath?

*Osr.* Sir?　　　　　　　　　　　　　　　130
*Hor.* Is't not possible to understand in another tongue?
You will do't, sir, really.

*Ham.* What imports the nomination of this gentleman?

*Osr.* Of Laertes?

*Hor.* His purse is empty already; all's golden words are
spent.

*Ham.* Of him, sir.

*Osr.* I know you are not ignorant—

*Ham.* I would you did, sir; yet, in faith, if you did, it
would not much approve me.　Well, sir?

*Osr.* You are not ignorant of what excellence Laertes is—

*Ham.* I dare not confess that, lest I should compare with
him in excellence; but, to know a man well, were to know
himself.

*Osr.* I mean, sir, for his weapon; but in the imputation
laid on him by them, in his meed he's unfellowed.　　　150

*Ham.* What's his weapon?

*Osr.* Rapier and dagger.

*Ham.* That's two of his weapons: but, well.

*Osr.* The king, sir, hath wagered with him six Barbary
horses: against the which he has imponed, as I take it,
six French rapiers and poniards, with their assigns, as girdle,
hangers, and so: three of the carriages, in faith, are very dear
to fancy, very responsive to the hilts, most delicate carriages,
and of very liberal conceit.　　　　　　　　160

*Ham.* What call you the carriages?

*Hor.* I knew you must be edified by the margent ere you
had done.

*Osr.* The carriages, sir, are the hangers.

*Ham.* The phrase would be more german to the matter,
if we could carry cannon by our sides: I would it might be
hangers till then.　But, on: six Barbary horses against six
French swords, their assigns, and three liberal-conceited
carriages; that's the French bet against the Danish.　Why
is this 'imponed', as you call it?　　　　　　171

*Osr.* The king, sir, hath laid, that in a dozen passes between yourself and him, he shall not exceed you three hits:
he hath laid on twelve for nine; and it would come to immediate trial, if your lordship would vouchsafe the answer.

*Ham.* How if I answer 'no'?

*Osr.* I mean, my lord, the opposition of your person in
trial.　　　　　　　　　　　　　　179

*Ham.* Sir, I will walk here in the hall: if it please his
majesty, 'tis the breathing time of day with me; let the foils

be brought, the gentleman willing, and the king hold his purpose, I will win for him an I can; if not, I will gain nothing but my shame and the odd hits.

*Osr.* Shall I re-deliver you e'en so?

*Ham.* To this effect, sir; after what flourish your nature will.

*Osr.* I commend my duty to your lordship.

*Ham.* Yours, yours. [*Exit Osric.*] He does well to commend it himself; there are no tongues else for's turn.

*Hor.* This lapwing runs away with the shell on his head.

*Ham.* He did comply with his dug, before he sucked it. Thus has he—and many more of the same breed that I know the drossy age dotes on—only got the tune of the time and outward habit of encounter; a kind of yesty collection, which carries them through and through the most fond and winnowed opinions; and do but blow them to their trial, the bubbles are out.

*Enter a* Lord.

*Lord.* My lord, his majesty commended him to you by young Osric, who brings back to him, that you attend him in the hall; he sends to know if your pleasure hold to play with Laertes, or that you will take longer time.

*Ham.* I am constant to my purposes; they follow the king's pleasure: if his fitness speaks, mine is ready; now or whensoever, provided I be so able as now.                    211

*Lord.* The king and queen and all are coming down.

*Ham.* In happy time.

*Lord.* The queen desires you to use some gentle entertainment to Laertes before you fall to play.

*Ham.* She well instructs me.                    [*Exit Lord.*

*Hor.* You will lose this wager, my lord.

*Ham.* I do not think so: since he went into France, I have been in continual practice; I shall win at the odds. But thou wouldst not think how ill all's here about my heart: but it is no matter.

*Hor.* Nay, good my lord,—

*Ham.* It is but foolery; but it is such a kind of gain-giving, as would perhaps trouble a woman.

*Hor.* If your mind dislike any thing, obey it: I will forestal their repair hither, and say you are not fit.                    229

*Ham.* Not a whit, we defy augury: there's a special providence in the fall of a sparrow. If it be now, 'tis not to come; if it be not to come, it will be now; if it be not now, *yet it will come:* the readiness is all: since no man knows *aught of what he leaves,* what is't to leave betimes?

*Enter* KING, QUEEN, LAERTES, Lords, OSRIC, *and*
     Attendants *with foils, &c.*

*King.* Come, Hamlet, come, and take this hand from me.
               [*The King puts Laertes' hand into Hamlet's.*
  *Ham.* Give me your pardon, sir: I 've done you wrong;
But pardon 't, as you are a gentleman.
This presence knows,
And you must needs have heard, how I am punish'd      240
With sore distraction.   What I have done,
That might your nature, honour and exception
Roughly awake, I here proclaim was madness.
Was 't Hamlet wrong'd Laertes?  Never Hamlet:
If Hamlet from himself be ta'en away,
And when he 's not himself does wrong Laertes,
Then Hamlet does it not, Hamlet denies it.
Who does it, then?   His madness: if 't be so,
Hamlet is of the faction that is wrong'd;
His madness is poor Hamlet's enemy.                  250
Sir, in this audience,
Let my disclaiming from a purposed evil
Free me so far in your most generous thoughts,
That I have shot mine arrow o'er the house,
And hurt my brother.
  *Laer.*           I am satisfied in nature,
Whose motive, in this case, should stir me most
To my revenge: but in my terms of honour
I stand aloof; and will no reconcilement,
Till by some elder masters, of known honour,
I have a voice and precedent of peace,               260
To keep my name ungored.   But till that time,
I do receive your offer'd love like love,
And will not wrong it.
  *Ham.*            I embrace it freely;
And will this brother's wager frankly play.
Give us the foils.   Come on.
  *Laer.*                  Come, one for me.
  *Ham.* I 'll be your foil, Laertes: in mine ignorance
Your skill shall, like a star i' the darkest night,
Stick fiery off indeed.
  *Laer.*          You mock me, sir.
  *Ham.* No, by this hand.
  *King.* Give them the foils, young Osric.   Cousin Hamlet,
You know the wager?                                   271
  *Ham.*                 Very well, my lord;

Your grace hath laid the odds o' the weaker side.
    *King.* I do not fear it; I have seen you both:
But since he is better'd, we have therefore odds.
    *Laer.* This is too heavy, let me see another.
    *Ham.* This likes me well. These foils have all a length?
                      [*They prepare to play.*
    *Osr.* Ay, my good lord.
    *King.* Set me the stoups of wine upon that table.
If Hamlet give the first or second hit,
Or quit in answer of the third exchange,          280
Let all the battlements their ordnance fire;
The king shall drink to Hamlet's better breath;
And in the cup an union shall he throw,
Richer than that which four successive kings
In Denmark's crown have worn. Give me the cups;
And let the kettle to the trumpet speak,
The trumpet to the cannoneer without,
The cannons to the heavens, the heavens to earth,
' Now the king drinks to Hamlet'. Come, begin:
And you, the judges, bear a wary eye.         290
    *Ham.* Come on, sir.
    *Laer.*             Come, my lord.        [*They play.*
    *Ham.*                 One.
    *Laer.*                   No.
    *Ham.*                      Judgement.
    *Osr.* A hit, a very palpable hit.
    *Laer.*                 Well; again.
    *King.* Stay; give me drink. Hamlet, this pearl is thine;
Here 's to thy health.
            [*Trumpets sound, and cannon shot off within.*
            Give him the cup.
    *Ham.* I 'll play this bout first; set it by awhile.
Come. [*They play.*] Another hit; what say you?
    *Laer.* A touch, a touch, I do confess.
    *King.* Our son shall win.
    *Queen.*               He 's fat, and scant of breath.
Here, Hamlet, take my napkin, rub thy brows:
The queen carouses to thy fortune, Hamlet.      300
    *Ham.* Good madam!
    *King.*            Gertrude, do not drink.
    *Queen.* I will, my lord; I pray you, pardon me.
    *King.* [*Aside*] It is the poison'd cup: it is too late.
    *Ham.* I dare not drink yet, madam; by and by.
    *Queen.* Come, let me wipe thy face.
    *Laer.* My lord, I 'll hit him now.

*King.*                    I do not think 't.
*Laer.* [*Aside*] And yet 't is almost 'gainst my conscience.
*Ham.* Come, for the third, Laertes: you but dally;
I pray you, pass with your best violence;
I am afeard you make a wanton of me.                    310
     *Laer.* Say you so? come on.          [*They play.*
*Osr.* Nothing, neither way.
*Laer.* Have at you now!
          [*Laertes wounds Hamlet; then, in scuffling, they
               change rapiers, and Hamlet wounds Laertes.*
*King.* Part them; they are incensed.
*Ham.* Nay, come, again.          [*The Queen falls.*
*Osr.*               Look to the queen there, ho!
*Hor.* They bleed on both sides.   How is it, my lord?
*Osr.* How is 't, Laertes?
*Laer.* Why, as a woodcock to mine own springe, Osric;
I am justly kill'd with mine own treachery.
*Ham.* How does the queen?
*King.*               She swounds to see them bleed.
*Queen.* No, no, the drink, the drink,—O my dear Hamlet,—
The drink, the drink! I am poison'd.          [*Dies.*
*Ham.* O villany!  Ho! let the door be lock'd:          322
Treachery!  Seek it out.
*Laer.* It is here, Hamlet: Hamlet, thou art slain;
No medicine in the world can do thee good;
In thee there is not half an hour of life;
The treacherous instrument is in thy hand,
Unbated and envenom'd: the foul practice
Hath turn'd itself on me; lo, here I lie,
Never to rise again: thy mother's poison'd:          330
I can no more: the king, the king's to blame.
*Ham.* The point envenom'd too!
Then, venom, to thy work.          [*Stabs the King.*
*All.* Treason! treason!
· *King.* O, yet defend me, friends; I am but hurt.
*Ham.* Here, thou incestuous, murderous, damned Dane,
Drink off this potion.   Is thy union here?
Follow my mother.          [*King dies.*
*Laer.*          He is justly served;
It is a poison temper'd by himself.
Exchange forgiveness with me, noble Hamlet:          340
Mine and my father's death come not upon thee,
Nor thine on me!          (*Dies.*
     *Ham.* Heaven make thee free of it!  I follow thee.
I am dead, Horatio.   Wretched queen, adieu!

You that look pale and tremble at this chance,
That are but mutes or audience to this act,
Had I but time—as this fell sergeant, death,
Is strict in his arrest—O, I could tell you—
But let it be.   Horatio, I am dead;
Thou livest; report me and my cause aright        350
To the unsatisfied.
   *Hor.*         Never believe it:
I am more an antique Roman than a Dane:
Here's yet some liquor left.
   *Ham.*         As thou 'rt a man,
Give me the cup: let go; by heaven, I 'll have 't.
O good Horatio, what a wounded name,
Things standing thus unknown, shall live behind me!
If thou didst ever hold me in thy heart,
Absent thee from felicity awhile,
And in this harsh world draw thy breath in pain,
To tell my story.         [*March afar off, and shot within.*
             What warlike noise is this?        360
   *Osr.*   Young Fortinbras, with conquest come from Poland,
To the ambassadors of England gives
This warlike volley.
   *Ham.*        O, I die, Horatio;
The potent poison quite o'er-crows my spirit:
I cannot live to hear the news from England;
But I do prophesy the election lights
On Fortinbras: he has my dying voice;
So tell him, with the occurrents, more and less,
Which have solicited.   The rest is silence.        [*Dies.*
   *Hor.*   Now cracks a noble heart.   Good night, sweet prince;
And flights of angels sing thee to thy rest!        371
Why does the drum come hither?        [*March within.*

   *Enter* FORTINBRAS, *the* English Ambassadors, *and others.*

   *Fort.*   Where is this sight?
   *Hor.*          What is it ye would see?
If aught of woe or wonder, cease your search.
   *Fort.*   This quarry cries on havoc.   O proud death,
What feast is toward in thine eternal cell,
That thou so many princes at a shot
So bloodily hast struck?
   *First Amb.*      The sight is dismal;
And our affairs from England come too late:
*The ears are senseless that should give us hearing,*        380
*To tell him his* commandment is fulfill'd,

That Rosencrantz and Guildenstern are dead:
Where should we have our thanks?
    *Hor.*                Not from his mouth,
Had it the ability of life to thank you:
He never gave commandment for their death.
But since, so jump upon this bloody question,
You from the Polack wars, and you from England,
Are here arrived, give order that these bodies
High on a stage be placed to the view;
And let me speak to the yet unknowing world      390
How these things came about: so shall you hear
Of carnal, bloody, and unnatural acts,
Of accidental judgements, casual slaughters,
Of deaths put on by cunning and forced cause,
And, in this upshot, purposes mistook
Fall'n on the inventors' heads: all this can I
Truly deliver.
    *Fort.*       Let us haste to hear it,
And call the noblest to the audience.
For me, with sorrow I embrace my fortune:
I have some rights of memory in this kingdom,     400
Which now to claim my vantage doth invite me.
    *Hor.* Of that I shall have also cause to speak,
And from his mouth whose voice will draw on more:
But let this same be presently perform'd,
Even while men's minds are wild; lest more mischance,
On plots and errors, happen.
    *Fort.*           Let four captains
Bear Hamlet, like a soldier, to the stage;
For he was likely, had he been put on,
To have proved most royally: and, for his passage,
The soldiers' music and the rites of war      410
Speak loudly for him.
Take up the bodies: such a sight as this
Becomes the field, but here shows much amiss.
Go, bid the soldiers shoot.
        [*A dead march.   Exeunt, bearing off the dead bodies;*
           *after which a peal of ordnance is shot off.*

# NOTES.

*These notes should be used with the Glossary, to which the student is referred for all matters of merely verbal interpretation.*

*Reference is made throughout to the lines of the Globe text. Where this might have caused any inconvenience, the lines of the present edition have been added in italics.*

The symbols Q 1, Q 2, Q 3, Q 4, Q 5, Q 6 denote the quarto editions of 1603 (first sketch), 1604, 1605, 1611, the undated fifth quarto, and 1637; F 1, F 2, F 3, F 4, the folio editions of 1623, 1632, 1664, 1685. Qq. denotes the consent of all the quartos except Q 1, Ff. that of all the folios.

Reference on points of grammar is made to the sections of the 3rd edition of Abbott's *Shakespearian Grammar*; for passages from other plays to Macmillan's *Globe* edition of the poet. The parallel text of Q 1, Q 2, and F 1 may be profitably studied in Vietor's edition (*Shakespeare Reprints*, Marburg, 1891).

*Dramatis Personæ.* This list is not in the Qq. or Ff. It was added by Rowe. The spelling adopted is that of F 1.

The division into Acts and Scenes is traditional; neither being given before the Players' Quarto of 1676, and in that only the Acts. The earlier Qq. have not got it, and in the Ff. it only extends as far as act ii. sc. 2. Mr. Rose (*New Shakspere Society Transactions, 1877-9*) has argued that the accepted division is incorrect ; but it would not be convenient to adopt any other here.

Mr. Rose's paper will, however, repay careful study. He would retain the present endings of acts i. and iv. Act ii. he would end with the present iii. 1, and act iii. with the present iv. 3. "Such an arrangement", he says, "is thoroughly Shakespearian; each act has its unity—the first is filled by the Ghost, the second by Hamlet's assumed madness and the king's attempts to fathom it, the third by the doings of one tremendous night, the fourth contains miscellaneous intermediate incidents, and the fifth ends all things."

## Act I.—Scene I.

*Elsinore. A platform before the castle.* Notes of locality are not given in the Qq. and Ff.; but Elsinore is mentioned in ii. 2. 278, and the platform, or terrace, in i. 2. 252.

The two opening scenes put the spectator in full possession of the situation of affairs in Denmark. The death and character of the late king, his reappearance to denote some unknown evil, the threats of war, and the consequent need for strong men, are emphasized in the first; the second adds the personal relations of Hamlet with the royal house, and depicts his state of mind at the beginning of the action. Coleridge has an excellent note on Shakespeare's first scenes. "With the single exception of *Cymbeline* they either place before us at one glance both the past and the future in some effect which implies the continuance and full agency of its cause, as in the feuds and party-spirit of the servants of the two houses in the first scene of *Romeo and Juliet*; or in the degrading passion for shows and public spectacles, and the overwhelming attachment for the newest successful war-chief in the Roman people, already become a populace, contrasted with the jealousy of the nobles in *Julius Cæsar*;—or they at once commence the action so as to excite a curiosity for the explanation in the following scenes, as in the storm of wind and waves, and the boatswain in *The Tempest*, instead of anticipating our curiosity, as in most other first scenes, and in too many other first acts; —or they act, by contrast of diction suited to the characters, at once to heighten the effect, and yet to give a naturalness to the language and rhythm of the principal personages, either in that of Prospero and Miranda by the appropriate lowness of the style, or, as in *King John*, by the equally appropriate stateliness of official harangues or narratives, so that the after blank verse seems to belong to the rank and quality of the speakers, and not to the poet;—or they strike at once the key-note and give the predominant spirit of the play, as in the *Twelfth Night* and in *Macbeth*;—or finally, the first scene comprises all these advantages at once, as in *Hamlet*."

Horatio is carefully differentiated from Marcellus, Bernardo, and Francisco: they are unlettered soldiers; he is a scholar, and, as such, has his touches both of imagination and scepticism.

**1.** The scene opens amid nervous suspense; there is a tradition that it was written in a charnel-house. "'T is bitter cold", and silent, and the watcher is "sick at heart". On two previous nights the ghost has appeared, to Bernardo and Marcellus. Bernardo's agitation shows itself in the way he challenges the guard, instead of waiting to be challenged.

**6. upon**, immediately after; cf. *Much Ado*, v. 1. 258, "And fled he is upon this villany", and Abbott, *Sh. Gr.* § 191.

**13. rivals.** Q 1 has *partners*, but the sense is the same. See Glossary, *s.v.*

**15. this ground**, the land of Denmark.

**16. Give you**, probably an ellipse for 'God give you', rather than for 'I give you'.

**19. A piece of him**, not merely a humorous answer, equivalent to 'something like him'. Horatio hints that although he is there in bodily presence, he is not in sympathy with his friend's expectation of seeing the ghost.

**21.** This line is given to Horatio in Q 2, to Marcellus in Q 1 and F 1. In the one case the actor will speak of 'this thing' with horror, in the other with derision.

**31. assail your ears** is followed somewhat irregularly by "what we have seen" because it is practically equivalent to 'tell you'. Cf. Abbott, *Sh. Gr.* § 252.

**36. yond same star,** probably the Great Bear, which swings round the pole. Shakespeare's diction is unfettered by any laws beyond those of his free-will. He says 'this time last night' if he pleases, or he expands the same idea in a descriptive and allusive fashion. Similarly in lines 118–9 he paraphrases the moon as

"the moist star
Upon whose influence Neptune's empire stands".

**42. a scholar.** Exorcisms were of course performed in Latin in the palindrome "Signa te signa, temere me tangis et angis". Cf. *Much Ado*, ii. 1. 264, "I would to God some scholar would conjure her".

**44. harrows.** So F 1. Q 1 has *horrors*, Q 2 *horrows*. Cf. Milton, *Comus*, 565, "Amaz'd I stood, harrowed with fear and grief". Horatio's scepticism has vanished once for all before "the sensible and true avouch" of his own eyes. Hamlet's persistent doubts and questionings do not occur to him, though, indeed, he is inclined to explain the spirit as an 'illusion' (line 127).

**46. usurp'st,** in the wide sense of 'usest without right', applicable equally to the 'time of night' and the appearance of the king.

**60.** For the difficulty of time suggested by Horatio's reminiscence, and connected with that of Hamlet's age, see v. 1. 154, note.

**62, 63.** The reading of Q 1, Q 2, F 1, is—

" when in an angry parle
He smote the sleaded (*sledded*, F 1) pollax on the ice".

The interpretation of the lines has puzzled commentators. There are two possible meanings: (i) We may read with Malone *the sledded Polacks, i.e.* 'the Poles who ride in sledges'. The form *Polack*" occurs in ii. 2. 63, 75; iv. 4. 23, and v. 3. 287. "An angry parle" will then mean 'a skirmish', and the allusion will be to some war, not with the Norwegians, but with the Poles. (ii) "The sledded poleaxe" may be a poleaxe weighted with a sledge or hammer at the back. I have preferred the second explanation for three reasons: (*a*) a 'parle' or parley elsewhere in Shakespeare always means a conference; (*b*) a conference is more likely than a battle to take place 'on the ice', *i.e.* on some bordering stream, which would be neutral ground; (*c*) Horatio only saw the elder Hamlet *once* (i. 2. 186), and presumably on a peaceful occasion, when his beaver was up, so that his appearance could be remembered; (*d*) the whole phrase suits best with some moment of sudden wrath, *and not with a day's fighting.* Moltke needlessly proposes to read *leaded, edged,* or *sledged poleaxe.*

**65. jump.** So Q 2. F 1 has the more commonplace *just*.

**68.** *i.e.* 'speaking generally'; 'Some evil is portended', says Horatio, 'though I know not precisely what'.

**70. Good,** an appellative, 'good sirs'; cf. Abbott, *Sh. Gr.* § 13.

**72. toils,** makes to toil; Shakespeare uses many verbs transitively, especially in a causal sense, which are now only used intransitively; cf. Abbott, *Sh. Gr.* §§ 290, 291.

**85. so,** *i.e.* as valiant; cf. *Macbeth*, i. 1. 16, "brave Macbeth— well he deserves that name".

**87. Well ratified by law and heraldry;** *i.e.* not only according to the civil law, but also according to the formalities of the court of chivalry. This court, a characteristic mediæval institution, took cognizance of matters of coat-armour or heraldry proper, and also, to some extent, of international law. See Appendix to my edition of *Richard II.* in the *Falcon Series.*

**90. a moiety competent,** an equivalent slice of territory.

**96. unapproved,** untried. Q 1 reads *inapproved*; Q 2 and F 1 *un-improved*, which might mean 'unemployed', 'not turned to account'; cf. *Julius Cæsar*, ii. 1. 159, "His means, if he improve them, may well stretch so far". But the idea of 'mettle of proof' is a common one.

**98. list.** Q 1 reads *sight*, in the modern slang sense.

**100. hath a stomach in 't,** gives an opportunity for courage.

**101. our state,** our rulers.

**108-125.** These lines are not in F 1.

**109.** The meaning ascribed by the watchers to the coming of the ghost shows that no suspicion of the king's murder had as yet been awaked in the court.

**112.** Horatio is not minimizing the importance of the apparition; it is a small thing, but it portends great trouble.

**114.** The prodigies in Rome are described in *Julius Cæsar*, act i. sc. 3, where Cassius speaks of them (line 70) as

"instruments of fear and warning
Unto some monstrous state".

The *Julius Cæsar* passage is taken from North's Plutarch; this in *Hamlet* perhaps partly from Lucan, *Pharsalia*, i. 526—

"Ignota obscuræ viderunt sidere noctes,
ardentemque polum flammis, cœloque volantes
obliquas per inane faces, crinemque timendi
sideris, et terris mutantem regna cometen".

Lucan mentions also the eclipse and the appearance of the dead in the streets.

**117.** The connection of this line with the preceding is so abrupt that some editors have thought that lines 121–125 should come between them.  Others insert a conjectural line, as Boaden's "*The heavens too spoke in silent prodigies*", or attempt to emend the text. Malone has—

> *Astres with trains of fire – and dews of blood*
> *Disastrous dimmed the sun.*

For the last line of this Staunton would substitute *Distempered the sun*, or *Discoloured the sun*.  But a comet cannot very well dim the sun, and *astres* is a very rare word, and "disasters in the sun" are clearly sun-spots.  The simplest explanation is that a line is missing, but it is useless to try and rewrite it.—Comets were supposed to cause the phenomenon of red dews, which is now said to proceed from innumerable butterflies, each of which lets fall a drop of red liquid as it emerges from the chrysalis.

**119.** The influence of the moon upon the tides is again alluded to in *Winter's Tale*, i. 2. 426—

> "you may as well
> Forbid the sea for to obey the moon".

Either because of this influence, or for the paleness of its radiance, especially as seen through clouds, Shakespeare frequently applies the epithet 'watery' to the moon. .

**120. almost to doomsday.**  In the description of the second coming of the Son of Man, given in *S. Matt.* xxiv. 29, it is prophesied that the sun shall "be darkened, and the moon not give her light".  Cf. also *Rev.* vi. 12, "the sun became black as sackcloth of hair, and the moon became as blood".

**127.** Crossing the spot where an apparition appeared was supposed to bring down its evil influence on the rash spectator.

**138. they say.**  Cf. lines 149, 165.   Horatio is a scholar and acquainted with theories of the supernatural.   He knows the common causes which make spirits walk.

**139.** The stage-directions, here and in line 127, are from Q 2.

**154. extravagant and erring.**  The Latin *extravagare* and *errare* both mean, in their radical sense, 'to wander abroad'.  Shakespeare is fond of such uses, which seem to suggest a larger measure, at least of Latin scholarship, than he is usually credited with.

**161. dare stir.**  So Q 2.  F 1 has *can walk*, Q 1 *dare walk*.

**162.** Planets, when in their malignant aspect, were supposed to injure the incautious traveller by night; cf. *Coriolanus*, ii. 2. 117—

> "with a sudden reinforcement struck
> Corioli like a planet".

We still use the phrase 'moonstruck'; see, *e.g.*, R. Browning, *One Word More*, xvi.

**163. takes.** So Q 1, Q 2. F 1 has *talks*. 'To *take*' is 'to affect', 'to charm'. See Glossary, *s.v.*

**165.** Horatio is half attracted by the imaginative theory, half sceptical.

**166. russet.** The earliest colour of dawn is not red but grey. Cf. *Much Ado*, v. 3. 29—

> "the gentle day
> Before the wheels of Phœbus, round about
> Dapples the drowsy east with spots of grey";

and *Romeo and Juliet*, iii. 5. 19, "I'll say yon grey is not the morning's eye".

**167. eastern.** So F 1. Q 2 has *eastward*. A comparison between this beautiful metaphor and the cruder version given in Q 1 will show the subtle art with which Shakespeare carried out his revision of the play. Q 1 has—

> "But see, the sun in russet mantle clad
> Walks o'er the dew of yon high mountain top".

The art consists in the rearrangement of the alliteration so as to connect the words in a more melodious fashion.

**170.** The first mention of Hamlet in the play, preparing us for the introduction of him in the next scene.

### Scene 2.

Hamlet's brief dialogue with the King and Queen and his subsequent soliloquy sufficiently acquaint us with his mood. He has no idea of his uncle's crime, though he detests his character; but his moral sense has received a severe shock from his mother's marriage. The whole world appears to him, in consequence, under the dominion of evil; he would gladly be quit of it. But that cannot be, and, moreover, he cannot do anything, nor even speak his feelings out. He must take refuge in irony and sarcasm, or, when possible, in silence.

Claudius is a hypocrite, but his hypocrisy is that of a statesman; he plays his part with a dignity and a keen insight into what is needful for the welfare of the state, which explain how the council came to choose him king.

The scene opens with a bridal procession. It is the custom of the stage for Hamlet to come on last, slowly and reluctantly, and clad in black, amongst the glittering draperies of the court.

The stage-direction is that of F 1; Q 2 has *Enter Claudius King of Denmark, Gertrad the Queen, Counsaile as Polonius and his son Laertes, Hamlet cum aliis.* I believe that the curious phrase *Counsaile as Polonius* contains a trace of the name *Corambis*, which occurs in the stage-direction of Q 1. If the name was somehow left in the MS. side by side with the substituted *Polonius*, the printer may have tried to make sense of it in his own way.  Cf. ii. 1. 1, note, and Appendix A.

7. This line explains the "wisest" of line 6.

11. an...a.  So Q 2; F 1 has *one...one.*  The F 1 reading rather strains the antithesis.  But cf. *Winter's Tale,* v. 2. 80, "She had one eye declined for the loss of her husband, another elevated that the oracle was fulfilled".  For the idea cf. the δακρυόεν γελάσασα ('laughing tearfully') of Homer, *Iliad,* vi. 484.  It is an oxymoron, which the grammarians describe as 'a contrast by juxtaposition of opposing ideas'.  Shakespeare is fond of the conceit; a good instance is in *Romeo and Juliet,* i. 1. 182—

> " Why, then, O brawling love! O loving hate!
> O anything, of nothing first create!
> O heavy lightness! serious vanity!
> Mis-shapen chaos of well-seeming forms!
> Feather of lead, bright smoke, cold fire, sick health!
> Still-waking sleep, that is not what it is ".

He burlesques it, however, in *Midsummer Night's Dream,* v. 1. 56.

17. that you know is parenthetical, 'that which you already know'.

18. a weak supposal of our worth, a supposal that our worth is weak.  Such transpositions of adjectives are common in Shakespeare; cf. *Macbeth,* ii. 1. 55, "Tarquin's ravishing strides".

21. His hope of gain is allied with his poor opinion of his adversary.

22. After a long parenthesis the foregoing subject is often recalled by a pronoun; cf. Abbott, *Sh. Gr.* § 242.

24. Cf. i. 1. 87.

25. Claudius mentions his brother three times in this carefully-prepared speech, and always with an epithet of affection or flattery.

31. in that gives the grounds for Norway's interference.

32. proportions, of the army, horse to foot, &c.

34. Q 1 has *Cornelia* and *Voltemar.*

38. delated.  So Q 2; F 1 has *dilated,* Q 1 *related.*  'Dilated articles' would mean 'articles set out at large'; 'delated articles' is 'articles setting forth what powers are delated, delegated, or made over to you'.

60. The metaphor is legal.  Laertes' will is like a deed, illegal until his father's hard-won consent has ratified it.  Lines 58–60, excep̃  ᵗ         ᷟh  my Lord ", are omitted in F 1.

e privileges of youth.

**65.** Hamlet is now Claudius' son, and therefore in a closer relationship to him than that of a mere kinsman.  But in feeling they are far from 'kind' or 'affectionate' towards each other.

**66. too much i' the sun.**  Hamlet ironically replies that he is too much in the sunshine of the royal presence to be gloomy.  There may also be a play of words between *sun* and *son* : 'You call me your son, and so I am, a mere prince, who should be a king'. Hamlet does not dwell on his loss of the crown, but it is one of the bitter drops in his cup; cf. v. 2. 65, "Popped in between the election and my hopes".  'To be i' the sun' appears also to be a proverbial phrase for 'to be miserable'.

**74.** Hamlet's reply means, 'it is common; but does it hurt the less?'  The same idea is repeated in *The Tempest*, ii. 1. 3—

> "Our hint of woe
> Is common ; every day some sailor's wife,
> The masters of some merchant and the merchant
> Have just our theme of woe".

And still more exactly in Tennyson, *In Memoriam*, vi. —

> "One writes, that 'Other friends remain',
> That 'Loss is common to the race '—
> And common is the commonplace,
> And vacant chaff well meant for grain.

> "That loss is common would not make
> My own less bitter, rather more :
> Too common !  Never morning wore
> To evening, but some heart did break".

**78. customary suits,** either 'the conventional garb of mourning' or 'the suits which I am accustomed to wear'.

**82. moods,** less the inner feelings than the outward poses or attitudes of grief.  Hamlet is contrasting the appearance with the reality. Therefore the *shows* of F 1 is better than the *shapes* of Q 2.

**92. obsequious sorrow,** in the double sense of 'dutiful sorrow' and 'sorrow as shown in obsequies, or funeral rites'.

**95. incorrect,** rather a participle than an adjective, referring more to the process than the result; 'not corrected', 'not trained into the right attitude'.

**97. unschool'd.**  Cf. *Merchant of Venice*, iii. 2. 161, "an unlessoned girl, unschooled, unpractised".  Shakespeare, like Milton, is fond of piling up negative adjectives in this way.

**99. any the most vulgar thing to sense.**  Cf. *Cymbeline*, i. 4. 65, "any the rarest"; *Henry VIII.* ii. 4. 48, "one the wisest"; and, for the transposition, Abbott, *Sh. Gr.* § 419a.

**110. nobility,** apparently in the sense of 'a high degree'.

**112. impart,** used intransitively, 'impart myself', 'offer myself'. Several emendations have been suggested to avoid the intransitive use, the best being Mason's, *Do I my part toward you.* .

**113. Wittenberg.** The university was really founded in 1502. It was made famous by Martin Luther.

**114.** The subject is repeated in the pronoun; cf. line 22, and Abbott, *Sh. Gr.* § 243.

**117. cousin,** the usual term of courtesy used by a king to his nobles.

**125.** "The king's intemperance is very strongly impressed; everything that happens to him gives him occasion to drink" (Johnson). Additional solemnity is to be imparted to the present revel by the firing of salutes; cf. v. 2. 278, *sqq.*

**126. tell** appears to be used intransitively for 'speak', without an object.

**129.** The idea of suicide, which occupies Hamlet's mind in iii. 1. 56 *sqq.*, has already occurred to him.

**too too.** Such reduplications have an intensive force, and are common in Elizabethan writers; cf. iii. 3. 8, and *Sonnet* cx. "Even to thy pure and most most loving breast".

**solid.** The contrast is with 'dew', and therefore the use of the word here need not imply that Hamlet is fat; cf. v. 2. 271, note. But *too too solid* is only the reading of F 1. Q 2 has *too too sallied* and Q 1 *too much griev'd and sallied.* I incline to think that *sallied* is right, in the sense of 'vexed'; cf. ii. 1. 39 (Q 2), and cf. Wordsworth, *Ode on the Intimations of Immortality,* vii. "fretted by sallies of his mother's kisses".

**132.** Cf. *Cymbeline,* iii. 4. 77—

> "Against self-slaughter
> There is a prohibition so divine
> That cravens my weak hand".

It need hardly be said that there is nothing about self-slaughter in the Bible. "Unless it be the Sixth Commandment, the 'canon' must be one of natural religion." (Bp. Wordsworth.)

**134. uses,** the customary, usual occupations of life.

**138. two months;** cf. iii. 2. 111.

**140.** Shakespeare, like Gray and Keats, accents Hypérion, instead of Hyperion. Hyperion was the Titanic Sun-god; cf. iii. 4. 56.

**149. Niobe,** a daughter of Tantalus, boasted that she had more sons and daughters than Leto. Consequently Apollo and Artemis slew her children with arrows, and she herself was turned by Zeus into a stone upon Mount Sipylus in Lydia, where she sheds tears all summer long; cf. Sophocles, *Antigone,* 823.

**150.** Q 1 has *devoid of reason.* Discourse is the Latin *discursus,* the process of the intellect from premises to conclusion in an argument.

**154.** unrighteous, because her subsequent conduct gave them the lie.

**158.** nor it cannot. The double negative is frequent in Shakespeare; cf. Abbott, *Sh. Gr.* § 406.

**159.** Hamlet does not speak of his mother's disgrace in public, nor, until the command of the Ghost is laid upon him, upbraid her in private.

**160.** The news of the apparition breaks in upon Hamlet's musings. It excites him, he eagerly questions concerning it, and jumps at once to the conclusion that there has been some foul play. This has not struck the others, but then Hamlet is ready to think the worst of his uncle.

**161.** Hamlet is full of thought when he first greets the new-comer, then he looks up, and recognizes his friend.

**163.** I 'll change...with you, either, 'I will be your servant, you my friend', or 'I will call you, and you me, friend'. Cf. line 254.

**167.** Good even, sir. This is spoken to Bernardo.

**175.** Satire; directly the surprise of seeing Horatio has worn off, the bitterness of Hamlet's heart rises to his lips. The reading is that of Q 1, F 1. Q 2 has *for to drink.*

**182.** my dearest foe. Shakespeare uses the epithet 'dear' of anything that nearly touches the emotions in any way. See Glossary, *s.v.*

**186.** Horatio is about to say, as he says in line 189, 'I saw him yesternight'. He breaks off nervously and substitutes 'once'. For that occasion cf. i. 1. 60–63, notes.

**187.** Cf. *Julius Cæsar,* v. 5. 73—

> "His life was gentle, and the elements
> So mixed in him that nature might stand up
> And say to all the world, 'This was a man!'"

**190.** who. Shakespeare often uses 'who' for 'whom'; cf. Abbott, *Sh. Gr.* § 274.

**193.** attent. In the transitional state of the language during the Elizabethan period, shortened forms of common words are frequently found. Cf. Abbott, *Sh. Gr.* § 22, and 'avouch' (i. 1. 37).

**198.** the dead waste. Q 2, F 1 have *wast,* which may represent 'waste' or 'waist'; Q 1 has *vast.* Both 'waste' and 'vast' have the sense of 'emptiness', 'stillness'. "The vast of night" occurs in *The Tempest,* i. 2. 327. "The waist of night" is found in Marston's

*Malecontent.* 'Waist' and 'middle' would here be tautologous, but such tautologies are frequent in Shakespeare's exuberant vocabulary.

**200. at point.** So Q 2; F 1 has *at all points.* In either case the meaning is 'completely'; cf. Glossary, *s.v. point.*

**202. slow and stately.** Adjectives are often used for adverbs; cf. Abbott, *Sh. Gr.* § 1.

**204. distill'd.** So Q 2; F 1 has *bestilled.* 'Distilled to jelly' is an odd phrase. To 'distil' is properly to convert into drops (Lat. *stilla*) of liquid; here it seems to mean 'softened', 'weakened'. Many emendations have been proposed, as, *be-chilled, dissolved. beth rilled.*
It is no doubt the quaking of jelly that Shakespeare has in mind.

**205. act,** like the Latin *actus*, is here used of the patient, rather than the agent.

**216. it.** Cf. **v. 1. 293.** In Shakespeare's time *his* was just beginning to give place to *its* as the genitive of *it.* Transition forms are *it*, as here, and *it's. It* occurs about fourteen times in F 1. In the Authorized Version of the Bible, *his* is almost invariable, but *it* occurs in *Leviticus,* xxv. 5, "of it own accord"; cf. Abbott, *Sh. Gr.* § 228; and Craik, *English of Shakespeare,* p. 91.

**222. writ down.** So Q 2, F 1; Q 1 has *right done.*

**226.** I do not think that Hamlet's rapid questions imply any doubt of his friend's good faith. He is immensely impressed with the story, and curious to know every detail.

**242.** Cf. *Sonnet* xii. 4, "And sable curls all silvered o'er with white".

**244.** Hamlet professes to think the ghost an 'illusion', as Horatio did. But to himself he calls it 'my father's spirit'. But the doubt comes back to him, and it is long before he can satisfy himself; cf. i. 4. 40; ii. 1. 580.
The belief that supernatural appearances were the work of evil spirits was common in Elizabethan times. In *Macbeth,* v. 8. 19, the witches are called "juggling fiends".

**248. tenable.** So Q 2; F 1 has *treble.*

**254.** Cf. line 163.

### Scene 3.

The principal elements in the situation of things at Elsinore have been put before us in the first two scenes; the need for a man of action, and the supernatural suggestion of some hidden evil in scene 1, the position and nature of Hamlet in scene 2. The present scene completes the picture by showing the contrast to Hamlet afforded by *the family of Polonius,* who may be taken as typical of the court at *Elsinore. All* are carefully drawn on a lower scale than his, shallow where he is subtle, commonplace where he is original. None the less, the portrait of the gentle maiden, Ophelia, is touched so as to win our sympathies. She is no mate for Hamlet; yet in her own sphere she is a beautiful and lovable character. Polonius is a politician without being a statesman, Laertes an apt representative of gilded youth as it existed at the court of Elizabeth. Both have low ideals; the father is consumed with the conceit of his own intellect and experience, which have shown him only the lower side of humanity; the son is 'Italianate', degraded in tone by his life in a foreign city; both are incredulous, not only of the purity and honour of Hamlet, but of that of Ophelia herself.

**2. as,** not 'because', but 'according as', 'whensoever'. Cf. Abbott, *Sh. Gr.* § 109.

**6. a toy in blood,** a passing fancy of youth. For the use of 'toy' cf. i. 4. 76, "toys of desperation".

**12.** The Scriptural metaphor of the temple of the body recurs in *Macbeth*, ii. 3. 72—

> "Most sacrilegious murder hath broke ope
> The Lord's anointed temple".

**21. safety.** So Q 2; F 1 has *sanctity*. 'Safety' must of course be scanned as a trisyllable; cf. Essay on Metre, § 6 (iii).

**26. act and place.** So Q 2; F 1 has *sect and force*.

Lines 36–39 are preceded by inverted commas in Q 2, perhaps because they are of the nature of maxims. Lines 61–77, and some lines which take the place of Polonius' speech 115, *sqq.*, are similarly printed in Q 1.

**45.** Laertes' advice is such as his own experience has taught him. Ophelia is partly impressed by her brother's worldly wisdom, yet she is not without an intimation of the shallowness of it.

**50.** Notice the change from the plural to the singular, characteristic of the loose Elizabethan syntax; and for the opposite construction, see iii. 2. 200. Cf. also Abbott, *Sh. Gr.* § 415.

**the primrose path.** Cf. *Macbeth*, ii. 3. 51, "Some of all professions that go the primrose way to the everlasting bonfire"; and *All's Well*, iv. 5. 56, "the flowery way that leads to the broad gate and the great fire". Also R. L. Stevenson, *Underwoods* I. xi.—

> "Life is over, life was gay;
> We have come the primrose way".

**57. There.** The natural explanation of the word is that Polonius lays his hand upon Laertes' head. But F 1 reads *you are stayed for there*.

**59.** The precepts of Polonius may be summed up in the Greek μηδὲν ἄγαν, 'Don't go too far; avoid excess; don't commit yourself'. They are *delivered* in the formal sententious way characteristic of the old man.

**64. dull thy palm, make thy friendliness too common.**

**65. comrade.** So F 1 ; Q 1, Q 2 both read *courage*.

**74. Are of a most select...in that.** This line is a well-known crux. The following are the readings of the three earliest editions :—

> Q 1. *And they of France of the chiefe rancke and station*
> *Are of a most select and generall chiefe in that.*

> Q 2. *And they in Fraunce of the best ranck and station*
> *Or of a most select and generous chiefe in that.*

> F 1. *And they in France of the best ranck and station*
> *Are of a most select and generous cheff in that.*

Evidently F 1 gives a nearer approach to a possible text than either of the Qq. Moreover it is shown by lines 65, 76, to afford a better version of this speech than Q 2. The principal explanations and emendations are—

(*a*) That given in the text, which is due to Collier. I think that the presence of *chiefe* in line 73 (Q 1 text) may have led to the erroneous substitution of *chiefe* for *choice* in line 74. When the play was revised the exact cause of the repetition may have been missed, *best* substituted for *chiefe* in line 73, and the wrong word left in line 74.

(*b*) *Chief* may be a substantive, meaning literally 'head', and so 'eminence' or 'superiority'.

(*c*) Both sense and scansion may be improved by reading, as the Cambridge editors suggest—

> *Are most select and generous, chief in that.*

Staunton and Ingleby read *sheaf*, in the sense of 'set', 'clique'; according to the Euphuistic phrase 'gentlemen of the best sheaf', which occurs in Jonson's *Magnetic Lady*, act iii. sc. 4. Ingleby also suggests that the *courage* of the Qq. in line 65 is Euphuistic for 'a gallant'.

**76. loan.** So F 1 ; Q 2 has *love*.

**78.** Polonius' last maxim appears so profoundly true, if taken in its highest sense of 'Be true to your own ideal', that critics have doubted whether he is meant to be altogether ridiculous. But it must be remembered that the phrase may also be interpreted as 'Look after yourself first, and you will find that honesty is the best policy'. And it would be a characteristic bit of Shakespeare's irony to put into Polonius' mouth words which really convey a great meaning, but which he only understands in a far lower sense.

**81.** 'May my blessing make my warnings the more acceptable.'

**88.** Neither Polonius nor Laertes conceives that Hamlet may be genuinely in love with Ophelia. They interpret him after their own *standard. And so* Ophelia's ignorance is poisoned; she becomes *ready to distrust* her lover, and to take her father's part against him.

**107.** Polonius' delight in playing upon words is one side of his supreme satisfaction with himself, and especially with his powers of expression. Cf. ii. 2. 85, *sqq.*

**109. Running it.** This is Collier's conjecture for the *Wrong it* of Q 2, and *Roaming it* of F 2. The phrase means 'hunting it through every twist and turn, as a greyhound hunts a hare'. Pope's *Wronging it* is nearer to Q 2, but less pointed. Warburton's *Wringing it* is another possible alternative.

**112. go to;** a common phrase of reproach, or, rarely, of encouragement. Cf. Abbott, *Sh. Gr.* § 185.

**115. springes to catch woodcocks,** a proverbial phrase for the entangling of a simpleton. Cf. v. 2. 317. Harting states that the woodcock was supposed to have no brains. The Clarendon Press editors quote Gosson, *School of Abuse*, p. 72 (ed. Arber), "When Comedy comes upon the stage, Cupid sets up a springe for woodcocks, which are entangled ere they descry the line, and caught before they mistrust the snare".

**116. prodigal,** adjective for adverb; cf. Abbott, *Sh. Gr.* § 1.

**122.** 'Do not entreat or entertain his suit so readily.'

**130. bonds.** This is the reading of the Qq. Ff., and there does not appear to be any reason to follow the majority of modern editors in accepting Theobald's emendation, *bawds*.

**131. This is for all,** once for all.

**133.** It is unnecessary to read *moment's* for the *moment* of Q 2 and F 1: for the use of 'moment' as an adjective cf. i. 5. 33, "Lethe wharf".

### Scene 4.

The elements of the tragedy are now before the mind of the spectator; the revelation of the ghost is the spark which sets them in motion. With this the first act, or prologue to the main action, naturally ends. Hamlet's problem is presented to him; the question is, "What will he make of it?" This must be decided in the course of the play by the laws of his character and circumstances. His first impulse is to believe and to revenge; yet, even so early as this, the hastily conceived design of simulating madness is a foretaste of what is to follow.

Scenes 4 and 5 are dramatically continuous; they are only separated scenically by the need for a slight change of locality.

**1. it is.** So Qq., F 2, 3; F 1, 2 have *is it*

**8.** Hamlet's speculative turn of mind is well illustrated in this passage. In the moment of nervous tension he finds a natural outlet in pursuing general reflections on an irrelevant matter, reflections which soon carry him into the deeps of philosophy.

9. **the swaggering up-spring reels.** Pope and Johnson referred 'up-spring' to Claudius, and interpreted it as 'upstart' or 'usurper'. It is more probably an epithet of 'reels', the whole expression being governed by 'keeps'. Elze points out that the word corresponds to *hüpfauf*, a wild German dance. There is a passage in Dekker's *Gull's Horn-book* worth quoting, "Teach me, thou sovereign skinker, how to take the German's upsy freeze, the Danish rousa".

11. The kettle-drum was a characteristically Danish instrument; cf. Cleveland, *Fuscara or the Bee Errant*—

> "Tuning his draughts with drowsy hums,
> As Danes carouse by kettle-drums".

12. **his pledge.** Cf. sc. 3, lines 124, *sqq.*

15. The English appear to have shared, in Shakespeare's time, a reputation for tippling with the nations of northern Europe. The drunkenness of the Germans is satirized in *Merchant of Venice*, act i. scene 2, and it appears from contemporary records that the Danes came under the same condemnation; cf. Howell's *Letters*, i. 6. 2 (1632), "The king [Christian IV.] feasted my lord [Leicester] once, and it lasted from eleven of the clock till towards the evening, during which time the king began thirty-five healths".

16. 'A custom which it is more honourable to break than to observe.'

Lines 18-37 are omitted in F 1.

19. **swinish phrase**, phrase that makes us out to be swine.

24. There is some irony in putting into Hamlet's mouth a truth which his own history is so notably to illustrate. It is 'by the o'ergrowth of some complexion', that is, the natural tendency to over-speculation in him, that he comes to failure.

32. **nature's livery or fortune's star.** Both phrases mean the same. The natural 'livery', 'temperament', or 'complexion' of a man depends on the star he chanced to be born under. Cf. *Much Ado*, ii. 1. 349, where Beatrice explains her lively nature, "Then there was a star danced, and under that was I born".

36, 37. These lines have puzzled commentators more than any other in the play. Furness, in his *Variorum* edition, devotes six pages to the criticism upon them, and the Cambridge editors enumerate some forty readings.
The Q 2 text is—

> *the dram of eale*
> *Doth all the noble substance of a doubt*
> *To his owne scandle.*

And the general sense is clearly, that a little leaven leavens the whole lump, a small fault brings scandal upon the whole of a noble character. But there can be little question that the Q 2 text is corrupt, and the wildest attempts have been made to emend it. It is hardly necessary for the purposes of this edition to catalogue these. They may be found in Furness, or in the *Cambridge Shakespeare.*

No explanation appears to me plausible which does not retain the word *eale.* "A dram of eale" may mean—

(1) A dram of a decoction of eels. Cf. Maplett, *Green Forest* (1567), quoted by Mr. W. M. Rossetti in *Notes and Queries* for October 30, 1869, "The eel being killed and addressed in wine, whosoever chaunceth to drinke of that wine so used shall ever afterwards lothe wine".

(2) A dram of reproach. Mr. T. Davies states in *Notes and Queries* for March 11, 1876, that 'eale' in the sense of 'reproach is still used in the western counties.

(3) Still more simply: a dram of e'il or evil. Very strong support is given to this interpretation by the Q 2 reading of *deale* for 'devil' in ii. 2. 627.

Then for the next line. It is surely desirable to make the slightest possible change in the Q 2 text that will afford a reasonable sense. The choice appears to me to lie between two emendations—

(1) *Doth all the noble substance offer doubt.*
(2) *Doth all the noble substance oft adoubt.*

In either case the meaning is the same, 'The dram of evil brings doubt upon the whole noble substance, lowering it to its own scandalous level'. The form 'adoubt' would be parallel to 'abase', the prefix giving it a causal sense.

In view of the uncertainty of the question I have thought it best to let the Q 2 reading stand in the text.

**38. his,** the ordinary possessive form both of 'he' and 'it' in Shakespeare. Cf. i. 2. 216, note, and Abbott, *Sh. Gr.* § 228.

**40. of health,** in opposition to 'damned'; an angel or spirit from heaven.

**43. questionable shape,** *i.e.* arousing obstinate questionings or problems in Hamlet's mind that need an answer.

**47. canonized,** not 'sainted', but 'buried according to the *canon* or ordinance of the church'.

**48. cerements.** Q 1 has *ceremonies.*

**49. inurn'd.** So F 1; Q 2 has the more commonplace *interr'd.*

**54. fools of nature,** the sport of nature.

The construction is rather cramped. "What may this mean" is followed by (*a*) "that thou...revisit'st", and (*b*) "to shake our disposition": "We fools of nature" is explanatory of the "our".

**71. his.** Cf. line 38, note.

**73. your sovereignty of reason.** Possibly 'your sovereignty' may be a courtier's phrase, like 'your highness'; but I think a better sense is got by taking the whole phrase as equivalent to 'reason, the sovereign quality in you'. Cf. i. 2. 110, "nobility of love". In that case 'deprive' is used in the rather exceptional sense of 'destroy'.

Lines 75–78 are not in F 1. The idea is further developed in *King Lear*, act iv. sc. 6.

83. **the Nemean lion,** one of the mythical monsters slain by Hercules.

**nerve.** Elizabethan usage inverts the senses now given to 'nerve' and 'sinew'. Cf. Glossary, *s.v.*

### Scene 5.

2. **My hour,** *i.e.* the hour of cock-crow; cf. i. 1. 147, *sqq.*

11. **to fast in fires.** 'Fast' appears to be used here in the very general sense of undergoing penance. Various emendations have been suggested, such as *to roast in fires; to waste in fires; to lasting fires.*

12. Cf. Vergil, *Aeneid*, vi. 739—

> "Ergo exercentur pœnis, veterumque malorum
> Supplicia expandunt. Aliæ panduntur inanes
> Suspensæ ad ventos; aliis sub gurgite vasto
> Infectum eluitur scelus, aut exuritur igni."

17. Cf. *Midsummer Night's Dream*, ii. 1. 153—

> "And certain stars shot madly from their spheres
> To hear the sea-maid's music".

19. **an end.** 'A' or 'an' appears to be often a dialectical form of 'on'. See Glossary, *s.v.*

20. **the fretful porpentine.** The porpentine or porcupine was supposed to shoot out its quills, like arrows, when fretted.

21. **eternal blazon,** revelation of the things belonging to eternity.

30. This is Hamlet's first impulse before the natural reaction of his character sets in. The speech is full of irony, considering the course the play is to take.

**meditation.** This does not seem to mean, as Warburton suggests, the mystical contemplation of God, or anything beyond 'thought' in the ordinary sense. 'As quick as thought' is a common phrase enough.

32. **the fat weed.** "If Shakespeare had any particular plant in mind, it must have been the asphodel, with its numerous bulbs, thick sown over the meadows of the lower regions." (Tschischwitz.) But the image seems rather to have been suggested by the heavy growth of shapeless weeds on wooden piles rising and falling with the motion of the water.

**33. roots.** So Q 2; F 1 has *rots*.

Lethe, a river or lake in the infernal regions of Greek mythology, whose waters gave forgetfulness of the past to those who drank. For the use of the substantive as an adjective cf. i. 3. 133, note.

**40.** Cf. i. 3. 256, 'I doubt some foul play'.

**42.** Shakespeare does not fall into the error of making his villains obviously mean, after the fashion of melodrama. Unless they had the gifts and powers to accomplish their ends, their success would appear unconvincing, and the whole motive of the play hollow.

**46. seeming-virtuous.** As to the extent of Gertrude's guilt see notes on act iii. sc. 4.

**47.** Cf. iii. 1. 53, *sqq.*, and the use of the same idea in Tennyson's *Locksley Hall*—

"Is it well to wish thee happy?—having known me—to decline
On a range of lower feelings and a narrower heart than mine!"

**53.** The natural order is 'as virtue never will be moved'. It is altered to bring out the antithesis of 'virtue' and 'lust'.

**56. sate.** So F 1; Q 2 has *sort*.

**61. secure,** in the sense of the Latin *securus*, implying less security itself, than a sense of security which may be mistaken.

**62. cursed Hebona.** So Q 2; F 1 has *cursed hebenon*. Hebona is generally supposed to be henbane (*Hyoscyamus niger*), which is a narcotic poison. Pliny (*Nat. Hist.* xxv. 4) states that the oil of it, dropped into the ears, stupefies the wits. On the other hand Dr. Brinsley Nicholson (New Sh. Soc. *Transactions*, 1880-2) argues that the plant meant is the yew. He shows that the name *ebenus* was applied to the yew; that Spenser's mention of "a heben bow" and "a heben lance" require a tough wood, and that, though the properties of neither plant exactly correspond to Shakespeare's description, the yew was supposed to curdle the blood, and so produce a kind of leprosy. Marlowe speaks of "the juice of hebon", but without showing which plant is meant. The *ebenus* or ebony is not poisonous.

**63.** Ambroise Paré, a surgeon, was suspected of having poured poison into the ear of Francis II. when he was dressing it.

**73.** The imperfect line allows a sufficient pause for Hamlet and the audience to realize the horror of the situation.

**75. dispatch'd,** suddenly bereft.

**76.** Cf. iii. 3. 81.

**77. disappointed.** Shakespeare, like Milton, is fond of piling up these picturesque negative adjectives and participles. 'Disappointed' is here used in its radical sense, 'not made ready'; cf. i. 1. 154, note. Capell proposed to read *unappointed*, but the more

varied rhythm appears preferable.   Pope's *unanointed* has the
additional defect of being identical in meaning with 'unaneled',
which, however, Pope interpreted as 'without a knell being rung'.

80. Many critics think that this line should be spoken by Hamlet,
but all the Qq. Ff. give it to the Ghost.

90. **uneffectual,** either because it is lost in the rays of the sun,
or, more probably, because it is light without heat.   Cf. Nash, *The
Unfortunate Traveller*, "The ostrich, the most burning-sighted bird
of all others, insomuch as the female of them hatcheth not her eggs
by covering them, but by the effectual rays of her eyes".

97. **this distracted globe.**   It is the stage tradition for the actor
to put his hand to his head at these words.

98. "Shakespeare alone could have produced the vow of Hamlet
to make his memory a blank of all maxims and generalized truths,
that 'observation had copied there'—followed immediately by the
speaker noting down the generalized fact, line 108." (Coleridge.)

105. Hamlet, already revolted by his mother's marriage, assumes,
as indeed the Ghost appears to do in line 85, that she had a share in
the greater crime.

107. **tables,** writing tablets of slate or ivory, often made in the
form of a book, with clasps.   They were perhaps covered with wax,
and written on with a sharp-pointed instrument.
Hamlet's action is symbolical of the scholar and philosopher, not
the man of deeds.

112. I cannot help thinking that some of the rude humour in the
latter part of this scene is a survival from the older play, and was
retained to please the groundlings.   It can, of course, be treated as
having a dramatic value.   It affords an outlet for Hamlet's excitement, and belongs to the exalted state of mind in which he conceives the idea of pretending madness.   This scheme has plainly
been formed by line 171.
The distribution of the speeches is that of Q 2; that of F 1 differs
slightly.

116. Hamlet parodies Horatio's call, by imitating that of a
falconer to his hawk.

124. Hamlet is on the point of saying 'but the king', when his
heart fails him, and he ingeniously turns off the sentence.

136. **S. Patrick,** according to Moberly the patron saint of
blunders and confusion, and therefore fitly invoked when 'the times
were out of joint'.   Or he may be thought of as concerned with un-
expiated crime.   Cf. Dekker, *The Honest Whore*, "S. Patrick, you
know, keeps Purgatory".

**there is,** not in Hamlet's words, but in Claudius' deeds.

**138. an honest ghost,** not a devil in his father's shape, as both Horatio and himself have thought possible.   Yet this very doubt recurs in ii. 2. 580.

**148.** Most European nations swore by the sword, in heathen times by the edge, in Christian by the cross hilt.

**156. Hic et ubique.**   Shakespeare rarely introduces Latin words in ordinary dialogue, which makes it the more likely that this scene contains fragments of an older play.

**167. our.**  So F 1; Q 2 has *your.*

**174.** One of the many lines which Shakespeare, as a practical playwright, leaves to be interpreted by the actor.

**189.** Hamlet's lurking sense of his own ineffectiveness bursts out in these lines.

The events of act i. are more or less continuous, from twelve o'clock on one night to dawn on the next.   An interval follows, as to the length of which see note on act ii. sc. 2 *ad fin.*

## Act II.—Scene I.

Act i. has been a sort of prologue; it contains the possibilities of which the remaining Acts show the tragic development.   As usual with Shakespeare, there is a crisis or turning-point at about the middle of the play, in the scene where Hamlet has a definite opportunity of killing the king and misses it (act iii. scene 3).   Up to that point we are concerned with the Cause of the tragedy, the action and reaction of the Ghost's injunction and Hamlet's character upon each other, the puttings off, the assumed madness.   After that, follows the Effect ; the successive fatal consequences due to that one cause are unrolled before us.

The first part of scene 1 is chiefly important as showing us at once that a considerable interval has elapsed.   Laertes has had time to reach Paris and make friends there.   It leads up to the more important question, 'What has become of Hamlet during the interval?   Is Claudius dead yet?'

The stage-direction of the text is that of F 1.   Q 2 has *Enter old Polonius with his man or two.*   This is interesting, because the words "*with his man or too*" look like an attempt to make sense of the name *Montano,* which was apparently left in the MS. side by side with the substituted *Reynaldo.*   Q 1 has *Enter Corambis and Montano.*   Cf. i. 2. 1, note, and Appendix A.

**7. Danskers.**  'Danske' is a common variant for 'Denmark'.

**10. encompassment and drift,** roundabout and gradual course; cf. the phrase 'to fetch a compass'.

**11. more nearer.**  The double comparative is not infrequent in Shakespeare; cf. iii. 2. 316; iii. 4. 167; v. 2. 119.

The thought is, 'You will get nearer by indirect than direct questions'. Polonius characteristically repeats this in other words in lines 65, 66.

**17.** The exactness and minuteness of Polonius' instructions is another sign of his self-conceit. He will leave nothing to the common-sense of his agent.

**20. forgeries,** in the general sense of 'false attributions'.

**28.** This speech shows at once the lowness of Polonius' moral tone and the futility of his intellect, with its love of nice and meaningless distinctions.

**35. Of general assault.** Dyce explains this as 'common to all young men'. But I think 'a savageness...of general assault' may also mean 'a passionate desire to assail all kinds of experience'.

**38. a fetch of warrant.** So F 1; Q 2 has *a fetch of wit*. A warranted or approved device.

**39. sullies.** So F 1; but Q 2 has *sallies*; cf. i. 2. 129, note.

**41.** Here Polonius nods wisely, and beckons with his forefinger to fill up the line.

**45. in this consequence,** with such words as follow.

**50.** Polonius' memory is something senile.

**59.** Is there an allusion here to the famous quarrel in a tennis-court between Sir Philip Sidney and the Earl of Oxford?

**64. of reach** is explained by i. 4. 56, "thoughts beyond the reaches of our souls".

**65. assays of bias,** attempts that resemble the curved roundabout course of a bowl; cf. Glossary, *s.v. bias*.

**68. have me,** understand me.

**71. in yourself,** personally, as well as by the report of others.

**73.** 'Let him go his own way without interference.'

**74.** Hamlet has not yet accomplished his purpose of revenge. The assumption of madness gives him time to consider the subject on every side, and the process fascinates him. One element in the situation is his utter solitariness; he needs the help of spiritual sympathy if he is to brace himself to the required effort. But where is it to come from? He turns naturally to his love Ophelia; yet he knows in his heart that she is not strong enough to give him what he wants. He makes one last attempt to disabuse himself of this impression, but her eyes only confirm it, and he reluctantly quits her for ever.

**85.** Hamlet is already regarded as mad in the court; the only question is, the reason? Polonius now jumps to the conclusion— *through love.* The disorder of Hamlet's attire, which may have been due either to intention or to preoccupation, also presents itself as a symptom of love-sickness; cf. *As You Like It*, iii. 2. 297, "your hose should be ungartered, your bonnet unbanded, your sleeve unbuttoned, your shoe untied, and everything about you demonstrating a careless desolation".

102. **the very ecstasy**, precisely the ecstasy.

103. **fordoes**, destroys. 'For' has the negative sense of 'to one's hurt', common in the German *ver*.

108. Cf. i. 3. 122.

114. This again must be taken as irony. Polonius is falling into this error even while he comments on it; cf. i. 5. 98, note.

118, 119. The expression is obscure. Probably Polonius is thinking of himself. His words seem to mean, 'If I make Hamlet's love for my daughter known, it may bring dislike on me; but probably, on the whole, more trouble would come out of keeping it dark'.

### Scene 2.

This long scene contains two main dramatic motives. In the latter part of it, from the entry of the players, we get the gradual approach to that crisis of the action which is brought about by the play-scene. The rest gives us, so to speak, a summary of the mental condition of Hamlet and of his attitude to the court during the months of delay. The points to notice are: (1) the assumption of madness, which deceives Gertrude, Ophelia, Polonius, Rosencrantz, Guildenstern, though the king, who has a better key to Hamlet's behaviour than any of these, is not without his suspicions; (2) the delight which Hamlet takes in the opportunity thus afforded him of pouring irony upon his enemies, and especially upon Polonius; (3) his invariable tendency to pass from the consideration of his own position into general satire and invective upon society. It is to be observed that Hamlet is not always acting the madman; he only does so, for instance, with Rosencrantz and Guildenstern, when he begins to suspect their good faith. And further, the pretence is easy to him. It only requires a slight exaggeration of his natural self. His thoughts and feelings, especially under conditions of nervous excitement, are always on a plane hardly intelligible to ordinary men. To appear mad he has only to relax the control which he normally keeps over them.

*Rosencrantz and Guildenstern.* Q 1 has *Rossencraft and Gilderstone.* The names are Danish; they occur as those of Danish students at Padua in 1587-9 and 1603 respectively, and a Danish courtier called Rosencrantz attended the coronation of James I.

2. **Moreover that**, besides the fact that; an unusual sense.

6. **Since**. So F 1 here and in line 13. Q 2 has the older form *Sith* in both cases.

**11. of,** applied to time, frequently takes the place of 'from'; cf. Abbott, *Sh. Gr.* § 167.

**12. humour.** So F 1; Q 2 has *haviour.*

**34.** Rosencrantz and Guildenstern are utterly commonplace men. The interchange of their names here is a subtle hint of their nonentity. They have been friends of Hamlet, superficially (lines 19, 228, 277), but they are not upon the same ethical or intellectual level as he is.

**40.** The introduction here of the Norway theme serves a double purpose. It marks the lapse of time since act i. sc. 2 (see note at end of this scene), and it again calls to our attention the need for a strong hand in Denmark, emphasized already in act i. sc. 1. This is done at intervals throughout the play.

**42.** The self-conceit of Polonius is only equalled by his effusive loyalty—to an usurper.

**still,** now as ever.

**47.** Polonius' statesmanship—a cunning both vulgar and shallow —is the point on which above all others he prides himself.

**52. the fruit.** So Q 2; F 1 has *the news,* of which Hunter would make *the nuts,* in the sense of 'It will be nuts to him' (!). The metaphor is only from the dessert, which comes *after* a feast.

**56. the main,** the obvious dominant fact in her life and that of her son.

**57.** There is no sign here that Gertrude knows anything of the nature of King Hamlet's death.

**61. Upon our first,** directly he had heard us.

**67. borne in hand,** handled, treated; cf. *Macbeth,* iii. 1. 81, 'How you were borne in hand'.

**73. three thousand.** So F 1; Q 2 has *three-score thousand,* but the F 1 reading is supported by the scansion and by Q 1.

**81. more consider'd time,** time more fit for consideration. Passive participles are often used in senses that are not exactly passive; cf. Abbott, *Sh. Gr.* § 374.

**90.** Again the irony of making a man utter his own condemnation.

**98. figure,** in the sense of rhetorical device.

**109.** This letter is no doubt a genuine love-letter of Hamlet's, written before the opening of the play, and before Ophelia had been instructed by her father to 'repel his letters' (i. 3. 122; ii. 1. 109). The terminology of it is no sign of madness. Love-letters have at all times been written in a nice and exalted vein; with an Elizabethan this would naturally result in such affectations and conceits as the Euphuists and Sir Philip Sidney had rendered popular. But to those who are not in love, love's language may well appear ridiculous or even insane. Cf. *Midsummer Night's Dream*, v. 1. 7—

> "The lunatic, the lover, and the poet
> Are of imagination all compact".

**110. beautified**, a fantastic variant for 'beautiful'; cf. Nash's dedication of *Christ's Tears over Jerusalem* (1594), "To the most beautified lady, the Lady Elizabeth Carey".

**111.** It is one of Polonius' absurdities to fancy himself a connoisseur of literature and the drama. His is one of those character-parts which gain incredibly by the voice and gesture of the actor.

**113.** "Women anciently had a pocket in the fore part of their stays, in which they not only carried love-letters and love-tokens, but even their money and their materials for needle-work." (Steevens.)

**123. this machine,** his earthly body.

**135. table-book,** note-book, the 'tables' of i. 5. 107. The idea is, 'If I had kept their secret as closely as a desk or table-book would have kept letters intrusted to them'.

**139. round,** not 'circuitously' but 'directly', 'straight out'; the common sense of 'roundly'; cf. *As You Like It*, v. 3. 11, "Shall we clap into it roundly, without hawking or spitting, or saying we are hoarse".

**141. out of thy star.** The idea is that persons in different ranks in life are under the influence of different stars, and therefore, like them, belong to different spheres; cf. *Twelfth Night*, ii. 5. 156, "in my stars I am above thee".

**146–50.** Considering that Hamlet was never mad, this chronicle of the stages of his malady is exquisite.

**160. four hours.** This is the reading of all the Qq. Ff.; at the same time I think that Hanmer's conjecture *for hours* is probably right.

**167.** The queen alone has any sympathy for Hamlet, whether in his love (line 114) or in his madness.

**171.** There is nothing corresponding to the remainder of this scene in the same place in Q 1, but a good deal of the matter follows the scene that corresponds to our act iii. sc. 1. Hamlet's dislike of Polonius is very marked; as the father of his love Ophelia, as the courtier of his uncle, as a man of the world, and as a fool, he is displeasing to the prince in every aspect.

**174. a fishmonger.** This taunt is purposely obscure, and conveys no meaning to Polonius. There are two possible explanations of what Hamlet may have intended by it. Coleridge gives one: "That is, you are sent to fish out my secret". Or 'fishmonger' may be used in a sense which it appears sometimes to bear, of a seller of women's chastity. Here and in lines 182 *sqq.*, Hamlet seems to suggest that Polonius would willingly make a market of his daughter.

**181.** Hamlet is still harping on Ophelia, so his irrelevance is not so great as it appears. Just as life comes out of carrion, so may she be the child of Polonius.

**182. a god kissing carrion.** Both Q 2 and F 1 read *a good kissing carrion*; the emendation is Warburton's. It may be justified by *1 Henry IV.* ii. 4. 113, "Didst thou never see Titan kiss a dish of butter?" and *Edward III.* (1596)—

> "The freshest summer's day doth sooner taint
> The loathed carrion that it seems to kiss".

If the reading of the Qq. Ff. is retained, the interpretation must be, ' If the sun can breed maggots of a dead dog, what will become of Ophelia? She too is 'good kissing carrion' (*i.e.* 'carrion good to kiss'). ' Therefore let her not walk i' the sun.'

**185. i' the sun,** in the sunshine of princely favours; cf. i. 2. 67.

**195.** There is no reason to find an allusion here to Juvenal, *Satire* x. 188, as Englished by Sir John Beaumont, or to any book in particular. Hamlet is clearly extemporizing on Polonius' peculiarities.

**214.** The words *and suddenly...between him* are left out in Q 2: probably it is an accidental omission.

**221.** Hamlet's transitions from banter to seriousness are frequent and pathetic. The effect, however, would be all the same upon his hearers.

Lines 244-274 (*245-271*) occur in F 1, but not in Q 2.

**256** (*254*). One of the startling sayings, which make one feel that Shakespeare has sounded the heights and depths of all philosophies.

**262. bad dreams,** the vision of his father, forcing him out of his favourite life of imagination and philosophy into the uncongenial world of action.

**270. outstretched.** "Hamlet is thinking of the strutting stage heroes." (Delius.)

Hamlet 'cannot reason'. The paradox he puts forward in this speech is not intended to suffer analysis.

**276. dreadfully attended,** not merely by his servants, but by his own ' bad dreams'.

**277. in the beaten way of friendship,** without ceremony, speaking as friend to friend.

**280** (*277*). Cf. i. 5. 185.

**282. too dear a halfpenny,** too dear at a halfpenny, valueless. For the omission of 'at' the Clarendon Press editors quote Chaucer, *Canterbury Tales*, 8875, "dere y-nough a jane"; and 12723, "dere y-nough a leeke".

Hamlet has not been playing the madman up to this point.  He
is unfeignedly glad to see his friends, and takes pleasure in a wit-
combat with them.  Suddenly his suspicions are aroused, and con-
firmed by their shuffling.  He at once glides into an extravagance of
speech, which easily convinces them of his insanity.

**304 &c.** There is nothing really mad in this speech of Hamlet's, it
is the natural expression of his pessimistic mood; but to the unphilo-
sophical mind—the plain man—all views of life that go in the least
beneath the surface will appear lunacy.

**322 (*318*).** Hamlet's thoughts are always returning to Ophelia.

**329. lenten.** Lent being a fast, 'lenten' is the reverse of joyous
or festive.

**332.** Hamlet's love of the drama is characteristic of his literary
temperament.  Shakespeare uses this episode of the players to introduce a certain amount of—what is unusual with him—topical allusion
to the fortunes of his company, and to vexed questions of dramatic
controversy.   We need not assume that all the literary criticism put
in Hamlet's mouth represents Shakespeare's own opinions.   It may
rather be that which would belong to the point of view of a scholar
and courtier, such, for instance, as we find in Sir Philip Sidney's
*Apologie for Poetrie.*
The players, however, are not merely incidental ; they have a share
in the working out of the plot.  Their coming suggests to Hamlet a
plan by which he may apply a crucial test to the king, and settle at
once all doubts as to the ghost's revelation.

**335. the humorous man,** the character part of the piece.  Cf.
the title-page of *Merry Wives*, Q 3, ' *The Merry Wives of Windsor,
with the humours of Sir John Falstaff*'.  Jonson's comedies, *Every
Man in his Humour, Every Man out of his Humour,* &c., are full of
such character studies.

**337. tickle o' the sere.**  F 1 has *tickled a' th' sere*.  The words
*the clown...sere* are omitted in Q 2.  The phrase occurs in Howard's
*Defensative against the poison of supposed prophecies* (1620), "Dis-
covering the moods and humours of the vulgar sort to be so loose
and tickle of the sere".  The meaning is pretty obvious—'easily
moved to laughter ', but how is it arrived at?  Perhaps the metaphor
is from a 'sere' or 'dry' throat, which is easily tickled.  An ingenious
explanation is given by Dr. Nicholson in *Notes and Queries* for July 22,
1871.  A 'sere' or 'sear' is part of the mechanism of a trigger.
Halliwell quotes in his *Archaic Dictionary* from Lombard (1596),
"Even as a pistol that is ready charged and bent will fly off by and
by, if a man do but touch the seare".  Thus "tickle o' the sere "
means ' ready to go off at once', like a hair-trigger.

**338.** ' The lady shall say her mind, even if she has to say more
than is set down for her, and so spoils the blank verse.'

**343-347.** On the 'travelling', the 'inhibition', the 'innovation', see Introduction, p. 15, and Appendix D.

Lines 352-379 occur in F 1, but not in Q 2.

**354-358.** On the 'aery of children' and the 'berattling of the common stages', see Introduction, p. 15, and Appendix D.

**355. cry out...question.** This is generally interpreted as 'cry out in a high childish treble' or 'cry out, dominating conversation'. I believe it really means, 'cry out on the burning question of the day, the question that is at the top, most prominent'.

**359. afraid of goose-quills,** afraid of being satirized.

**363. the quality,** the profession of actors.

**366. if their means are no better.** This phrase seems to support the belief that the profession of an actor was looked on with some contempt, even by literary men. Shakespeare is supposed to refer to this in *Sonnet* cxi.—

" O, for my sake do you with Fortune chide,
   The guilty goddess of my harmful deeds,
   That did not better for my life provide
   Than public means which public manners breeds,
   Thence comes it that my name receives a brand ", &c.

**378. Hercules and his load,** perhaps an allusion to the sign of the Globe Theatre, Hercules bearing the world for Atlas.

**381.** Hamlet quotes the case of his uncle as another instance of the change of fashion. His choice of an illustration shows the preoccupation of his thoughts.

**383. his picture in little.** Does this mean a miniature, or his picture on a coin?

**396. I am but mad north-north-west,** I am only mad when the wind is in one point of the compass, only touched with madness.

**397. a handsaw.** So Q 2, F 1. Hanmer proposed *hernshaw*, or 'heron', but the phrase as spelt in the text is proverbial. But very likely 'handsaw' may be a corruption of 'heronshaw'. Authorities on falconry say that the birds fly with the wind, and therefore, when it is from the south, the sportsman would have his back to the sun and be able to distinguish them without being dazzled. 'Hawk', however, is said to be a name given to a kind of tool used by plasterers.

**406. o' Monday morning.** I do not think there is any special point in this phrase. Hamlet affects to be talking of indifferent matters, that Polonius may not think any attention has been paid to his approach.

**410.** Hamlet maliciously spoils the effect of Polonius' announcement by being the first to speak of actors.

**412. Buz, buz,** according to Blackstone an interjection used at Oxford, equivalent to 'Stale news!'

**414.** *i.e.* 'Have they come 'upon your honour'?    Then your honour is—an ass.'

**416.** A satire on the numerous subdivisions of the drama. The licence given to the King's Company in 1603 entitles them "freely to use and exercise the art and faculty of playing Comedies, Tragedies, Histories, Enterludes, Moralls, Pastoralls, Stage plays, and such other like ".

**418. scene individable, or poem unlimited.** Delius explains these as referring respectively to plays that observed and that disregarded the Unity of Place.

**419, 420.** Seneca was the fashionable Latin model for tragedy, Plautus for comedy; Shakespeare's *Comedy of Errors* is based upon the *Menaechmi* of Plautus. A translation of this play by Warner appeared in 1595. All the plays of Seneca had been translated by 1581. *The Influence of Seneca on Elizabethan Tragedy* is the title of an interesting book by Dr. J. Cunliffe.

**420. Plautus.** Q 1 has the curious reading *Plato.*

**the law of writ and the liberty.** This again means pieces written according to rules and without rules, 'classical' and 'romantic' dramas. Collier, however, explains it 'written and extemporized plays'.

**422. Jephthah** had a daughter, and was ready to sacrifice her, as Polonius would Ophelia; cf. line 174, note.

**426.** A ballad entitled *Jesphas Dovgther at his death* was entered on the Stationers' Register in 1567-8, and another, or perhaps the same, entitled *Jepha Judge of Israel* in 1624. Various forms are in existence; in one the first stanza runs as follows:—

> "I red that many years ago,
>     When Jepha Judge of Israel,
> Had one fair daughter and no more,
>     Whom he loved so passing well.    *
> And as by lot God wot,
> It came to pass so like it was,
> Great war there should be,
>     And who should be the chief, but he, but he".

In 1602 a drama was written for Henslowe on the same subject by Dekker and Chettle.

**438. the first row...chanson.** So Q 2, and the reading is supported and explained by that of Q 1, *the first verse of the godly ballet.* F 1, however, has *Pons Chanson,* explained by Hunter as equivalent to *chanson du pont neuf,* 'a popular ballad'.

**439. my abridgement,** the players, who are "the abstract and brief chronicles of the time" (line 548). But Hamlet may also mean that the coming of the players cuts short or abridges his discourse; or again, that they serve as an entertainment to abridge or while away the time. Cf. *Midsummer Night's Dream*, v. i. 39, "Say, what abridgement have you for this evening?"

**442. valanced,** with a beard. This is the Q 2 reading; F 1 has *valiant*.

**445.** It should be remembered that on the Elizabethan stage female parts were taken by boys.

**448. cracked within the ring.** "There was a ring on the coin, within which the sovereign's head was placed; if the crack extended from the edge beyond this ring, the coin was rendered unfit for currency." (Douce.)

**450.** The French appear to have had an unenviable reputation as sportsmen, of pursuing all birds, and not only the nobler game.

**454 (452). me,** the ethic dative, introducing a person interested in the action of the verb; cf. ii. 1. 6, and Abbott, *Sh. Gr.* § 220.

**457. caviare,** a Russian delicacy, made of sturgeons' roes.

**the general,** the multitude.

The phrase may be illustrated by a quotation from Nicholas Breton's *The Courtier and the Countryman* (1597): "Another of the fine dishes...was a little barrel of caviary; which was no sooner opened and tasted, but quickly made up again, and was sent back with this message: 'Commend me to my good lady, and thank her honour, and tell her we have black soap enough already; but if it be any better thing, I beseech her ladyship to bestow it upon a better friend that can better tell how to use it'. Now if such be your fine dishes, I pray you let me alone with my country fare."

**459. in the top of mine,** with greater authority than mine.

**460. well digested in the scenes,** the scenes carefully arranged to advance the plot.

**461. modesty,** correctness, propriety, the opposite of extravagance, a common sense of the Latin *modestia*.

**466. by very much more handsome than fine,** *i.e.* its beauty was not that of elaborate ornament, but that of order and proportion.

**468. Æneas' tale to Dido.** There are many critical difficulties in understanding exactly what Shakespeare meant by this recitation episode; but they can only be briefly touched on here.

To begin with, there can be no doubt that Hamlet, at least, does not quote the lines in irony; they are not, to him, mere burlesque. The speech which introduces them is clearly intended for serious criticism, and, moreover, if they were burlesque, the point of the

episode in leading up to Hamlet's comparison of himself with the
player (lines 576, sqq.) would be dulled. Nevertheless, the lines as
they stand do read to me as the most absolute burlesque. Compare
them with the passage, with which they were obviously meant to
challenge comparison, the tale of Aeneas to Dido in Marlowe and
Nash's *Dido, Queen of Carthage*, ii. 1. 214, sqq. (Cf. Appendix E.)
The work of the earlier writer is inflated enough, but surely Shakespeare, with his 'coagulate gore' and his 'eyes like carbuncles',
excels him in bombast and extravagance. I am aware that this is
not the view of all critics, and it is opposed to the high æsthetic
authority of Coleridge, who writes: "The fancy that a burlesque
was intended sinks below criticism ; the lines, as epic narrative, are
superb". Perhaps Schlegel's explanation is the true one, that the
bombast is necessary to a play within a play. He says: "This extract must not be judged of by itself, but in connection with the place
where it is introduced. To distinguish it as dramatic poetry in the
play itself, it was necessary that it should rise above its dignified
poetry in the same proportion that the theatrical elevation does above
simple nature." Or perhaps we must not confuse Shakespeare with
Hamlet ; the actor-playwright, the romanticist *par excellence*, may be
gently satirizing the point of view of the university and court wit and
scholar, with his 'law of writ', his unities and classical models. But
there are further difficulties in this explanation. It agrees well enough
with the criticism which is put into Hamlet's mouth. The play is
said to be characterized by order and proportion, "well digested in
the scenes", free from irrelevancies and affectations, and therefore
"caviare to the general". This is exactly what might be said of
any 'classical' play, such as *Ferrex and Porrex*. But when we
come to the speech itself, all this is forgotten. The style is that of
an early turgid romantic play, full of affectations, and indeed the
play of *Dido, Queen of Carthage*, which it imitates, is essentially
romantic and not classical in character. So that it is impossible to
say that any quite satisfactory solution of the difficulty has been
arrived at.

472. the **Hyrcanian beast**, the tiger; an obvious reference to
Virgil, *Aeneid*, iv. 266—

"duris genuit te cautibus horrens
Caucasus, Hyrcanæque admôrunt ubera tigres".

492. **Rebellious to his arm.** Does this explain the sense of
*Macbeth*, i. 2. 56, "Point against point rebellious"?

495. This line affords the nearest verbal parallel between this
passage and the corresponding one in *Dido, Queen of Carthage*; cf.
that play, ii. 1. 254—

"Which he disdaining, whisked his sword about,
And with the wind thereof the king fell down".

Mr. Fleay suggested in *Macmillan's Magazine* for Dec. 1874, that
this scene was one of Nash's additions to Marlowe's play, and that

Shakespeare wrote his speech in rivalry.  In a later work, however, he assigns the scene to Marlowe.

**496.** The last three lines are represented by a blank in Q 2.

**502. a painted tyrant,** a tyrant in a picture.

**503.** 'Indifferent to his own will and the matter he had in hand.'

**517. fellies.**  Q 2 has *follies*, F 1 *fallies*.

**522. a jig,** a humorous performance by a clown, given after the fall of the curtain.  It included music, dancing, and coarse humour, and probably resembled some of the 'turns' at a modern music-hall more than anything else.  The titles of jigs by Kempe and others occur in the Stationers' Registers.

**525, 526. mobled.**  So Q 2 ; F 1 has *inobled*.

**527.** Polonius is rather bored, but he thinks it well to interpolate a criticism, in order to keep up his character as a judge of literature. The criticism is rather an unfortunate one, however.

**531. o'er-teemed,** worn out with bearing children.

**540.** Dryden did not know that 'milch' only meant 'moist', and wrote of this passage in the preface to his *Troilus and Cressida*, "His making milch the burning eyes of heaven was a pretty tolerable flight too; and I think no man ever drew milk out of eyes before him".

**541. passion,** like 'milch', is governed by 'made'.

**549.** Cf. line 439, note.

**550.** This line, like line 359, appears to show that personal satire was a considerable feature of the Elizabethan stage.

**564. a speech of some dozen or sixteen lines.**  There is a mare's-nest controversy on these lines in the *Transactions* of the New Shakspere Society for 1874.  I have no doubt that they are to be found in Lucianus' speech (iii. 2. 266, *sqq.*).  They are interrupted by the king's sudden rising.  Others think that they are to be found in the Player King's speech (iii. 2. 196, *sqq.*), because this speech is philosophical and therefore characteristic of Hamlet.  But the only object of altering the play could be to introduce a scene exactly parallel to Claudius' crime.

**570.** The suggestion that the player could only refrain from mocking Polonius out of courtesy to Hamlet is delicious.

**576.** Hamlet has been smitten by the player's emotion, obvious even to Polonius (line 542), into a consciousness of his own weakness. As a student of the drama he is aware of the profound influence of acting upon the minds of the spectators.  Hitherto he has been, so he thinks, deterred from action by doubts as to the genuineness of the ghost.  Now he makes the play, altered for the purpose, a test of the king's guilt,—and then, no more hesitation.

**580. wann'd.** So Q 2; F 1 has *warm'd.*

**584.** The pauses in this speech (cf. lines 593, 603, 610, 616) are filled up by intervals of meditation.

**595. John - a - dreams.** The word recurs in Armin's *Nest of Ninnies* (1608), "His name is John, indeed, says the cynic; but neither John-a-nods, nor John-a-dreams, yet either as you take it".

**601.** Cf. *Richard II.* i. 1. 44, "With a foul traitor's name stuft I thy throat"; and i. 1. 124—

"as low as to thy heart,
through the false passage of thy throat, thou liest".

**605.** For the belief that pigeons were gentle because they had no gall cf. Drayton, *Eclogue* lx.—

"a milk-white dove
About whose neck was in a collar wrought
Only like me my mistress hath no gall".

**617. About,** about it, to business.

**627.** This was a common explanation of the supernatural. It is that put forward by James the First's *Demonologie,* and is found also in Sir T. Browne's *Religio Medici:* "I believe...that these apparitions and ghosts of departed persons are not the wandering souls of men, but the unquiet walks of devils, prompting and suggesting unto us murder blood and villainy, instilling and stealing into our hearts, that the blessed spirits are not at rest in their graves, but wander solicitous of the affairs of the world".

**631. such spirits,** such humours, as melancholy.

**633. More relative,** more closely related, more definite.

**this,** *i.e.* the story of the ghost. Hamlet has taken out his tablets to compose the 'dozen or sixteen lines'; in these same tablets he has written his note after the ghost's departure (i. 5. 109), and he now taps them significantly. He is happy now, for he can put off his whole problem, with a good conscience, until the result of his congenial device is made clear.

An interval of at least a month has elapsed between acts i. and ii. There has been time for Laertes to reach France and want fresh supplies (ii. 1. 1), for the ambassadors to return from Norway (ii. 2. 40), for Hamlet's reputation for madness to be established, and for Rosencrantz and Guildenstern to be sent for (ii. 2. 3). Cf. also iii. 2. 136 and note *ad loc.* with i. 2. 147. From the beginning of act ii. the action is fairly continuous to the end of act iv. sc. 3. Act iii. sc. 2 is on the 'morrow night' to act ii. sc. 2 (ii. 2. 563), and act iii. sc. 1 is doubtless on the morrow morning. It will be remembered that Mr. Rose has shown reason for supposing that act iii. sc. 1 is really part of act ii.

### Act III.—Scene I.

This short scene sums up the precise situation of affairs at the moment when the crisis is coming on. There are three points to be noticed.

(1) Hamlet has resolved to make the play the solution of all his doubts; if that test shows the king guilty, he shall die. Even as he forms this determination, his heart fails him. He turns to an alternative which has dimly presented itself before (i. 2. 132), and deliberately considers the desirability of suicide. But such a way out of the difficulty is too simple, too easy for his over-speculative nature. He sees the future filled with countless possibilities, which puzzle his will, and this enterprise also loses the name of action.

(2) Hamlet has long known that no help is to be had from Ophelia. Yet when she appears before him, his old tenderness revives. He speaks gently to her, and then—discovers that she is deceiving him, acting as a decoy for Polonius. This obliges him to play the madman again, and his paradoxes express a feeling of revulsion from the poor foolish girl. His mother's sin has already made him lose faith in womanhood, and now he sees Ophelia, too, spotted with all the vileness of her sex. He assails her with reproaches so inappropriate to herself that she can only take them as the sign of a shattered mind.

(3) With Polonius and the like Hamlet's acting is successful; but the king is shrewder. His suspicions are awaked, and he at once plots to get his nephew out of the way. Hamlet has, therefore, gone too far on the path of delay, and though he does not know it, the opportunities of revenge are fast slipping away from him.

1. **drift of circumstance**, roundabout methods; cf. i. 5. 127; ii. 1. 10.

5. Cf. ii. 2. 304.

13. This hardly appears to give a fair account of what really took place, unless indeed we accept Clarke's somewhat strained interpretation ' He was sparing in speech when we questioned him; but of demands respecting ourselves he was very free in return'. Warburton proposed to read—

> *Most free in question, but of our demands*
> *Niggard in his reply.*

32. The phrase **lawful espials** is not found in Q 2.

43. Polonius and the king hide behind an arras. The book given to Ophelia is doubtless a prayer-book; cf. the following lines and the word 'orisons' in line 89.

46. Here again the truth of Polonius' words affords an ironical contrast to the meanness of his actions.

49. This speech is the first hint of any sting of conscience in Claudius; cf. act iii. sc. 3.

**52. the thing that helps it,** the waiting-maid; cf. the well-known saying, ' No man is a hero to his *valet-de-chambre*'.

Lines 57, 58 are an expansion of the idea ' to be'; lines 59, 60 of ' not to be'. Hamlet may propose to take arms either by attacking the king, and so exposing himself to probable death, or, more likely, by killing himself. The metaphor contained in "take arms against a sea of troubles" has been criticised as being confused and absurd; but the difficulty, if there is any, disappears when it is shown that there is an allusion to a custom attributed to the Kelts by many classical writers. Shakespeare may have read of it in Aristotle or Strabo or Nicolas Damascenus, but most probably in Abraham Fleming's translation of Aelian's *Histories* (1576), book xii.: "Some of them are so bold, or rather desperate, that they throw themselves into the foaming floods with their swords drawn in their hands, and shaking their javelins, as though they were of force and violence to withstand the rough waves, to resist the strength of the stream, and to make the floods afraid lest they should be wounded with their weapons".

**61. to say.** Bailey objected to these words as breaking the sense, and proposed *straightway*. But I think they are meant as a hint that it is not a real end.

**67. this mortal coil.** 'Coil' generally means 'turmoil'; cf. Glossary, *s.v.*; but it is often explained here as 'body', and the phrase is compared to *Merchant of Venice*, v. I. 64, "this muddy vesture of decay", and to Beaumont and Fletcher's *Bonduca*, iv. 4, "the case of flesh". The body is conceived of as wound round the soul like a coil of rope. Various editors have suggested *clay*, *soil*, *veil*, *spoil* ( = 'slough').

**69. of so long life,** so long lived.

**70. the whips and scorns of time,** *i.e.* of the temporal world. In Armin's *Nest of Ninnies* (1608) occurs the phrase, "there are, as Hamlet says, things called whips in store". If the reference is to Shakespeare's *Hamlet*, it may either be a misquotation of this passage, or it may preserve a reading not found in any of the Qq. Ff. But of course it may refer to the older *Hamlet*.

**76. a bare bodkin;** the sense is probably ' a mere bodkin', rather than ' an unsheathed bodkin'.

**80. No traveller returns.** "Then how about the Ghost?", asked Theobald; to which Coleridge replied, "If it be necessary to remove the apparent contradiction—if it be not rather a great beauty—surely it were easy to say that no traveller returns to this world as to his home or abiding place".

**83. conscience,** the exercise of conscious thought, speculation on the future. This speech is not merely ironical. Hamlet has become aware of the flaw in his own character, though he attributes it to humanity in general.

**86. pitch.** So Q 2; F 1 has *pith* (cf. i. 4. 22, "pith and marrow"). 'Pitch' is 'height', the metaphor being from falconry.

**96.** 'I may have given you love-tokens, but never my life, my very self.'

**103.** At this moment Hamlet hears a rustle behind the arras, and immediately suspects Ophelia's good faith. He begins to speak cynically out of the disbelief in women which his mother has now taught him. For the antithesis between 'honest' and 'fair' cf. the dialogue between Touchstone and Audrey in *As You Like It*, act iii. sc. 3.

**119. inoculate.** The metaphor is of course from gardening; cf. Glossary, *s.v.*

**120. of it,** of our old stock.

**122.** Hamlet again becomes tender to Ophelia; he tries by self-accusation to persuade her that his love was little loss. He is not entirely insincere; he feels that those evil tendencies are really dormant in him, though they will very likely never come into action. He is 'crawling between earth and heaven', without the strength to take definitely the way either of good or of evil. And, as often in the crises of life, he feels compelled to confess what is worst in him. Cf. the self-accusations of Malcolm in *Macbeth*, act iv. sc. 3.

**132 (*130*).** Hamlet suddenly determines to test Ophelia by the question, 'Where's your father?' She lies to him, and he then bursts into a partly genuine, partly assumed extravagance of invective against womankind, unfairly enough applying it all to her.

**142 (*137*). Get thee to a nunnery,** *i.e.* 'breed no children'. In line 122 the implied reason was the wickedness of man; now it is the falseness of woman.

**148 (*142*). paintings...face.** So Q 2; F 1 has *prattlings...pace*. Line 51 supports the Q 2 reading; cf. also *Merchant of Venice*, iii. 2. 88, *sqq.*—

"Look on beauty
And you shall see 't is purchased by the weight".

**151 (*144*).** Hamlet is satirizing various forms of feminine affectation or unreality, the painted face, the affected speech and walk, the use of dubious words in pretended innocence. What particular affectation is meant by 'nick-name God's creatures'? Perhaps such discourse as that of Beatrice to Benedick in the first scene of *Much Ado*, a merely superficial raillery, covering other feelings.

**155. all but one.** Claudius is the one.

**157.** Ophelia sinks down in a chair, her face buried in her hands. Hamlet is just leaving the stage, when he turns round, gently ~~approaches~~ her, raises a lock of her hair, and presses it to his lips, ~~goes~~.—So Mr. Beerbohm Tree plays the part, and ~~ar~~ business.

**161. mould of form,** model on which all formed themselves.

**167. blown,** in full blossom.

**171.** The double negative is common in Shakespeare and Elizabethan writers generally. Cf. Abbott, *Sh. Gr.* § 406.

**175. for to.** When 'to' lost its prepositional force and became merely the sign of the infinitive, 'for' was added to strengthen the sense of motion or purpose. Cf. Abbott, *Sh. Gr.* § 152.

**178. tribute.** Aethelred the Unready (994) began the practice of buying off the Danish invaders of England. Hence arose the tax known as Danegelt, which was levied long after the invasions had ceased, though it was no longer paid to the Danes.

**184.** Polonius still sticks to his own theory.

**192.** Eaves-dropping appears to be Polonius' one conception of statesmanship.

### Scene 2.

This important scene finally convinces Hamlet of the king's guilt; it closes with a resolution to 'do bitter business'. Hamlet is throughout in a state of extreme nervous tension; at the success of his plot he breaks into the wildest excitement. Hence the nonsense he talks to Ophelia, and his riotous fooling of the courtiers. The episodes with the players and Horatio serve partly as a quiet opening to the turbulent emotions of the play-scene, partly to show that Hamlet's action is fundamentally sane and rational. It is characteristic of him to be able to interest himself at such a critical moment in the niceties of the actor's art.

**1.** The effectiveness of restraint, of the middle course between ranting and tameness—that is the gist of Hamlet's counsel.

**10 (8).** Cf. *Every Woman in her Humour* (1609), "As none wear hoods but monks and ladies, and feathers but forehorses...none periwigs but players and pictures".

**12. the groundlings,** the inferior part of the audience, who paid a penny for standing room in the yard or 'pit' of the theatre. Cf. Jonson, *Bartholomew Fair*, Induction, "The understanding gentlemen of the ground here asked my judgment".

**15. Termagant,** supposed to be a god of the Saracens, a boisterous character often represented in the mysteries. Cf. *Guy of Warwick*, where the Sultan says—

"So help me Mahoun of might
And Termagaunt my god so bright";

and Bale, *Acts of English Votaries* (*Reliques*, i. 77), "Grennyng upon her lyke Termagauntas in a play". In *1 Henry IV.* v. 4. 114 the word is used as an adjective, "that hot termagant Scot". Skeat derives it from the Ital. *Trivigante*, the moon who wanders (Lat. *vagari*) through the heavens in a threefold aspect (Lat. *ter*), as Hecate, Selene, Artemis.

16. **Herod**, another common character in the mysteries. It was traditionally played with as much noise and rant as possible. Cf. the stage-direction in the Coventry play of *The Nativity*, "Here Erode ragis in thys pagond, and in the strete also". In the Chester play of *The Slaughter of the Innocents* (ed. Sh. Soc. p. 153) he is made to say—

> "For I am kinge of all mankinde,
>  I byde, I beate, I lose, I bynde,
>  I maister the moone, take this in mynde,
>      That I am moste of mighte,
>  I am the greatest above degree,
>  That is, that was, that ever shalbe".

Chaucer (*Miller's Tale*, 3384) says of the parish clerk, Absolon, "He pleyeth Herodes up on a scaffold hye".

24 (*20*). The saying that the stage should hold the mirror up to nature should be taken strictly in accordance with the context; it is not a pronouncement in favour of realism on the stage, but only a plea for naturalness of gesture and speech in acting.

50 (*48*). The following lines are inserted here in Q 1. There is nothing corresponding to them in Q 2 or F 1 :—

> "And then you have some again, that keeps one suit
>  Of jests, as a man is known by one suit of
>  Apparell, and gentlemen quotes his jests down
>  In their tables, before they come to the play, as thus:
>  'Cannot you stay till I eat my porridge?' and, 'You owe me
>  A quarter's wages'; and, 'My coat wants a cullison';
>  And, 'Your beer is sour'; and blabbering with his lips,
>  And thus keeping in his cinque-pace of jests,
>  When, God knows, the warm Clown cannot make a jest
>  Unless by chance, as the blind man catches a hare;
>  Masters! tell him of it".

It seems to have been the common practice of the clowns to insert 'gag' in their parts, like a modern actor of Gaiety burlesque. Stowe praises the 'extemporal wit' of Thomas Wilson and Richard Tarlton. It has been suggested that the passage in Q 1 was aimed especially at the famous comic actor, William Kempe, who probably acted the serving-men of Shakespeare's earlier comedies. He appears to have left the Chamberlain's company in 1599, but in 1602 he had returned to them, and this may well explain the omission of the passage in Q 2 and F 1. Cf. Introduction, page 16.

59. Hamlet's admiration for Horatio, a man of such opposite *character to himself*, is very natural. Apparently he has confided

in him to some extent, though probably Horatio was hardly capable of fully understanding or helping Hamlet in his difficulties.

**66. pregnant,** because the fawning courtesy may lead to 'thrift' or 'profit'.

**74.** "According to the doctrine of the four humours, desire and confidence were seated in the blood, and judgment in the phlegm, and the due mixture of the humours made a perfect character." (Johnson.)

**75.** Doubtless Hamlet recurs to the idea suggested here in the episode of the recorders.

**81. One scene,** the 'dozen or sixteen lines' of ii. 2. 565. See note *ad loc.*

**84.** *i.e.* 'make a mental note of every action'.

**95. idle.** If this really means 'mad', it is a pretty clear proof that the madness is assumed. Cf. Glossary, *s.v.*

**98. the chameleon's dish.** Cf. *Two Gentlemen of Verona,* ii. 1. 178, "Though the chameleon Love can feed on the air"; and Sir T. Browne, *Pseudodoxia Epidemica,* iii. xx. "Concerning the chameleon, there generally passeth an opinion that it liveth only upon air, and is sustained by no other aliment".

**99. promise-crammed.** Claudius has promised Hamlet that he shall be his 'son', when he should be king (i. 2. 64); and Hamlet has promised to slay Claudius, but does not do it.

**102. are not mine,** do not refer to my question.

**108. Julius Cæsar.** There are numerous records of performances of plays, both in Latin and English, in the colleges of Oxford and Cambridge. In 1607 *Cæsar and Pompey* or *Cæsar's Revenge* was acted at Trinity, Oxford; this was in English. A Latin play on Cæsar's death was acted at Christ Church in 1582. It will be remembered that Shakespeare's own *Julius Cæsar* appeared about 1601, the probable date of the first version of *Hamlet.*

**109. i' the Capitol.** The murder of Cæsar actually took place in the Theatre of Pompey, which stood in the Campus Martius. Here, as in *Julius Cæsar* and *Antony and Cleopatra,* Shakespeare transfers the scene of it to the Capitol.

**132.** Hamlet means that 'your only jig-maker' is what would have been expected to cause sorrow, the death of a husband and father.

**136. two months.** In i. 2. 138 it was 'not two', and in i. 2. 153 the marriage of Claudius and Gertrude was said to have taken place 'within a month'. This leaves about a month for the interval between acts i. and ii. Cf. act ii. sc. 2, note, *ad fin.*

*138. I'll have a suit of sables.* The obvious sense is, 'I'll give up mourning, throw off my inky cloak'. But 'sable' certainly means as a rule black. Probably the meaning here is 'robes trimmed with the fur of sables', which were sumptuous and expensive, and not regarded as mourning. Others take the word as equivalent to the French *isabelle* or 'flame-colour'.

**144.** Apparently this is a line from a ballad. It is again quoted in *Love's Labour's Lost*, iii. 1. 30. The 'hobby-horse' was a character in the may-games and morris-dances. It was represented by a man astride upon a stick with a horse's head upon it. It appears to have been suppressed at the Reformation, and to this fact the ballad probably referred.

**145.** It was common for the action of a play to be briefly represented in dumb-show at the beginning, not, however, on the English stage, but on that of Denmark. Hunter quotes a description of such a performance given by Danish soldiers in 1688, from the diary of Abraham de la Pryme. It would seem, however, that in this case the device rather gives away Hamlet's design to surprise the king. The dumb-show must have prepared him for what followed.

**147. miching mallecho**, 'secret mischief' (cf. Glossary, *s.vv.*), in a double sense, of the poisoner's crime, and of Hamlet's own secret plot. There is a similar *double-entendre* in the use of the title 'The Mousetrap' (line 247).

**165.** Here at least, whatever may have been his purpose in act ii. sc. 2, Shakespeare imitates the cruder style of the earlier English tragic drama. Both the rhymes and the stilted language are characteristic thereof. Cf. the laboured periphrases by which lines 165 to 168 express the fact that thirty years have passed, with Shakespeare's own parallel phrase in i. 1. 36.

**175. distrust you**, am distrustful for you; cf. i. 3. 51, "fear me not".

**177. holds quantity**, are proportionate to each other. For the use of a singular verb with a double substantive cf. Abbott, *Sh. Gr.* § 336.

**178.** 'They have naught either of fear and love, or they have both in extremity.'

**240.** Note the irony of putting this in the Queen's mouth.

**249. Vienna.** Q 1 has *Guyana.*

**Gonzago.** In Q 1 the name is given as *Albertus.* Moreover in Q 1 Albertus and Baptista are throughout called *Duke* and *Duchess*; in Q 2, except for this line, they are always *King* and *Queen.* The retention of the titles of Q 1, even in one place only, betrays that a change has been made.

**253.** A proverbial expression, found in Lyly, and in *Damon and Pythias* (1582), "I know the gall'd horse will soonest wince".

**255. a chorus.** In *Winter's Tale, Romeo and Juliet, Henry V.*, a chorus is introduced to explain the progress of the action.

**257. the puppets,** the He and She, the actors in the comedy of love. At 'puppet shows' or 'motion', as in the modern Punch and Judy show, the dialogue was spoken by some one on or behind the stage. Cf. *Two Gentlemen of Verona*, ii. 1. 100, "O excellent motion! O exceeding puppet! Now will he interpret to her". So Greene, in his *Groatsworth of Wit*, says of himself, "It was I that ... for seven years' space was absolute interpreter of the puppets". And Nash, in his *Pierce Penniless*, "the puling accent of her voice is like a feigned treble, or one's voice that interprets to the puppets". Hamlet wantonly insults Ophelia with cynical talk of love.

**262. mistake,** *i.e.* take amiss. So Q 2, F 1, with an obvious reference to the Marriage Service. Many editors adopt Pope's *must take*.

**265.** Cf. *The True Tragedie of Richard the Third* (p. 61, Sh. Soc. reprint)—

"The screeking raven sits croaking for revenge,
    Whole herds of beasts comes bellowing for revenge".

**266.** This speech is doubtless Hamlet's 'dozen or sixteen lines': cf. ii. 2. 565, note.

**268. midnight weeds.** Cf. iv. 7. 143, and *Macbeth*, iv. 1. 25, "Root of hemlock digged i' the dark".

**269. Hecate,** or Diana in her aspect as an infernal goddess, was regarded in the Middle Ages as the queen of witches.

**274.** No such Italian form of the story can be identified.

**277.** This line is omitted in Q 2, probably by accident, as it occurs in Q 1. As Mr. Beerbohm Tree plays the part, Hamlet's excitement increases during the delivery of Lucianus'—his own—speech. He creeps across the floor of the hall, muttering the words from a written paper, and as the King rises, he leaps up wildly, tears the paper, and scatters the fragments in the air.

**282.** In the rest of the scene, Hamlet indulges the excitement which he has held pent up during the play. But his elation is, at any rate at first, less at knowing the truth than at the artistic success of his dramatic venture. The source of Hamlet's quatrain is unknown, if it is a quotation at all.

**go weep;** cf. the passage on Jaques and the weeping deer in *As You Like It*, act ii. sc. 1.

**286. this,** this specimen of play writing.

**287. turn Turk,** go to the bad; the phrase recurs in *Much Ado*, iii. 4. 57. Cf. Cooke, *Greene's Tu Quoque* (1614), "This it is to turn Turk, from an absolute and most complete gentleman, to a most absurd and ridiculous lover".

**288. Provincial roses,** the double damask rose, Gerard's *Rosa provincialis*, so called either from Provence, or from Provins, a town forty miles from Paris.

**290. Half a share.** A collection of papers of the year 1635, printed by Mr. Halliwell-Phillipps in his *Outlines of the Life of Shakespeare*, vol. i. p. 312, throws much light on the internal economy of the King's Company. The profits were divided between the 'actors' and the 'housekeepers' or proprietors, some of whom were actors also—witness the following extract, "That the house of the Globe was formerly divided into sixteen partes, whereof Mr. Cuthbert Burbidge and his sisters had eight, Mrs. Condell four, and Mr. Heminges four. That Mr. Tailor and Mr. Lowen were long since admitted to purchase four partes between them from the rest, viz., one part from Mr. Heminges, two partes from Mrs. Condell, and halfe a part a peece from Mr. Burbidge and his sister".

**292.** The friendship of Damon and Pythias was famous in antiquity.

**294. Jove himself;** cf. iii. 4. 46.

**295. A very, very—pajock.** The word 'pajock' is humorously substituted for 'ass', which would—more or less—have rhymed. Many explanations of it have been given, but Dyce has shown that in Scotland the peacock is often called a 'peajock', just as the turkey is a 'bubbly-jock'. Therefore we may be content, with Pope, to see an allusion to the fable of the birds choosing the peacock as king instead of the eagle. Mr. Irving adds a point by looking at a peacock-feather fan which he has taken from Ophelia's lap. Skeat, however, derives 'pajock' from 'patch', 'a pied fool', and this explanation is supported by Spenser's use of 'patchocke' for ragamuffin. Claudius is called 'a king of shreds and patches' in iii. 4. 102. Prof. Leo suggests that Hamlet leaves his sentence unfinished, and that *pajock* is a misprint for a stage-direction *Hiccups*!

**303. A recorder** appears to have been a flute with a hole bored in the side, and covered with gold-beaters' skin, so as to approach the effect of the human voice.

**316. more richer.** Cf. ii. 1. 11, note.

**345. were she ten times our mother.** This sounds mere folly to Rosencrantz, but Hamlet intends to reproach, not to be reproached.

**348. these pickers and stealers,** these hands, in allusion to the phrase in the catechism, "Keep my hands from picking and stealing". Cf. *As You Like It*, iv. 1. 111, "By this hand, it will not kill a fly".

**354.** Hamlet ironically suggests a cause for his distemper which Rosencrantz will understand. As a matter of fact the loss of the crown is a small item in his score against Claudius. More is made
    Belleforest.

**358.** Malone quotes from Whetstone, *Promos and Cassandra* (1578), "Whylst grass doth growe, oft sterves the seely steede"; and from *The Paradise of Dainty Devices* (1578), "While grass doth growe, the silly horse he sterves".

**360. To withdraw with you.** He beckons Guildenstern aside, as if to impart a secret to him.

**365.** Guildenstern's speech was mere words, with no intelligible meaning.

**372. as lying,** at which Guildenstern has shown himself proficient.

**373. and thumb.** So F 1; Q 2 has *and the umber.*

**385. this little organ,** himself, rather than the recorder.

**397. backed like a weasel.** The full absurdity of Polonius' complaisance is only realized by remembering that the back of a camel is its most conspicuous part, and quite unlike that of a weasel.

| **412.** Nero was the murderer of his mother Agrippina.

**417. seals,** the seal of deeds.

*f* Hamlet ends the scene on a note of the firmest resolution.

### Scene 3.

Hamlet has his opportunity to translate resolution into action and misses it. Critics have objected to what they regard as the cold-blooded cruelty of his reasons for not killing the king while he is praying. But they do not observe that these are not reasons, only excuses. Hamlet would kill the king if he could, but he has delayed so long that he cannot now commit himself to the definite immediate act. But the hour is slipping from him. Claudius, in spite of his momentary weakness of contrition, is determined to be quit, in one way or another, of this dangerous prince.

**5. The terms of our estate,** the conditions on which the safety of our crown depends.

**7. lunacies.** So F 1; Q 2 has *browes.*

**9. many many.** Cf. i. 2. 129, "too too solid flesh"

**11.** Cf. Laertes' speech, i. 3. 10, *sqq.*

**15. The cease...dies** is a somewhat tautological expression. Bailey proposed to read *Deceasing majesty.*

**30.** As a matter of fact, it was Polonius' own suggestion. Cf. iii. 1. 184.

**33. of vantage,** from a point of vantage.

**35. dear my lord.** 'My lord', 'my liege', become practically a *single noun,* like the French *milord.*

| 37. Claudius' better self is strong enough to make him repent his crime, not to lead him to give up the fruits of it. The touch of remorse is artistically necessary to prevent his becoming a mere abstract character, beyond the reach of our understanding and sympathy.

37. **the primal eldest curse**, the curse of Cain

39. **as sharp as will**, sharp enough, if nothing were in the way, to determine the will. Theobald proposed *as 'twill*.

45. Cf. Lady Macbeth's washing of her hands in *Macbeth*, v. 1. 31, and ii. 3. 60—
> "Will all great Neptune's ocean wash this blood
> Clean from my hand?"

62. For the omission of the auxiliary verb with *compelled* cf. i. 2. 90, and Abbott, *Sh. Gr.* § 403.
Claudius' confession removes the last vestige of doubt from the spectators' minds as to the truth of the ghost's story.

75. Once Hamlet begins to ' scan ' and speculate he is lost.

78. A pause, while Hamlet reflects in silence.

80. Cf. i. 5. 76, *sqq.*

**full of bread.** Cf. *Ezekiel*, xvi. 49, " Behold, this was the iniquity of thy sister Sodom ; pride, fulness of bread, and abundance of idleness was in her and her daughters ".

83. ' So far as we can tell by inference, not direct knowledge.'

93, 94. This passage "recalls very forcibly some of those painfully realistic representations of the torments of the damned, which are to be found in various illustrated books of the sixteenth and seventeenth centuries " (Marshall). The damned souls in the miracle plays were always represented with black faces. Cf. *Henry V.* ii. 3. 42, " Do you not remember, a' saw a flea stick upon Bardolph's nose, and a' said it was a black soul burning in hell-fire ". Mr. Symons quotes R. Browning, *Soliloquy of the Spanish Cloister*—

> " If I trip him just a dying
> Sure of heaven as sure can be,
> Spin him round, and send him flying
> Off to hell, a Manichee ".

96. This line is terribly ironical; Hamlet's delay only prolongs the days of his ineffectiveness and failure.

### Scene 4.

Much critical controversy has been spent on the question of Gertrude's guilt or innocence in the matter of her husband's murder. I think the natural inference from this scene (especially line 30), and

from the Ghost's story in act ·i. scene 5, is that she knew nothing of
it. She was guilty of a sinful love for Claudius, but was not an accom ·
plice in his greater crime. Hamlet, indeed, assumes throughout that
the stain of murder as well as of adultery is upon her, but he is naturally inclined to take the blackest view. It is noteworthy that in the
First Quarto the Queen's innocence is much more definitely declared
(cf. Appendix A).

In any case, it is his mother's faithlessness in love that is most
bitterly in Hamlet's mind, and with this he chiefly upbraids her. At
first he is successful; the stings of remorse begin to make themselves
felt. Then comes the ghost, and she is convinced that Hamlet is
mad. From that moment she is overcome with fear, and his words
pass over her unheeded. For the rest of the play her heart is cleft
in twain; she vacillates to the end between good and evil, between
her son and her lover.

**4. silence.** So Q 2, F 1. Many editors accept Hanmer's emendation *sconce*.

**9, 10. thy father** ... **my father,** Claudius ... the elder Hamlet.

**24.** Hamlet evidently thinks that the king is concealed behind the
arras. He aims a blow at him out of pure impulse, without waiting
to consider. And thus in the death of Polonius comes the first
tragic result of his delay.

**33.** Hamlet is too intent on the business in hand to give Polonius
more than a brief epitaph.

**42. the rose, the charm, the grace;** cf. iii. 1. 160. The idea is
that Gertrude's wicked love makes the purest love seem a shameful
'thing.

**44. sets a blister there.** Harlots were branded in the forehead;
cf. iv. 5. 119, and *Comedy of Errors*, ii. 2. 138, "tear the stained
skin off my harlot-brow".

**49 this solidity and compound mass,** the earth itself. For
the idea of the whole universe being affected by a sin, cf. Milton,
*Paradise Lost*, ix. 1000 —

> " Earth trembled from her entrails, as again
> In pangs, and nature gave a second groan;
> Sky loured, and, muttering thunder, some sad drops
> Wept at completing of the mortal sin
> Original".

**53.** Opinions differ as to the action that should accompany this
line on the stage. I have very little doubt that Hamlet draws a
miniature, a ' picture in little ' (ii. 2. 384), of his father from his
pocket, and then turns to point at one of Claudius that hangs on the
wall of the closet. Both Irving and Salvini suppose the pictures to
be seen with the mind's eye only.

**95.** Cf. iii. 2. 414.

**98. a vice of kings.** The Vice was a stock character in the Moralities; he appears to have personified the weaker side of human nature (hence his name); but practically he was a buffoon, and supplied the comic element in the dramas. Thus he is one of the ancestors of Shakespeare's fools. Several allusions to the Vice and his dagger of lath appear in the plays; cf. *e.g. Twelfth Night,* iv. 2. 132—

> "I'll be with you again
> In a trice
> Like to the old Vice,
> Your need to sustain;
>
> Who, with dagger of lath,
> In his rage and his wrath,
> Cries, ah, ha! to the devil".

Thus "a vice of kings" means practically 'a king *pour rire'*.

**102. shreds and patches.** The Vice, like his successor the Fool, appears to have been often dressed in motley. Cf. Mr. Skeat's interpretation of 'pajock' in iii. 2. 295, note.

**103.** At his previous apparition the Ghost was visible to all those present, now he only allows himself to be seen by Hamlet, just as the ghost in *Macbeth* appears to the king only.

**106.** Here, as in ii. 2. 593, *sqq.*, Hamlet is quite conscious of his own weakness.

**107. lapsed in time and passion,** having allowed both time and the passion of revenge to slip by.

**122. start up and stand.** 'Hair', partly perhaps owing to the influence of 'soldiers', is treated as a plural.

**126.** A reminiscence of the biblical phrase, "I say unto you, If these should hold their peace, the very stones should cry out".

**133.** Cf. iii. 1. 171, note.

**139 &c.** Those who believe that Hamlet was really mad get over this speech by pointing out that nearly all insane patients are prepared to solemnly assert their own sanity.

**150. avoid what is to come,** not 'avoid the future', but 'avoid sin in the future'.

**151.** 'Do not, by any new indulgence, heighten your former offences.'

**152.** Even in his tenderness Hamlet cannot quite forget the bitterness of cynicism.

**157. the worser;** cf. iii. 2. 316, note.

**160. Assume,** not 'pretend', but 'acquire'.

Lines 161-165 are not in F 1.

**161. all sense,** all consciousness or sinning.

**162. Of habits devil,** the evil genius of our habits.    Q 2 has no comma after 'eat', and Theobald proposed to read—

> *Who all sense doth eat*
> *Of habits evil.*

Lines 168-170 ( down to the word *potency*) are not in F 1.

**169. And either...the devil.**   Q 2 has *And either the devil,* an obvious misprint.   Some such emendation as *lay, curb, quell, shame,* or perhaps *house, throne,* is necessary.

**172. same** is used sarcastically, as so often in Shakespeare.

**182.** The rest of this speech is meant ironically.

**bloat.**   So Theobald for the *blowt* of Q 2, *blunt* of F 1.

**183. mouse,** a term of endearment.   Cf. *Love's Labour's Lost,* v. 2. 19, and *Twelfth Night,* i. 5. 69, " Good my mouse of virtue, answer me ".

**194.** The only other possible allusion to this lost story is in a letter of Sir John Suckling, " It is the story of the jackanapes and the partridges ; thou starest after a beauty till it be lost to thee, and then let'st out another, and starest after that till it is gone too."

**195. To try conclusions,** to see what will happen.

**200. I must to England.**   How does Hamlet know this? The scheme was imparted to Polonius in iii. 1. 177, to Rosencrantz and Guildenstern in iii. 3. 4.   Hamlet has had no chance of learning it from them ; and if he knew of it, he must have seen the danger of leaving the king alive.   Moreover in iv. 3. 48 he expresses surprise at the news of his intended voyage.

**210.** Hamlet puns on the two senses of ' craft ', viz. ' ship ' and ' guile '.

**211. packing,** plotting ; perhaps also with reference to the other sense of ' being off '.

**213.** Hamlet has always a keen scent for the ironies of life.

I am inclined to accept Mr. Rose's suggestion that the first three scenes of the traditional act iv. should really be regarded as part of act iii.   Then if with him we give act iii. sc. 1 to act ii., the events of act iii. will be those of ' one tremendous night '.   Act iv. will cover Hamlet's absence, and act v., as now, begin with his return.   By this arrangement we get well set on foot in act iii. two chains of effects springing from Hamlet's critical failure in act iii. sc. 3.   These are the attempt of Claudius upon his life, and the death of Polonius, with its results.   For the working out of these chains see note to act iv. sc. 4, *init.*

### Act IV.—Scene I.

This scene is practically continuous with act iii. sc. 4. As soon as Hamlet has left his mother's closet, Claudius enters, to know the result of the interview. He finds the Queen overwhelmed and hardly able to speak—the combined effect of her son's reproaches and of her grief at his ecstasy.

**12. good old man**, for so, in spite of his tediousness (ii. 2. 95), Polonius appeared to those gifted with less keen perceptions than Hamlet's. Even Claudius had faith in him (ii. 2. 154).

**27. he weeps.** There does not seem to be anything in the last scene to justify this statement. Some critics think that Gertrude is henceforward on Hamlet's side, and is here doing her best to put his conduct in a favourable light. I doubt this; when in the presence of Claudius, she seems to be under his influence still.

**40.** This line is apparently incomplete in Q 2. F 1 omits lines 41-5, and ends the scene with—

> And what's untimely done. Oh come away,
> My soul is full of discord and dismay.

The most likely emendation of the Q 2 text is Capell's *so, haply, slander.* Tschischwitz suggests *by this, suspicion.*

### Scene 2.

In this scene and the following, Hamlet continues his assumption of madness. He is not at all unwilling to be sent to England; it will oblige him to a further delay; and he promises himself an intellectual treat in checkmating any design which his companions may have against him.

**12. a sponge**; cf. Barnabe Rich, *Faults, Faults, and Nothing else but Faults* (1606), "Vespasian, when reproached for bestowing high office upon persons most rapacious, answered 'that he served his turn with such officers as with spunges, which, when they had drunk their fill, were then the fittest to be pressed". Both Shakespeare and Rich are indebted for the idea to Suetonius, *Vita Vesp.* c. 16. In Q 1 this passage occurs near the end of act iii. sc. 2.

**19. like an ape.** So F 1; but the Q 2 reading, *like an apple*, is nearly as good. Q 1 has *as an Ape doth nuts.*

**29.** Here, as in ii. 2. 269, Hamlet is probably talking deliberate nonsense. But the interpretations of various grave editors may be found in Furness' *Variorum* edition.

**32. Cf. Psalm** cxliv. "Man is like a thing of naught", and the of the phrase in *Midsummer Night's Dream*, iv. 2. nd bless us, a thing of naught ".

**Hide fox, and all after.** This phrase is omitted in Q 2: it is said to be a name for 'hide and seek'. Perhaps Hamlet rushes from the room, leaving the rest to pursue him; or perhaps the fox is Polonius, who, if he does not now, will soon stink liké one. Cf. iv. 3. 37.

### Scene 3.

9. Cf. Lyly, *Euphues* (p. 67. ed. Arber), "A desperate disease is to be committed to a desperate doctor".

21-23. **worms...emperor...diet.** There is an allusion to the famous Diet or convocation of the dignities of the German Empire held at Worms in 1521. It was before this that Luther was summoned to appear.

The thought here is very similar to that of v. 1. 218, *sqq.*

33. **a progress,** the technical term for a royal journey of state through the provinces.

48. Cf. iii. 4. 200, note.

50. 'Whatever your purposes are, the angels are fighting on my side.'

63. **free awe,** awe which does not need compulsion.

66. **congruing.** So Q 2; F 1 has *conjuring*.

70. **were ne'er begun.** So F 1; Q 2 has *will ne'er begin*.

### Scene 4.

The present Act works out the results of Hamlet's failure until they bring about the catastrophe of act v. There are two main threads of incident. Firstly, there is the failure of the plot against Hamlet's life, which leads to his return to England, and drives Claudius to new devices; and secondly, Hamlet's unkindness to Ophelia, together with the death of Polonius, sends her mad. Laertes returns, burning for revenge, and readily becomes the king's accomplice.

The stress laid upon the fortunes of Ophelia in the latter part of the play has its dramatic purpose. It impresses us with the fact that Hamlet's ineffectiveness has its tragic results outside his own life; and at the same time the pathos of the situation makes us feel pity rather than anger towards him, since his deep affection for Ophelia is manifest throughout. And it is essential to the effect of tragedy that the sympathies of the spectator should be at the end with the hero.

The scene with the captain serves as a transition to the new Act; and at the same time strikes the note of contrast between Hamlet and Fortinbras, the strong practical man. The perception of this contrast is characteristically put in Hamlet's own mouth.

Attempts have been made, without much success, to find an allusion in the expedition of Fortinbras to some enterprise of Raleigh or Essex or some other Elizabethan worthy.

**3. Craves.** So Q2; F1 has *claims*.

**6. in his eye.** Cf. iv. 7. 46, and *Antony and Cleopatra*, ii. 2. 212—

> " Her gentlewomen, like the Nereides,
> So many mermaids, tended her i' the eyes ".

The phrase occurs as a technical one for 'in the royal presence' in the household books of James the First's reign. In F1 the scene ends with line 8.

**36.** Cf. i. 2. 150.

**40, 41. some craven scruple...on the event.** Hamlet describes his own weakness better than anyone can do it for him.

**50. Makes mouths at,** mocks at.

**53.** Is it by irony that Hamlet repeats Polonius' counsel? Cf. i. 3. 65.

**60. twenty thousand.** It was only 'two thousand' in line 25.

**66. my thoughts,** always thoughts, never deeds.

A comparison of ii. 2. 58, *sqq.*, with line 2 of this scene points to an interval of a few days between scenes 3 and 4, in order that Claudius' 'license' may reach Fortinbras. These must be spent by Hamlet in travelling from Elsinore—though it is on the sea (i. 4. 71) —to the port. Yet both i. 3. 1 and iv. 3. 43 imply that the port is close at hand. But iv. 3. 54 shows that Hamlet started directly after scene 3.

In any case, a longer interval follows this scene, during which Laertes returns from France.

### Scene 5.

The interest of scenes 5 and 7 lies partly in the ingenuity with which the king turns Laertes to his purposes, partly in the pathos of Ophelia's madness and death. Laertes is a youth of high spirit and true emotions, but his French training has left him without high principle, and he is weak enough to be easily led. The genuine insanity of Ophelia is a pendant to that assumed by Hamlet; the immediate cause is her father's death, yet the loss of her lover must also have affected her deeply. The character of the songs she sings —they are not given in full in this edition—is not inconsistent with perfect purity; all who have had experience of mad patients can confirm this; and therefore it gives no support to the curious theory, held by no less a critic than Goethe, that she had been Hamlet's *mistress*.

**2.** *Gent.* So Q2; these speeches are given in F1 to Horatio, and lines 14, 15 to the Queen.

**9.** **to collection,** to collect some meaning from it.

**11.** **which;** the antecedent appears to be 'the words'.

**17.** Gertrude is still weakly remorseful.

**23.** The music used for Ophelia's songs upon the stage is said to have been handed down by tradition from Shakespeare's time. It is printed in Furness' *Variorum* edition, and in Chappell's *Popular Music of the Olden Time*, vol. i.
D. G. Rossetti used this first stanza as the opening of a beautiful little poem called *An Old Song Ended*.

**26.** The cockle hat, staff, and sandals were the guise of a pilgrim, often the disguise of a lover. Notice the confusion in Ophelia's mind throughout between her father and her sweetheart. She hardly knows which is dead. Of course she never had any conception of how Polonius came by his death. That was kept a profound secret in the court, and Claudius himself was suspected in consequence.

**38.** **did go.** Both Q2 and F1 read *did not go*, surely in error.

**41.** There is a monkish legend that a baker's daughter was turned into an owl for refusing bread to our Saviour. It is said by Douce to be well known in Gloucestershire, and Mr. Leland (*The English Gipsies*) found it among the gipsies, among whom the name for an owl is Māromengro's Chavi, or Baker's Daughter. The connection in Ophelia's mind is simply the idea of a sudden transformation, or change of circumstances, such as her father's death and Hamlet's absence have brought about for her.

**48.** It was the custom for the first girl seen by a man on the morning of Feb. 14th to be regarded as his valentine, or true-love, for the year.

**89.** **in clouds,** in mysterious reserve; the emendation *inclosed* is quite superfluous.

**95.** **a murdering-piece.** This is generally explained as a piece of artillery, the French *meurtrière*. But may it not mean a play representing murder? for Claudius' present situation affects him, as such a play would do, through the imagination. And what more likely than that he explained, to Gertrude, his perturbation of act iii. sc. 2 as due solely to the power of imagination?

**97.** **Switzers.** The kings of France had long a Swiss body-guard; so that the term 'Switzers' became really equivalent to 'guards'.

**105.** This may mean that the rabble supports every word that Laertes utters; but I think it refers rather to 'custom' and 'antiquity'; *unless* the word 'king' is used as these direct, it is meaningless.

**119.** Cf. iii. 4. 44, note.

**brows.**  Both Q 2 and F 1 read *brow*.

**123.** Such sentiments are common in Shakespeare (cf. *e.g. Richard II.* passim), but they are generally put in the mouths of kings them-selves, or their supporters.

**130.** Laertes' vigour of revenge is no doubt an intentional contrast to the languor of the quite equally sincere Hamlet.

**142. swoopstake.**  Both Q 2 and F 1 have *soopstake*; Q 1 has *swoopstake-like.*  In a swoopstake or sweepstake the winner draws all the stakes from the board; so the king suggests that Laertes means to make a general clearance of friend and foe.  The ' winner and loser' of line 143 is, of course, not the same metaphor, only suggested by it.

**146. the kind life-rendering pelican.**  F 1 reads ludicrously *politician.*  It was a common belief that the pelican either fed its young or restored them to life when dead, with its own blood.  Many attempts have been made to explain the origin of this story, but it appears to be a pure legend.  Moreover, it originally belonged to the vulture—the pelican of heraldry is really a kind of vulture—and was only transferred to the pelican by a mistake of the compilers of the Vulgate.  (See the *Academy*, xxv. 97. 243.)  In the Middle Ages the pelican symbolized first the Resurrection, then the Eucharist. A curious change took place at the Reformation.  Both the Catholic conceptions of the Eucharist and the use of symbolism in religion fell into disfavour, and the pelican became thenceforward an emblem of self-sacrifice generally, an i, in especial, of true kingship.  The emblem-books of the period illustrate this abundantly.  So does Lyly, of whose curious Euphuism the display of fantastic similes from unreal natural history is characteristic.  He calls Elizabeth "that good Pelican that to feede hir people spareth not to rend hir owne personne".  From Lyly the tradition passed to Shakespeare. For Shakespeare, the young of the pelican represent filial ingrati-tude.  Goneril and Regan are called "these pelican daughters" (*Lear*, iii. 4. 77); and John of Gaunt, in his rebuke to Richard II. (*R'.. I and II*, ii. 1. 120), says

> " That blood already, like the pelican,
> Hast thou tapped out and drunkenly caroused ".

In *Edward III.* iii. 5. 111, which may or may not be by Shakespeare. Edward asks the meaning of the device on some colours, and the Black Prince :

> -. my lord,
> r crooked beak,
> may be fed
> from her heart.
> — so should you ".

**153. Let her come in.** In Q 2 this is given to Laertes; F 1 has it as part of a stage-direction. *A noise within. Let her come in.*

**157. rose of May.** Cf. iii. 1. 160; iii. 4. 42.

**160.** Neither here nor in act i. sc. 3 is Laertes, in spite of his affection for Ophelia, quite able to understand her.

**161–163.** These lines are not in Q 2. Nature, at its finest in Ophelia's love, has sent her wits after Polonius.

**165. Hey non nonny.** Such meaningless refrains are common in old songs; cf. the 'adown adown' of line 170, and the 'down, adown, adowna' of *Merry Wives*, i. 4. 44. 'Hey, nonny, nonny' occurs in Balthazar's song "Sigh no more ladies, Sigh no more" (*Much Ado*, ii. 3. 64), and "With a hey, and a ho, and a hey nonino" in "It was a lover and his lass" (*As You Like It*, v. 3. 17).

**172. how the wheel becomes it.** These are old-fashioned ballads, which Ophelia has heard to the music of her nurse's spinning-wheel. Steevens' statement that 'wheel' means a refrain is probably purely imaginary.

The story or ballad of 'the false steward' and 'his master's daughter' is unknown.

**174. more,** more touching.

**175.** Ophelia distributes her flowers appropriately, the rosemary and pansies to Laertes, the fennel and columbine to Claudius, the rue and daisy to the queen.

**rosemary,** often strewn on biers, to signify remembrance; cf. *Romeo and Juliet*, iv. 5. 79—

> "Dry up your tears, and stick your rosemary
> On this fair corse";

also *Winter's Tale*, iv. 4. 74—

> "For you there's rosemary and rue; these keep
> Seeming and savour all the winter long;
> Grace and remembrance be to you both".

**176. pansies** are for thoughts, because of their name, the French *pensées*. The flower is also a country emblem of love and courtship.

**178.** Laertes uses **thoughts** in a sense it sometimes has, of 'melancholy'.

**180. fennel** symbolizes flattery and **columbine** ingratitude; cf. Chapman, *All Fools*, ii. 1—

> "What's that? a columbine?
> No; that thankless flower fits not my garden".

**181. rue,** a bitter plant with medicinal virtues. It was symbolical of repentance, and was therefore usually mingled with the holy water, and known as 'herb of grace', or 'herbygrass'. This name was also sometimes given to wormwood, another symbol of remorse (cf. iii. 2. 19). When Ophelia says to the queen, 'You must wear your rue with a difference', she probably means, 'For you it signifies repentance, for me only regret'. Cf. *Richard II.* iii. 4. 104—

> " Here did she fall a tear; here in this place
> I 'll set a bank of rue, sour herb of grace;
> Rue, even for ruth, shall shortly here be seen,
> In the remembrance of a weeping queen ".

**183. a difference** is properly an heraldic bearing, meant to distinguish the arms of one branch of the same family from another.

**184. a daisy,** for faithlessness, as *violets* are for faithfulness; cf. Greene, *Quips for an Upstart Courtier*, "Next them grew the dissembling daisy to warn such light-of-love wenches not to trust every fair promise that such amorous bachelors make them".

**they withered all.** Faithfulness, says Ophelia, left the world with my father. Yet here, too, Hamlet must be in her thoughts; cf. i. 3. 7, where Laertes compared his love for her to 'A violet in the youth of primy nature'.

**187. bonny sweet Robin.** Cf. *Two Noble Kinsmen,* iv. 1. 107—

> "I can sing the Broome
> And Bonny Robin".

The tune is found in several Elizabethan song-books; the words are lost, but they appear to have been a ballad on Robin Hood.

**190.** This is a song known in the song-books as *The Merry Milkmaids,* or *The Milkmaids' Dumps.*

**195.** This scene is ridiculed in Jonson, Chapman, and Marston's *Eastward Hoe* (1604), iii. 1—

> " His head as white as milk,
> All flaxen was his hair;
> But now he is dead,
> And laid in his bed,
> And never will come again".

Hamlet is introduced in the same scene as a half-mad footman.

**213. burial.** So F 1; Q 2 has *funeral.*

**216. Cf.** *Genesis,* iv. 10, "The voice of thy brother's blood crieth unto me from the ground"; and *Richard II.* i. 1. 104—

> ...d. like sacrificing Abel's, cries
> tongueless caverns of the earth,
> and rough chastisement ".

### Scene 6.

This scene serves to keep the fortunes of Hamlet in our mind during the period of his absence.    It is simultaneous with scenes 5 and 7, the action of which is practically continuous, and in a modern play it would probably be made to take place in a corner of the same hall, while the King and Laertes whisper apart.

**2. Sea-faring men.** So Q 2; F 1 has *sailors*.

**21. thieves of mercy,** merciful thieves; cf. " brow of woe ", for ' woeful brow ', in i. 2. 4.

**they knew what they did.** A theory has been founded on this phrase, coupled with Hamlet's mysterious allusion to two crafts meeting in one line, and his expressed intention to delve one yard below his enemies' mines (iii. 4. 210), that the pirate was of his own procuring.    But surely Hamlet's mine was merely the altering of the letters.    (See v. 2. 12, *sqq.*)

**26. the bore of the matter.** The metaphor is from a gun that will carry heavy shot.

### Scene 7.

The Laertes motive and the Ophelia motive of scene 5 are continued here.   Laertes proves an easy tool for the king's ingenious villany.    His naturally impetuous temper, made degenerate by such a life in France as is suggested in act iii. sc. 1, snatches at even an ignoble chance of revenge.    It is noteworthy that in Q 1 the proposal to use a poisoned foil comes from Claudius.

**15. his sphere.** The Ptolemaic astronomy regarded the universe as composed of ten orbs or hollow spheres, one within the other. In the inmost seven of these the planets had their courses; in the eighth the fixed stars; the other two were the Crystalline and the Primum Mobile.    There are many allusions to this arrangement in Shakespeare; *e.g. Midsummer Night's Dream*, ii. 1. 153—

" And certain stars shot madly from their spheres
     To hear the sea-maid's music ".

**18.** Cf. iv. 3. 4.

**20. that turneth wood to stone.** Springs whose water is highly charged with lime will petrify with a deposit of it any object put into them.    Harrison, *Description of England* (ed. New Sh. Soc. pp. 334, 349), mentions several such, one at King's Newnham in Warwickshire.    There is a famous one also at Knaresborough. The Clarendon Press editors quote Lyly, *Euphues* (ed. Arber, p. 63), " Would I had sipped of that river in Caria, which turneth those that drink of it to stone ".

**21. Convert his gyves to graces.** I suppose the idea in ' gyves ' is ' faults which should be fetters on his popularity '.

Clarke interprets, "turn all my attempts to restrain him into so many injuries perpetrated against his innocence and good qualities". Theobald proposed *gybes*, Daniel *gyres*.

**22. so loud a wind.** So F 1; Q 2 has *so loved Arm'd*.

**28. of all the age,** qualifies 'challenger', not 'mount'. Moberly points out that the King of Hungary, at his coronation, stands on the Mount of Defiance at Presburg and challenges the world to dispute his claim.

**30. sleeps.** The plural form occurs in Phaer's *Aeneid*, ii. "in Sleepes and drinking drownd".

**33.** Claudius hopes to hear from England of the success of his plot against Hamlet's life. He is ironically made to express this hope just before Hamlet's letter is brought in.

**34. I loved...we love.** Claudius' affection for Polonius was personal, not merely official.

**37. this to the queen.** Nothing more is said of this letter, but Q 1 has a scene where Horatio tells the Queen of Hamlet's danger, and she acknowledges that her husband is a villain.

**59.** 'How can Hamlet be returning, and yet—it is his own character—how otherwise?' But several critics would read *How should it not be so?*

**63. checking at.** The metaphor is from falconry; the hawk is said to check when she leaves her proper game for some other bird.

**68. shall uncharge,** *i.e.* shall not charge or accuse.

**69-82.** These lines, from "My lord" to "graveness", are not in F 1.

**73.** Hamlet is by no means a bookworm; which accounts for his popularity with the common people, and for Ophelia's description of him in iii. 1. 159, *sqq.*

**82. Importing health and graveness.** Warburton proposed *wealth*, and Malone explained 'health' as meaning 'attention to health'; but probably it refers back to 'careless livery'; cf. a similar construction in iii. 1. 159, "the courtier's, soldier's, scholar's, eye, tongue, sword".

**84.** One remembers the feats of chivalry at Elizabeth's court, in which Sidney contended with 'that sweet enemy, France'.

**86.** The mythical Centaur was doubtless in Shakespeare's mind.

**93. Lamond.** So F 1; Q 2 has *Lamord*. Mr. Elliot Browne suggests an allusion to a famous swordsman, Pietro Monte, who was instructor to Louis the Seventh's Master of Horse. In the English translation of Castiglione's *Il Cortegiano*, bk. i., he is called Peter Mount.

**112-119.** 'Love is a thing of time, not of eternity; it has a beginning and an end.'

**123.** The recognition of a ' should ' when it is too late is like a spendthrift's sigh for his squandered estate, a bitter-sweet sensation. It was a belief that sighing drew blood from the heart ; cf. *Romeo and Juliet*, iii. 5. 59, " Dry sorrow drinks our blood ".

**139. a pass of practice,** either ' a treacherous pass ' (cf. line 68), or, ' a pass in which you are practised', or, ' a pass by way of friendly exercise '.

**146. Under the moon;** cf. iii. 2. 268, note.

**151. shape,** design.

**163.** The scenic apparatus of Shakespeare's time would have been inadequate to represent Ophelia's death upon the stage; even now it would be difficult. Even in Ibsen's *Rosmersholm*, which ends with a suicide by drowning, the event is only reported by a witness who sees it from a window.

**164.** Cf. *Locrine*, v. 5—

> " One mischief follows on another's neck.
> Who would have thought so young a maid as she
> With such a courage would have sought her death ".

**168. his hoar leaves.** The willow leaf with its silvery underside is always a conspicuous object in river scenery; cf. Lowell, *Among My Books*, " Shakespeare understood perfectly the charm of indirectness, of making his readers seem to discover for themselves what he means to show them. If he wishes to tell that the leaves of the willow are gray on the underside, he does not make it a mere fact of observation by bluntly saying so, but makes it picturesquely reveal itself to us as it might in nature ".

**170. crow-flowers,** generally the buttercups, sometimes the *Lychnis Flos cuculi*, or Ragged Robin.

**long purples,** the country name for various species of *Orchis*, the *Orchis mascula* or *Orchis maculata*.

**178. tunes.** So F 1 and Q 1; Q 2 has *lauds*, *i.e.* chants, so called from the psalm *Laudate Dominum*. The F 1 reading suits better the character of Ophelia's songs in scene 5.

This scene is ridiculed in Beaumont and Fletcher's *The Scornful Lady*, ii. 3—

> " I will run mad first, and if that get not pity,
> I 'll drown myself to a most dismal ditty ".

**189. these,** the tears, for which he is apologizing.

**192. douts.** So Knight for the *doubts* of F 1; Q 2 has *drowns*.

An interval of a very few days separates the Acts; leaving time for Hamlet to return from the seaport (cf. iv. 4, note, ad fin.), and for preparation to be made for Ophelia's burial.

## Act V.—Scene I.

This scene does not advance the action much, for Hamlet's quarrel with Laertes has very little to do with their subsequent encounter; it only serves to bring into contrast the opposing characters of the two men. But we want a moment or two of relief before the breathless rush with which the play closes, and this the grim humour of the grave-diggers and Hamlet's moralizing afford. The solemnity of Ophelia's burial helps us to realize the pathos of her fate, and therein the tragedy of Hamlet's failure.

The dialogue between the clowns affords an example of Shakespeare's unrivalled power of insight into the mental habits and modes of reasoning of uneducated people.

9. **se offendendo**, a mistake of the clown's for *se defendendo*, a phrase used not in suicide cases, but in verdicts of justifiable homicide. It has been suggested that the reasoning in this speech and the next is a parody of the arguments used in the inquest on a certain Sir James Hales, reported in Plowden's *Commentaries* (3 Eliz.).

14. **goodman delver.** The First Clown, who takes the lead, is the sexton; the Second an ordinary labourer.

32. **even Christian,** fellow Christian. But there is, of course, an allusion to the supposed equality of all Christians in the sight of the Church.

35. **Adam's profession.** Cf. Tennyson's *Lady Clara Vere de Vere*, "the grand old gardener and his wife", and the well-known couplet —

> "When Adam delved and Eve span,
> Who was then the gentleman?"

38. This must be satire on the ludicrous statements of writers on heraldry, as to the antiquity of their science. The Q 2 text here runs: '*A was the first that ever bore arms. I'll put another question to thee.* The printer's eye seems to have slipped from one *arms* to another.

44. **confess thyself—** It is a proverb 'Confess thyself, and be hanged'. Hence the idea of a gallows-maker in the Second Clown's mind.

45. **Go to.** The phrase here expresses the Second Clown's vague sense that he is being chaffed. It corresponds to the 'Garn, who are you a gitting at?' of the modern Londoner.

59. **and unyoke,** and then thy task is done.

68. **get thee to Yaughan.** So F 1; Q 2 has *get thee in.* Collier proposed *Get thee to—(Yawns)*! Yaughan is a Welsh name, and there is therefore no need to regard it as a corruption of the *German Johan.* Probably the allusion is to some well-known tavern-

keeper. That there was a tavern attached to the Globe theatre is proved by the sonnet on the burning of that playhouse (Collier, *Annals of the Stage*, i. 388). The passage looks like one of the bits of clown's gag satirized in iii. 2. 42 (see quotation from Q 1 in note *ad loc.*).

69. The Clown's song is an inaccurate version of three stanzas of *The aged lover renounceth love*, from *Tottel's Miscellany* (1557). It is attributed in Gascoigne's *Epistle to a Young Gentleman*, prefatory to his poems, and in Harl. MS. 1703, to Lord Vaux. In *Tottel's Miscellany* (ed. Arber, p. 173) the verses run as follows—

> 'I lothe that I did loue,
>   In youth that I thought swete:
> As time requires for my behove
>   Me thinkes they are not mete.
>
> For age with steyling steppes,
>   Hath clawed me with his crowche,
> And lusty life away she leapes,
>   As there had bene none such.
>
> A pikeax and a spade
>   And eke a shrowdyng shete
> A house of clay for to be made,
>   For such a gest most mete."

75. 'Custom hath made it proper or natural to him to take his employment easily.'

90. Cf. *Timon of Athens*, i. 2. 216—

> "And now I remember, my lord, you gave
> Good words the other day of a bay courser
> I rode on; it is yours, because you liked it".

100. loggats, a game resembling bowls, but played on a floor instead of a green. The loggats are pear-shaped pieces of wood, and are pitched, not rolled.

103. for and, a strong form of 'and', equivalent to the earlier 'and eke'.

106 &c. The exact interpretation of these law-terms is not of much importance to the interpretation of the play, but, according to Lord Campbell, they are "all used seemingly with a full knowledge of their import".

115 (*113*). the fine of his fines. The first 'fine' has the sense of end. This line is omitted in Q 2. The printer's eye has apparently slipped from the first *his recoveries* to the second; cf. line 38, *note*.

**126.** in that, *i.e.* in legal parchments, which give no assurance against death.

**149. by the card,** with precision; the origin of the expression being probably from the accuracy with which charts are drawn out. Staunton, however, refers it to the 'card' of etiquette, or book of good manners; cf. v. 2. 114. Yet a third explanation is that it refers to the card or 'plat' on which an actor's 'part' was copied out for him. Some of these Elizabethan 'plats' are still preserved. Cf. Appendix A.

**170.** Cf. Marston, *Malcontent*, iii. 1, "your lordship shall ever finde...amongst a hundred Englishmen fourscore and ten madmen".

**177. thirty years.** This statement, coupled with that in line 160 that the Sexton 'came to 't' on the day of Hamlet's birth, is on the face of it conclusive that Hamlet is a man of thirty. This is consistent with the thirty years of married life of the Player King and Queen (iii. 2. 165), and also, as it seems to me, with Hamlet's developed character and philosophy. Several critics, however, point to considerations which lead them to regard him as nearer twenty than thirty; Professor Minto would treat him as a youth of seventeen. The chief of these considerations are :

(i) Hamlet's mother is still young enough to love and be loved. But so was the Player Queen; and iii. 3. 68, 83 imply that Gertrude is a middle-aged matron.

(ii) Hamlet is called 'young Hamlet' (i. 3. 123), and his love for Ophelia spoken of as "a violet in the youth of primy nature", &c. (i. 3. 7, *sqq.*). But Henry V., who is made by Shakespeare at least twenty-six when he comes to the throne, is spoken of as "in the very May-morn of his youth". Cf. also the phrase in *Much Ado*, iii. 3. 140, " How giddily 'a turns about all the hot bloods between fourteen and five and thirty".

(iii) Hamlet has barely left Wittenberg, and the Elizabethan noble rarely stayed at the University beyond seventeen. Certainly, in England, but not in Denmark. Cf. Nash, *Pierce Penniless' Supplication to the Devil* (Sh. Soc. p. 27), " For fashion sake some [Danes] will put their children to school, but they set them not to it till they are fourteen years old, so that you shall see a great boy with a beard learn his A B C, and sit weeping under the rod when he is thirty years old ".

The fact is that many men among the northern nations are no older at thirty than Hamlet is represented. Mr. Furnivall thinks that Shakespeare meant Hamlet to be about twenty when he began the play, but found it necessary to make him older as he went on! Mr. Marshall suggests that this bit, and the " fat and scant of breath " bit (v. 2. 298), were put in to make the part fit the personality of Burbage.

*190. three and twenty years.* This date, together with Hamlet's boyish reminiscences of Yorick, is quite consistent with the 'thirty years' of line 177. Q 1, however, has, in place of both the other two passages—

> " Look you, here's a skull hath been here this dozen years,
> Let me see, ay, ever since our last King Hamlet
> Slew Fortinbras in combat, young Hamlet's father,
> He that's mad ".

**198. Yorick.** Dr. Nicholson finds in this passage a compliment to Tarlton, Kempe's great predecessor as a comic actor. The name may be a corruption of the Danish *Jörg*, or of the *Roricus* of Saxo-Grammaticus. This Roricus was Hamlet's grandfather. Mr. Latham identifies Yorick with the Eric who plays Claudius' part in the German version of the play; and suggests that the idea of his being a jester may be a confusion due to existence of some *Gesta Erici Regis*. Is not this a little far-fetched?

**211. on a roar.** The nearest parallel is *Rape of Lucrece*, 1494—

> " For sorrow, like a heavy-hanging bell
> Once set on ringing, with his own weight goes ".

**213.** Cf. iii. 1. 148.

**240.** The personal note of the remainder of the scene is a curious contrast to the impersonal generalized tone of the speculations in which Hamlet has just been indulging. Observe that he has only just reached Elsinore and knows nothing of Ophelia's fate. It is not revealed to him until line 264, where Laertes speaks of 'my sister'.

All the dialogue that follows has the rhythmical dignity of a dirge; see, *e.g.*, the speeches beginning with lines 249, 261, 266, 277, 292.

**244. it**; cf. ii. 1. 216, note.

**250. doubtful.** There is nothing in the description of Ophelia's death given by Gertrude in iv. 7. 163, *sqq.*, to show that it was voluntary.

**255. her virgin crants.** Q 2 has *crants*, F 1 *rites*. Warburton proposed *chants*, but 'crants' is probably the same word as the 'corances' of Chapman's *Alphonsus*. It signifies 'crowns' or 'garlands', and refers here to the garlands which it was customary to carry before the biers of unmarried women and then to hang up in the church.

**256. the bringing home.** A funeral is here compared to the procession of a bride from church. The same idea is the motive of a beautiful *Elegy* by Mr. Robert Bridges (*Shorter Poems*, p. 16). Cf. also *Romeo and Juliet*, iv. 1. 84.

**261.** Even Laertes, shallow and debauched boy as he is, is dignified and ennobled by sorrow. His love for his sister is the redeeming point in him.

**263. violets** are Ophelia's flowers throughout; cf. i. 3. 7; iv. 5. 184.

Cf. also Persius, *Satire* i.

> "e tumulo fortunataque favilla
> Nascentur violæ";

and Tennyson, *In Memoriam*, xviii.—

> "'T is well; 't is something; we may stand
> Where he in English earth is laid,
> And from his ashes may be made
> The violets of his native land".

**269. treble woe.** So Q 2; F 1 has *terrible woer*.

**276.** Olympus, Pelion, and Ossa are three mountains in the north of Thessaly. The Giants, warring with the Gods, are said to have piled them upon each other in an attempt to scale heaven.

**277. blue,** again the 'picturesque' epithet.

**279. the wandering stars,** the planets.

**290.** Hamlet has forgotten everything else, his delayed revenge, his mother's sin, his own danger, even his pessimism, everything but just the love which he had put from him. He is a philosopher, but his action is usually swayed by impulse.

**292. I loved Ophelia.** Cf. the denial of iii. 1. 115, 120, 'I loved you once...I loved you not'.

**299. Woo't drink up eisel.** This line is one of the half-dozen cruces of the play. Q 1 reads *vessels*, Q 2 *Esill*, F 1 *Esile*. There are two plausible explanations, between which the reader may choose:

(i) Some river may be intended, and if so, it is probably the *Yssel*, a northern branch of the Rhine, which runs not far from Denmark. Steevens, however, conjectured *Weissel*, Hanmer *Nile*, and Elze *Nilus*, the two latter being probably led by the mention of crocodiles.

(ii) Theobald proposed *eisel*, meaning 'vinegar'; cf. Glossary, *s.v.* The advantage of this explanation is that it suggests a nasty drink, corresponding to such an unsavoury food as a crocodile, rather than an impossibly huge one.

**305.** Almost insensibly Hamlet has slipped from the expression of real feeling into the half-simulated extravagances, the 'wild and whirling words' that have become almost a second nature to him.

**306. Ossa;** cf. line 276, note.

**307-311.** Q 2 gives these lines to the Queen; F 1, in error, to

**310. her golden couplets.** The dove never lays more than two eggs, and the young, when first hatched, are covered with a golden down.

**315.** The idea is, 'Nothing can prevent inferior creatures, such as Laertes, from following their nature, and now and then they get a chance to come to the front'. The proverbial expression, 'Every dog hath his day' is found in four other places in Elizabethan literature. In spite of this the emendation proposed by Mr. Street, *dog will have his bay*, is so plausible that I incline to adopt it.

### Scene 2.

It is necessary first that Hamlet's reappearance should be explained. This is done by his narrative to Horatio. Then follows the brief scene with Osric, which declares Hamlet's character to be fundamentally unchanged; and then comes the end. Hamlet's revenge is accomplished at last, not deliberately, but by a sudden impulse, and at what a cost! Claudius died justly, but—over and beyond Ophelia—the blood that is shed is at Hamlet's door. 'The rest is silence', and the entry of Fortinbras and Hamlet's dying submission symbolize the triumph of another order of mind.

**1. this,** the fate of Ophelia; **the other,** Hamlet's adventures.

**6. Rashly.** This is more characteristic of Hamlet than he knows: if he is effective at all, it is always rashly, from impulse, and not from a ' deep plot '.

**9. pall.** So Q 2; F 1 has *parle*; Pope suggested *fail*.

**10.** The metaphor is from the making of skewers or some such thing.

**21.** Cf. iv. 3. 60, *sqq.*

**22.** This is generally explained, ' With the suggestion of such dangers, if I am allowed to live '. I think it means rather ' With such exaggeration of the actual facts of my life '.

**31. they,** not ' my enemies ' but ' my brains '. Hamlet means that under the stress of circumstances he acted without stopping to think it over.

**33.** A piece of affectation which only a clever young man of Hamlet's type could be guilty of. Cf. Montaigne (tr. Florio, 1603, p. 125) " I have in my time seen some, who by writing did earnestly get both their titles and living, to disavow their apprentisage, mar their pen, and affect the ignorance of so vulgar a quality ".

**42. a comma 'tween their amities.** I think Johnson explains this rightly, " A comma is the note of connection and continuity of sentences; the period is the note of abruption and disjunction ". But various editors have thought it necessary to conjecture *commere*, *comate*, *cement*, and so forth.

**47.** Cf. i. 5. 77.

**57.** I doubt if we have the materials to say whether Rosencrantz and Guildenstern were fully aware of the tenor of their commission to England. In the *Hystorie of Hamblett* they are certainly guilty. But in any case they had already (ii. 2. 282, *sqq.*) given Hamlet proof of their willingness to sacrifice friendship to the bidding of the king.

**61. the pass and fell incensed points.** These are merely two ways of expressing the same idea. In fencing you make the pass with the point.

**63. Does it not...stand me now upon.** Is it not imperative upon me? Cf. *Richard III.* iv. 2. 59—

> " It stands me much upon
> To stop all hopes " ;

and *Richard II.* ii. 3. 138, " It stands your grace upon ". The similar phrase ' It lies on ' occurs in *Coriolanus*, iii. 2. 52, " It lies you on to speak ". See Abbott, *Sh. Gr.* § 204.

**65.** One of Hamlet's few allusions to his disinheritance.

**68-82.** These lines are not in Q 2.

**73. the interim is mine.** A reflection likely to give Hamlet satisfaction; an interim—a further chance of delay.

**78. court.** So Rowe for the *count* of Qq. Ff. I think that the emendation is justified by line 237.

**80.** Osric, a type of the empty-headed courtier or man about town, the affected fribble, parleying Euphuism or the Sidneian tongue, and so covering his nothingness with a nicety of borrowed phrase.

**84. this water-fly,** this ephemeral frail creature that flits so idly over the surface of a tragic pool.

**89. a chough.** The idea is probably rather ' an ignorant provincial ' than ' a chattering crow '. See Glossary, *s.v.*

**94.** Cf. the scene with Polonius, iii. 2. 391, *sqq.* Theobald quotes Juvenal, *Satire* iii.

> " igniculum brumæ si tempore poscas,
> Accipit endromidem ; si dixeris, æstuas, sudet ".

**108.** Cf. *Love's Labour's Lost*, v. 1. 103, " I do beseech thee remember thy courtesy ; I beseech thee apparel thy head ". The phrase is a curious one. It was etiquette or courtesy to stand bareheaded before a superior, and yet perhaps a higher courtesy to omit the ceremony when requested. But this refinement is not in Osric.

*109-142 (108-140).* These lines are omitted in F 1.

**112. differences,** qualities that distinguish him from ordinary men; cf. the heraldic use (iv. 5. 183, note).

**113. feelingly,** with insight and nice perception.

**114. the card or calendar of gentry.** The metaphor may be from the shipman's card (*Macbeth*, i. 3. 17) or chart, by which a ship's course is directed; or more likely from some card or booklet giving rules of etiquette. So in Lyly a 'card' is a set of moral precepts or examples.

**117.** Hamlet parodies Osric, and succeeds in making himselt quite unintelligible to him in his own tongue.

**120. yet but yaw neither,** and yet but stagger in the attempt to overtake his perfections; cf. Glossary, *s.v. yaw.* Q 3 has *yet but raw.* Staunton suggested *and wit but yaw*; Tschischwitz *and yet but row.*

**131. in another tongue.** Horatio is sarcastic. 'What! you can chatter in a jargon that is certainly not English; can't you understand in it too? pray try'.

**162.** 'You want a comment in the margin to explain the text.'

**172.** It is difficult to make out from Osric exactly what the wager is. Probably 'a dozen' is a vague general term. The king bets that Laertes will not make as much as twelve hits for Hamlet's nine. It might of course take twenty-one passes to decide this.

**190 (*188*).** Hamlet's courtesies are becoming a little irritable.

**196 (*192*).** So Q 2. F 1 has *mine (nine* F 2) *more of the same bevy.* I am inclined to suggest *many more of the same bread*, to help out the 'yesty' metaphor below.

**200. fond and winnowed.** So F 1. Q 2 has *prophane and trennowed*; Warburton proposed *fanned and winnowed*, Johnson *sane and renowned*, Tschischwitz *profound and winnowed*; Nicholson thinks that the second word is *vinewed* or *fenowed* (*i.e.* 'rotten'). The F 1 text may stand, in the sense of 'foolish and over-refined'. The whole speech is obscure. Osric is a type of the foolish young man about town, who picks up the phrases and tricks of style fashionable at the moment, and uses them without any originality or understanding; who parleys Euphuism after Lyly, and Arcadianism after Sidney. Hamlet says of him and his kind that they have only got the slang of the day and its manner of dialogue. These borrowings (or 'collection') act as yeast to 'raise' or fill with bubbles the bread of their absurd and fantastic opinions: if you blow them to their trial (*i.e.* talk to them with any originality in their own vein) the bubbles burst, their golden words are spent.

**203-218 (*198-216*).** These lines are omitted in F 1.

**222.** With Hamlet's presentiment of coming evil compare that of Antonio in *Merchant of Venice*, i. 1, and that of Hermione in *The Winter's Tale*, ii. 1.

**231.** Cf. *S. Matthew*, x. 29, "Are not two sparrows sold for a farthing? and one of them shall not fall on the ground without your Father".

**234.** The text is Johnson's. Q 2 reads *since no man of ought he leaves, knowes what ist to leave betimes, let be*; and F 1 *since no man ha's ought of what he leaves. What is't to leave betimes?*

**260.** 'An opinion and precedent to show that I am justified in making peace.' The wish to be right with the public opinion of his world is characteristic of Laertes.

**266.** For the double meaning of foil, see Glossary, *s.v.* The use of the pun, to produce a grimly ironical effect, is quite in Shakespeare's later manner, after the mere delight in punning for its own sake had disappeared.

**274. he is better'd,** he has the better reputation. The odds have been really laid on Laertes, so the phrase 'laid the odds' in line 272 must be taken in the general sense of 'made a bet'.

**283. union.** So F 1. Q 2 has *unice*; Q 3 *onixe.*

**285.** Cf. i. 2. 285. Commentators quote several illustrations of this noisy Danish custom.

**293.** The so-called 'union' is doubtless poison in reality.

**298. fat, and scant of breath.** It has been thought that this is an unpoetic description of "the glass of fashion and the mould of form", and that it is to be explained by the physical peculiarities of the actor Burbage. Very probably 'fat' means little more than 'out of training'.

**310.** 'You trifle with me as if I were a child.'

**312.** *They change rapiers.* This stage-direction may be explained in three ways:—

(1) Both swords may be knocked out of the combatants' hands, and in the hurry each may pick up his opponent's; or

(2) Laertes only may drop his sword; Hamlet may put his foot on it, and courteously offer his own. This was Salvini's way of playing the scene; or

(3) Laertes may try to disarm Hamlet by gripping the hilt of his sword at close quarters. In a fencing school Hamlet's proper reply would be to perform the same manœuvre, and so the two would change weapons.

*317.* Cf. i. 3. 115, note.

*343. of it,* of Hamlet's death.

347. Cf. Sylvester, *Translation of Du Bartas*—

> " And death, dread serjeant of the th' eternal Judge,
> Comes very late to his sole-seated lodge ".

**as,** an ellipse, ' Had I but time—which I have not, as '.

352. Cf. *Macbeth*, v. 8. 1—

> " Why should I play the Roman fool, and die
> On mine own sword?"

354. **a wounded name;** cf. line 261, " to keep my name un-gored ".

358. **felicity,** the felicity of death, the "consummation devoutly to be wished ".

375. **cries on havoc,** cries out against the butchery.

376. **eternal.** It is suggested that here, and in i. 5. 21, *Julius Cæsar*, i. 2. 160, *Othello*, iv. 2. 130, ' eternal ' is used for ' infernal '. But the usual sense of ' eternal ' world at least fit this passage and that in *Julius Cæsar*.

383. **his mouth,** the king's.

400. **rights of memory,** claims which are not forgotten.

# APPENDIX A.

## THE FIRST QUARTO OF 1603.

It is difficult, without actually reprinting the Q 1 version of *Hamlet*, to give an exact idea of its character and its divergencies from the received text. The student should by all means read it for himself in Griggs' facsimile, or better still, in Dr. Wilhelm Vietor's parallel text edition (No. 2 of *Shakespeare Reprints*, Marburg, 1891). It is also to be found in Furness' *New Variorum Hamlet*, vol. ii., and in the *Cambridge Shakespeare*, vol. ix. I propose, however, in this Appendix to briefly mention the points on the consideration of which the theory as to the nature of Q 1 given in the Introduction is based. They appear to me to justify the three following propositions:—

A.  Q 1 is an imperfect and mutilated copy of the play.

B.  The version from which it was taken was different from that represented by Q 2 and F 1.

C.  This version, as well as the later one, was the work of Shakespeare.

I will take these in their turn.

A. There can be no doubt that whatever Q 1 represents it represents it very badly. In many places it is so garbled and mutilated that it would be unintelligible without a knowledge of the later texts. It is most probably one of the 'stolen and surreptitious copies' mentioned in the preface to the folio of 1623. And I think we may assume that it was not stolen from any written copy of the play. No combination of an imperfect draft and a mole-eyed printer would be sufficient to account for the result. Moreover, the errors are in many cases manifestly due to mishearing and not to misreading. The more probable hypothesis is that the printer sent an agent to the theatre while *Hamlet* was being acted, and that he, with or without the aid of shorthand, took down such notes as he could of the dialogue[1]. These were afterwards strung together

*[in left margin: Q 1 a mutilated copy.]*

---

[1] Shorthand was invented before 1602. The schemes proposed in Timothy Bright's *Characterie* (1588) and Bales' *Art of Brachygraphie* (1590) are not of much use; but John Willis' *Art of Stenographie* (1602) is more practical. The method was certainly used for pirating plays. Heywood complains of it in two or three places. In the prologue to the *Rape of Lucrece* (1608), he speaks of it being only 'copied by the ear', and in that to *If you know me, you know Nobody*, he says that the audience—

> " Did throng the seats, the boxes, and the stage
> So much that some by stenography drew
> The plot : put it in print : scarce one word true ".

Cf. also Marston's *Malecontent*, and Webster's *The Devil's Law Case* (1623)—
"Do you hear, officers !
*You must take great care that you let in no brachygraphy men to take notes*".
See Levy, *Shakespeare and Shorthand*.

into something resembling a play.  They were in parts extremely
scanty, and were either left incomplete or else very roughly pieced
out.   It has been suggested that some hack-poet was employed to
revise them; but that is extremely unlikely.   Not Chettle, nor
Munday, nor any of Henslowe's crew of scribblers could have produced quite such an *indigesta moles*.  Their lines might have lacked
wit and imagination, but they would at least have made sense, and
to some extent have scanned.   And the same reasons which make it
unlikely that Q 1 was printed from a written text dispose of the idea
that a sight of the 'prompter's copy' was obtained for the revision;
it is, however, just possible that two or three of the subordinate
actors may have lent their 'parts'.[1]  The speeches belonging to
Horatio, Marcellus, and Voltemar are perhaps better represented than
the rest.

Those characteristics of Q 1 which may fairly be attributed to the
shortcomings of the reporter fell under four main heads.

i.  He appears to have left out bits of the dialogue here and there.
In a few places this can be shown almost with certainty.   Thus, for
i. 4. 69-71 Q 1 has—

> " What if it tempt you toward the flood my Lord,
> That beckles ore his bace into the sea ".

Here it is pretty obvious that the line

> "Or to the dreadful summit of the cliff "

has been dropped out.   This being so, it is natural to suppose that
the same thing has occurred in other passages, and especially where
Q 1 only gives a line or two at the beginning and another line or two
at the end of what appears as a long speech in Q 2.  The shortness of
the play in Q 1 confirms this view.   It contains only 2143 lines to the
3891 of the Globe text.  But it is impossible to say how much of this
is due to omissions, and how much to a fuller expansion in Q 2 of
the first form of the play.

ii.  In many passages the words have been taken down nearly
right, but the reporter has failed to observe the proper distribution
into lines, and has replaced it by one of his own.   Thus part of
Hamlet's soliloquy in i. 2 becomes—

> " O God within two moneths ; no not two ; maried,
> Mine uncle : O let me not thinke of it,
> My father's brother: but no more like
> My father, then I to *Hercules*.
> Within two months ere yet the salt of most
> Unrighteous teares had left their flushing
> In her galled eyes: she married, O God, a beast
> Devoyd of reson would not have made
> Such speede: Frailtie, thy name is Woman,
> Why she would hang on him, as if increase
> Of appetite had growne by what it looked on ".

[1] Actors' parts appear to have been copied for them on pasteboards, known as
'plats' or 'cards' (cf. v. 1. 149, note).   Some of these are still extant: three, The
*Battle of Alcazar, Frederick and Basilea*, and *The Dead Man's Fortune*, have
been facsimiled for Mr. Halliwell-Phillipps.

Similarly prose is often printed as if it were verse, and verse sometimes as prose.

iii. Often the reporter's hearing has failed him, and he has put
down, instead of the words actually spoken, others resembling them
in sound. This is the origin of such mistakes as 'impudent' for 'impotent' (i. 2. 29), 'right done' for 'writ down' (i. 2. 223), 'ceremonies' for 'cerements' (i. 4. 48), 'martin' for 'matin' (i. 5. 89).

iv. Where the notes are very scanty and the reporter has forgotten
the context, he has strung them together with words of his own. The
result is a curious medley of Shakespearian phrases bereft of their
meaning like a church-window filled with fragments of glass from
some shattered design. Thus, for i. 2. 101 *sqq.* Q 2 has—

> " It is a fault gainst heaven, fault gainst the dead,
> A fault gainst nature, and in reason's
> Common course most certain
> None lives on earth, but he is born to die ".

Here the reporter seems to have been misled by some note of the
words 'from the first corpse (course Q 2)', and to have turned reason's
'common theme' into 'common course'.

B. After making all allowance for the reporter's haphazard way
of working, I cannot persuade myself that the *Hamlet* which he saw
Q 1 a different at the theatre and tried to reproduce was the *Hamlet* of
version to Q 2   Q 2. There are wide differences between the two ver-
and F 1.      sions which none of the blundering mental processes
just enumerated are adequate to explain. They are, however, quite
consistent with the theory that we have in Q 1 a slovenly version of
an early and crude form of the play.

i. The order of the scenes is slightly different from that of Q 2.
The chief variation is that the 'To be or not to be' soliloquy and
the interview between Hamlet and Ophelia (iii. 1 in Q 2) precede
in Q 1 the 'fishmonger' scene with Polonius and the entry of the
players (ii. 2 in Q 2).

ii. Many of the names of the characters are different. *Leartes,
Ofelia, Gertred, Cornelia, Voltemar, Rossencraft, Gilderstone,* may
be mere corruptions aided by mishearing for the *Laertes, Ophelia,
Gertrard* or *Gertrad* (*Gertrude,* F 1), *Cornelius, Voltemand, Rosen-
crans* or *Rosencraus* (*Rosincrance* F 1), *Guildensterne* of Q 2. *Duke* and
*Duchess* for *King* and *Queen* (iii. 2. 165) are of no importance. But
some further explanation is needful of the substitution of *Gonzago* for
*Albertus* (iii. 2. 250), and of *Polonius* and *Reynaldo* for *Corambis*
and *Montano.* Let alone the *Corambus* in the German play (Introduction, pp. 12, 13, and Appendix C) and the traces of the old names
in the stage-directions of Q 2 (cf. notes to i. 2. 1 and ii. 1. 1), nothing will persuade me to the theory gravely held by Dr. Tanger
that these are mere mistakes due to similarity of sound. Other
instances of the change of names at the revision of a play are to be
found in the *Petruchio* and *Grumio* of *The Taming of the Shrew,*
which replace the *Ferando* and *Sander* of *The Taming of a Shrew,*

and in Ben Jonson's *Every Man out of his Humour*, where the Italian names of the first version give way to English ones in the second.

iii. There are passages where the Q 1 text does not appear to be corrupt, but where it yet differs widely from Q 2, and as a rule is markedly inferior in richness of vocabulary and depth of thought. Such differences appear to point directly to revision. Excellent instances may be found in Ophelia's two speeches concerning Hamlet. Cf. with the iii. 1. 158 *sqq.* of Q 2, the following of Q 1 :—

> " Great God of heaven, what a quick change is this?
> The Courtier Scholar Soldier, all in him
> All dasht and splintered thence, O woe is me,
> To a seene what I a seene, see what I see ".

And this with the ii. 1. 77 *sqq.* of Q 2—

> " O young Prince Hamlet, the only floure of Denmark,
> Hee is bereft of all the wealth he had,
> The Jewell that adorn'd his feature most
> Is filcht and stolne away, his wit's bereft him.
> Hee found mee walking in the gallery all alone,
> There comes hee to mee with a distracted looke,
> His garters lagging downe, his shooes untide,
> And fixt his eyes so stedfast on my face
> As if they had vow'd, this is their latest object.
> Small while he stoode, but gripes me by the wrist,
> And there he holdes my pulse till with a sigh
> He doth unclaspe his holde, and parts away
> Silent, as is the mid time of the night:
> And as he went, his eie was still on mee,
> For thus his head ouer his shoulder looked,
> He seemed to finde the way without his eies:
> For out of doores he went without their helpe,
> And so did leave me."

I do not think that the same hand which garbled the other parts out of the play is likely to have produced these neat paraphrases.

iv. There are other passages in Q 1 which have no representatives at all in Q 2. Only a few of these are of any length. One is given in the notes to iii. 2. 52; another is a scene between Horatio and Gertrude which comes between iv. 5 and iv. 6 of the received text. It is hard to see how these can have come into existence if they were not part of the play as heard by the reporter.

v. In several important respects the characterization of Q 1 is different from that of Q 2. I do not dwell on the point that Hamlet himself is far less subtly represented. This may be merely the result of the accidental omission by the reporter of some of the delicate touches in the delineation of the complete play. But there are at least two variations which must surely be deliberate. One is that our sense of Laertes' guilt is diminished by the fact that in Q 1 the proposal to use a poisoned foil comes not from him, but from Claudius. The other, that the character of Gertrude is put in quite a different light. In Q 2 the extent of her guilt is left vague and doubtful, and to the end she wavers between husband and son. In Q 1 she is made *to protest* very definitely her innocence of the murder, *and thenceforward to* show herself a strong partisan of Hamlet's.

This is her position in the *Historie of Hamlet* also, and the modification of it shown in Q 2 seems to me clearly the result of design. It was Shakespeare's intention that Hamlet should stand alone.

C. Assuming then that Q 1 and Q 2 represent two successive forms of *Hamlet*, a first sketch and a revision, are we justified in treating them both as the work of Shakespeare; or ought we to suppose that the first sketch contains any appreciable amount of the pre-Shakespearian *Hamlet*, in the existence of which we have good reason to believe (Appendix B)? I prefer the former view, although the Clarendon Press editors give the weight of their authority to a theory that Q 1 is the early *Hamlet* partly revised by Shakespeare, and that this revision had not gone much beyond act ii. I do not accept this. I believe that Q 1 is Shakespeare's independent treatment of the subject suggested to him by the older play. If he borrowed anything beyond the outline of the plot, it was probably the fooling, meant to tickle the groundlings, at the end of i. 5. It is true that the three last acts are not only more incoherent in themselves than the two earlier, but also that they depart more from Q 2; but this is capable of many explanations. The reporter may have grown tired of his task. So far as the dialogue goes, in the few places where we get it uncorrupted there is nothing inconsistent with its being Shakespeare's. It is not all at his highest level; it may have been hastily written for a provincial tour, and one need hardly be surprised that what is retained in Q 2 is better than what is rejected; but it does not, any of it, appear to have any affinity with the kind of thing that the pre-Shakespearian *Hamlet* probably was. I do not want, however, to lay too much stress on this question of style, for after all, the passages in question are necessarily the more colourless and commonplace, and I do not believe that I or anyone else have a sufficiently acute critical sense to say definitely of such that they are or are not Shakespeare's. Much more important is the essential identity, in other respects than style, of even the last three acts of Q 1 with Q 2. Almost all the details, the incidents and touches of characterization, the deep and imaginative sayings, are there at least in germ. I need only endorse Mr. Furnivall's remark, that if Q 1 is not Shakespeare's, then " the credit of three-fifths of the character of Hamlet, and about one-half of the working out of it, belong to the author of the old *Hamlet*".[1]

(Marginal note: *Both versions by Shakespeare.*)

---

# APPENDIX B.

## THE PRE-SHAKESPEARIAN HAMLET.

There are several allusions in contemporary literature to a play on Hamlet, which can hardly have been Shakespeare's, at the close of

[1] *Forewords to Quarto 2*, 1604. (Griggs' Facsimile.)

the sixteenth and beginning of the seventeenth centuries.   It is worth while to collect them here.

1. From an epistle by Thomas Nash, prefixed to Greene's *Menaphon: Camilla's alarm to slumbering Euphues*, 1589—

"Ile turne backe to my first text, of studies of delight, and talke a little in friendship with a few of our triviall translators.   It is a common practice now a daies amongst a sort of shifting companions, that runne through every arte and thrive by none to leave the trade of *Noverint* whereto they were borne, and busie themselves with the endevours of art, that could scarcelie latinize their necke verse if they should have neede; yet English Seneca read by candle-light yeeldes manie good sentences, as *Blould is a beggar*, and so foorth: and if you intreate him faire in a frostie morning, he will afoord you whole *Hamlets*, I should say Handfulls of tragical speaches.   But O grief! *Tempus edax rerum*;—what is it that will last always?   The sea exhaled by drops will in continuance be drie; and Seneca, let bloud line by line, and page by page, at length must needs die to our stage."

It has been thought possible that although *Menaphon* was not published until 1589, Nash's *Epistle* may have been written as early as 1587.

2. From the *Diary* of Philip Henslowe for 1594, while the Lord Chamberlain's and the Lord Admiral's men were playing for him at Newington Butts—

"9. of June 1594.   Rd. at hamlet.   viijs."

The play appears only to have been played once at this time, and is not marked n[ew] e[nterlude].

3. From Lodge's *Wit's miserie, and the World's madnesse*, 1596—

"[Hate Virtue is] a foul lubber, and looks as pale as the wisard of the ghost, which cried so miserally at the theator, like an oyster-wife, *Hamlet revenge*".

4. The following, though subsequent to the First Quarto of 1603, may possibly refer to the early play.   The actual phrase " Hamlet revenge," does not occur in the text of Shakespeare's play, as it has reached us, though the exhortation to revenge is given in other words in i. 5. 8, and i. 5. 25.

From Dekker's *Satiromastix*, 1602—

"*Asinius*. Wod I were hanged if I can call you any names but Capitaine and Tucca.

*Tucca*. No. Fye'st; my name's Hamlet revenge: thou hast been at Parris garden, hast not?"

Tucca comes on "his boy after him, with two pictures under his cloak"; cf. iii. 4. 53.

5. From *Westward Hoe*, 1607—

"I, but when light wives make heavy husbands, let these husbands play mad *Hamlet*; and crie *revenge*".

6. From Armin's *Nest of Ninnies*, 1608—

"*ther are*, as Hamlet saies, things cald whips in store" .

C₁. iii. 1. 70, note.

7. From Rowland's *The Night Raven*, 1618—
"I will not cry *Hamlet Reuenge* my greeves, But I will call *Hang-man Reuenge* on theeves".

An attempt has been made to show that Shakespeare's play belongs to the sixteenth century, on the strength of the following MS. note in Gabriel Harvey's copy of Speght's Chaucer—

"The younger sort take much delight in Shakespeare's *Venus and Adonis*, but his *Lucrece* and his tragedy of *Hamlet Prince of Denmarke*, have it in them to please the wiser sort".

But though Harvey doubtless purchased the volume in 1598, as this date occurs both at the beginning and end of it, the MS. notes therein appear to have been written at various subsequent times.

We may gather from the above passages that the play was known at least as early as 1589 (possibly 1587); that it was played at the Theater, at Newington Butts, and at Paris Garden; that it contained the ghost; and that the phrase, "Hamlet revenge", made an impression on the popular imagination.

Mr. Fleay (*Biographical Chronicle of the English Drama, s.v.* Kyd, ii. 26) suggests that the author of this older *Hamlet* was Thomas Kyd. It certainly appears likely that the attack in Nash's epistle to *Menaphon* was aimed at him.

---

# APPENDIX C.

## "FRATRICIDE PUNISHED."

Most of our information respecting the early performances of English plays in Germany is derived from Cohn's invaluable *Shakespeare in Germany*, to which the student is referred for further information. The following facts bear upon the relations of *Fratricide Punished* to our *Hamlet*.

(1) In Heywood's *Apology for Actors* (ed. Shakesp. Soc. p. 40) it is stated that "the King of Denmarke, father to him that now reigneth, entertained into his service a company of English comedians, commended unto him by the honourable the Earle of Leicester".

(2) Cohn shows that this king was Frederick II., who died 1588. Leicester's players went to the court of the Elector of Saxony in 1586, subsequently returned to England and became the nucleus of the company with which Shakespeare was connected throughout his dramatic career. See Fleay, *Chronicle of the London Stage*, passim.

(3) There is a diary kept by an officer of the Saxon court at Dresden in 1626, which contains a list of plays performed by 'the English actors'. Amongst these occurs *Hamlet a Prince in Denmarck.*

(4) The existing text of *Fratricide Punished* is from a MS. dated 'Pretz, den 27 October, 1710'. It is printed by Cohn, and translated in Furness' *New Variorum Hamlet*, ii. 121.

Dr. Latham (*Two Dissertations on Hamlet*, 1872) argues, but not, I think, very conclusively, that the date of *Fratricide Punished* can be fixed to about 1589, by an allusion to the expedition to Portugal in that year.

---

# APPENDIX D.

### THE 'TRAVELLING' OF THE PLAYERS (Act ii. scene 2, line 343).

The passage in which Rosencrantz explains the reasons why Hamlet's favourite company of tragedians are 'travelling' appears in a different form in each of the three versions. They may here be given together for purposes of comparison.

#### FIRST QUARTO.

*Ham.* How comes it that they trauell? Do they grow restie?
*Gil.* No my lord, their reputation holds as it was wont.
*Ham.* How then?
*Gil.* Yfaith my Lord, noueltie carries it away,
For the principall publike audience that
Came to them, are turned to private playes,
And to the humour of children.

#### SECOND QUARTO.

*Ham.* How chances it they trauaile? their residence both in reputation, and profit was better both wayes.
*Ros.* I thinke their inhibition, comes by the means of the late innouasion.
*Ham.* Doe they hold the same estimation they did when I was in the City; are they so followed?
*Ros.* No indeede are they not.

#### FIRST FOLIO.

*Ham.* How chances it they trauaile? their residence both in reputation and profit was better both wayes.
*Rosin.* I thinke their Inhibition comes by the meanes of the late Innouation?
*Ham.* Doe they hold the same estimation they did when I was in the City? Are they so follow'd?
*Rosin.* No indeed, they are not.
*Ham.* How comes it? Doe they grow rusty?
*Rosin.* Nay, their indeauour keepes in the wonted pace; But there is Sir an ayrie of Children, little Yases, that crye out on the top of question; and are most tyrannically clap't for 't: these are now the fashion, and so be-ratled the common Stages (so they call them) that many wearing Rapiers, are affraide of Goose-quils, and dare scarce come thither.

It will be seen that the reason for the 'travelling' assigned in Q 1 is the popularity of a rival company, of children; in Q 2 an 'inhibition' due to an 'innovation'; in F 2, both these causes are mentioned.

*The title-page of Q 1 shows us that Hamlet,* in the early days of its career, was acted out of London. It is not unnatural, therefore, to seek in this passage an allusion to some 'travelling' of Shakespeare's own company, which may help to determine the date of the play. It will be well to take the two points separately.

i. *The 'Inhibition' and 'Innovation'.*—It would appear that 'inhibition' was a technical term for an order restraining theatrical performances, or the performances of a particular company, 'from taking place in London. The 'inhibition' here spoken of has been identified with various such orders issued at different times during the long struggle between the theatrical or court and the anti-theatrical or city parties, represented respectively by the Privy Council and the Corporation. (See Halliwell-Phillipps, *Outlines of the Life of Shakespeare*, and Fleay, *Chronicle History of the London Stage.*) So, too, the 'innovation' has been interpreted as 'the new practice of introducing polemical matter on the stage', or 'the new morals of the Puritan party'. But we are helped to a better explanation by the fuller knowledge of the history of the Globe company, which is due chiefly to Mr. Fleay. In 1601 the company was in disgrace at court owing to the share they had taken in the conspiracy of Essex and Southampton. A performance of *Richard II.* had been given by them to encourage the conspirators.[1] For the only time during a long period of years they were not invited to take part in the Christmas festivities. Probably they travelled during the autumn; they seem to have been at Aberdeen in October[2] and at Cambridge about the same date;[3] and if so, this is most likely the 'travelling' alluded to in the play. Then the 'inhibition' will be the refusal of permission to act at court, and the 'innovation', the political innovation or conspiracy which led to it.

ii. *The Aery of Children.*—Can this allusion also be referred to this same year, 1601? It was just at this time that the children of the Chapel Royal were acting at the Blackfriars. They took a prominent part in the stage-controversy known as the 'war of the theatres', and amongst other plays they produced between 1597 and 1603, Ben Jonson's *Cynthia's Revels* and his *Poetaster*, satirical plays, full of attacks on rival poets and players, and answering well to the description given in the text. Moreover, the Q I phrase, 'the humours of children', seems to point to Jonson's fondness for painting 'humours' or comic types. Witness the titles of his earlier plays, *Every Man in his Humour* and *Every Man out of his Humour.* If the allusion has been correctly identified, *Hamlet* may be the play in which Shakespeare 'put down' Ben Jonson.[4]

---

[1] See Mr. Hales' *Notes and Essays*, and the Introduction to my edition of *Richard II.* (Falcon Series).

[2] Cf. *Macbeth* (Warwick Series), Introduction, p. 11, and the excursus on Shakespeare in Scotland in Knight's Shakespeare.

[3] Kempe and Burbage are introduced in the 2nd part of *The Returne from Parnassus*, a Cambridge play with a local scene, probably written in 1601. (Cf. Macray's edition of the play, and Fleay, *Biographical Chronicle of the English Drama*, ii. 349.)

[4] Cf. *The Returne from Parnassus.* Mr. Fleay, however, thinks that the play meant was *Troilus and Cressida.*

The question remains, why was the point about the 'innovation' omitted in Q 1, and that about the children in Q 2? The first difficulty is easily explained. When the reporter went to the theatre,—probably early in 1602, as the book was entered in the Stationers' Registers in July of that year,—Elizabeth was still on the throne. Whatever the Globe company chose to do in the provinces, they would have been ill-advised to allow any allusion to the facts of their disgrace to stand in the play when it was acted in town. Just in the same way, the most objectionable scene of *Richard II.*, from a political point of view, was omitted from the two editions of the play published in Elizabeth's lifetime. In 1604, however, the date of Q 2, she was dead, and such nice caution became no longer necessary. At the same time another change of circumstances led to the omission of the attack on the player-children. By 1604 the so-called 'war of the theatres' was over, Jonson and Shakespeare were probably friends again, and the latter had no desire to print anything discourteous to the former.[1] In the meantime, however, the passage had been elaborated at the general revision of the play to the form in which it is found in F 1. As to the re-appearance of both the allusions in 1623, probably they had remained throughout in the theatre copy of the play. When F 1 was published, both the matters to which they referred had become ancient history, and there was no reason why they should be suppressed.

---

# APPENDIX E.

### "DIDO, QUEEN OF CARTHAGE."

It is worth while to reprint the passage from *Dido, Queen of Carthage*, parodied in *Hamlet*, act ii. sc. 2. The play was published, as by Marlowe and Nash, in 1594, the year after Marlowe's death. It is usually supposed to have been left incomplete by him, and finished by Nash. Mr. Fleay, however, thinks that it was an early play, written by the two in collaboration. The passage in question is from act ii. sc. 1 :—

*Æn.* . . . . . . . .
At last came Pyrrhus, fell and full of ire,
His harness dropping blood, and on his spear
The mangled head of Priam's youngest son ;
And, after him, his band of Myrmidons,
With balls of wild-fire in their murdering paws,
Which made the funeral flame that burnt fair Troy ;
All which hemmed me about, crying, "This is he ' "
*Dido.* Ah, how could poor Æneas scape their hands?

[1] Cf. the omission, probably for similar reasons, in Q 2 of the attack upon Kempe, which appeared in Q 1—iii. 2. 50, note.

*Æn.* My mother Venus, jealous of my health,
    Convey'd me from their crooked nets and bands;
    So I escaped the furious Pyrrhus' wrath:
    Who then ran to the palace of the king,
    And at Jove's altar finding Priamus,
    About whose withered neck hung Hecuba,
    Folding his hand in hers, and jointly both
    Beating their breasts, and falling on the ground,
    He, with his falchion's point raised up at once,
    And with Megæra's eyes, star'd in their face,
    Threatening a thousand deaths at every glance:
    To whom the agèd king thus, trembling, spoke;
    "Achilles' son, remember what I was,
    Father of fifty sons, but they are slain;
    Lord of my fortune, but my fortune's turned:
    King of this city, but my Troy is fired;
    And now am neither father, lord, nor king:
    Yet who so wretched but desires to live?
    O, let me live, great Neoptolemus!"
    Not moved at all, but smiling at his tears,
    This butcher, whilst his hands were yet held up,
    Treading upon his breast, struck off his hands.
*Dido.* O, end, Æneas! I can hear no more.
*Æn.* At which the frantic queen leaped on his face,
    And in his eyelids hanging by the nails,
    A little while prolonged her husband's life.
    At last, the soldiers pull'd her by the heels,
    And swung her howling in the empty air,
    Which sent an echo to the wounded king:
    Whereat he lifted up his bed-rid limbs,
    And would have grappled with Achilles' son,
    Forgetting both his want of strength and hands;
    Which he disdaining, whisk'd his sword about,
    And with the wind thereof the king fell down;
    Then from the navel to the throat at once
    He ripp'd old Priam; at whose latter gasp
    Jove's marble statue gan to bend the brow,
    As loathing Pyrrhus for this wicked act.
    Yet he, undaunted, took his father's flag,
    And dipp'd it in the old king's chill-cold blood,
    And then in triumph ran into the streets,
    Through which he could not pass for slaughter'd men;
    So, leaning on his sword, he stood stone-still,
    Viewing the fire where with rich Ilion burnt.

---

# APPENDIX F.

## GOETHE AND COLERIDGE ON HAMLET.

These two passages are the foundation of modern Shakespeare criticism:—

(1) From Goethe's *Wilhelm Meister* (1795).

"I sought for every indication of what the character of Hamlet was *before the death of his* father; I took note of all that this interesting *youth had been*, independently of that sad event, independently of the subsequent terrible occurrences, and I imagined what he might have been without them.

"Tender and nobly descended, this royal flower grew up under the direct influences of majesty; the idea of the right and of princely dignity, the feeling for the good and the graceful, with the consciousness of his high birth, were unfolded in him together. He was a prince, a born prince. Pleasing in figure, polished by nature, courteous from the heart, he was to be the model of youth and the delight of the world.

"Without any supreme passion, his love for Ophelia was a presentiment of sweet needs. His zeal for knightly exercises was not entirely his own, not altogether natural to him; it had rather to be quickened and inflamed by praise bestowed upon another. Pure in sentiment, he knew the honourable-minded, and would prize the repose which an upright spirit enjoys, resting on the frank bosom of a friend. To a certain degree he had learned to discern and value the good and the beautiful in arts and sciences; the vulgar was offensive to him; and if hatred could take root in his tender soul, it was only so far as to make him despise the false and fickle courtiers, and scornfully to play with them. He was calm in his temper, simple in his behaviour, neither content in idleness, nor yet too eager for employment. An academic routine he seemed to continue even at court. He possessed more mirth of humour than of heart; he was a good companion, compliant, modest, discreet, and could forget and forgive an injury; yet never able to unite himself with one who overstept the limits of the right, the good, and the becoming.

"Figure to yourselves this youth, this son of princes, conceive him vividly, bring his condition before your eyes, and then observe him when he learns that his father's spirit walks; stand by him in the terrible night when the venerable ghost itself appears before him. A horrid shudder seizes him: he speaks to the mysterious form; he sees it beckon him; he follows it and hearkens. The fearful accusation of his uncle rings in his ears; the summons to revenge, and the piercing reiterated prayer: 'Remember me!'

⁄ "And when the ghost has vanished, whom is it we see standing before us? A young hero panting for vengeance? A born prince, feeling himself favoured in being summoned to punish the usurper of his crown? No! Amazement and sorrow overwhelm the solitary young man; he becomes bitter against smiling villains, swears never to forget the departed, and concludes with the significant ejaculation: 'The time is out of joint: O cursed spite, that ever I was born to set it right!'

"In these words, I imagine, is the key to Hamlet's whole procedure. To me it is clear that Shakespeare sought to depict a great deed laid upon a soul unequal to the performance of it. In this view I find the piece composed throughout. Here is an oak tree planted in a costly vase, which should have received into its bosom only lovely flowers; the roots spread out, the vase is shivered to pieces.

"A beautiful, pure, noble, and most moral nature, without the strength of nerve which makes the hero, sinks beneath a burden which it can neither bear nor throw off; every duty is holy to him, —this too hard. The impossible is required of him,—not the impossible in itself, but the impossible to him. He winds, turns, agonizes, advances, and recoils, ever reminded, ever reminding himself, and at last almost loses his purpose from his thoughts, without ever again recovering his peace of mind."

(2) From Coleridge's *Notes and Lectures upon Shakespeare* (1808).

"I believe the character of Hamlet may be traced to Shakespeare's deep and accurate science in mental philosophy. Indeed, that this character must have some connection with the common fundamental laws of our nature may be assumed from the fact that Hamlet has been the darling of every country in which the literature of England has been fostered. In order to understand him, it is essential that we should reflect on the constitution of our own minds. Man is distinguished from the brute animals in proportion as thought prevails over sense; but in the healthy processes of the mind, a balance is constantly maintained between the impressions from outward objects and the inward operations of the intellect; for if there be an overbalance in the contemplative faculty, man thereby becomes the creature of mere meditation, and loses his natural power of action. Now, one of Shakespeare's modes of creating characters is to conceive any one intellectual or moral faculty in morbid excess, and then to place himself, Shakespeare, thus mutilated or diseased, under given circumstances. In Hamlet he seems to have wished to exemplify the moral necessity of a due balance between our attention to the objects of our senses and our meditation on the working of our minds,—an *equilibrium* between the real and the imaginary worlds. In Hamlet this balance is disturbed; his thoughts and the images of his fancy are far more vivid than his actual perceptions, and his very perceptions, instantly passing through the *medium* of his contemplations, acquire, as they pass, a form and a colour not naturally their own. Hence we see a great, an almost enormous, intellectual activity, and a proportionate aversion to real action consequent upon it, with all its symptoms and accompanying qualities. This character Shakespeare places in circumstances under which it is obliged to act on the spur of the moment. Hamlet is brave and careless of death; but he vacillates from sensibility, and procrastinates from thought, and loses the power of action in the energy of resolve. Thus it is that the tragedy presents a direct contrast to that of *Macbeth* ; the one proceeds with the utmost slowness, the other with a crowded and breathless rapidity."

# ESSAY ON METRE.[1]

## § 1. Metre as an indication of Date.

English blank verse did not come into use till the sixteenth century: and at the commencement of its career, the rules which regulated its employment were strict. It was only when the instrument was becoming familiar that experiments could be ventured upon, and variations and modifications freely introduced. The changes in the structure of blank verse between the time when Shakespeare commenced writing and the time of his retirement are great; and the variations in this respect are among the most important indications of the date of any given play. That is to say, broadly speaking, the less strictly regular the metre, the later the play.

In the same way, a gradually increasing disregard of other kindred conventions marks the later plays as compared with the earlier. A good deal of rhyme survives in the dialogue in the earlier plays; later it is only to be found occasionally at the close of a scene or a speech to round it off—probably a concession to stage tradition analogous to the similar use of 'gnomae' in Greek plays, and of a 'sentiment' in modern melodrama.

In the present play, the general characteristics of the metre appear to be those of Shakespeare's middle period; but there are an unusual number of irregularities; the intense excitement constantly finds vent in rapid dialogue which overflows the bounds of metre.

The extensive use of prose in the play is worth careful notice. Prose was at first used by Shakespeare for comic passages only, and even when this limitation ceased to be observed, it continued as a rule to be the medium of a lower plane of emotion than that represented by blank verse. Thus in the present play it is appropriate to the discourse between Hamlet and the players (ii. 2 and iii. 2), between Hamlet and the clowns (v. 1), between Hamlet and Osric (v. 2). It is also, of course, used for letters (ii. 2; iv. 7), and the speech of servants. But it is also used exceptionally in the middle and later plays to produce special and peculiar effects, *e.g.* for the sleep-walking scene (v. 1) in *Macbeth*, and for Ophelia's madness (iv. 5). Similarly, I think, Hamlet speaks in prose wherever he is playing the madman; where he is not so acting, in the soliloquies, in the scenes with Horatio (iii. 2; v. 2), in the interview with his mother (iii. 4), in the lament over Ophelia (v. 1), then in blank verse.

[1] This *outline of Shakespeare's Prosody* is adapted, by the kind permission of Mr. A. D. Innes, from the one written by him for his edition of *Julius Cæsar*, in this series.

In the scene with Ophelia (iii. 1) he passes from blank verse to prose just at the point where he begins to suspect her good faith. Of course while Hamlet speaks prose, personages of less dignity must do the same ; the King, however, is not so bound (iv. 3).

The 'plays within the play' (ii. 2; iii. 2) are written in a stilted and archaic style of blank verse, in order to produce an artificial effect in comparison with the ordinary dialogue, as that itself is artificial when compared with the natural speech of ordinary life. (Cf. notes *ad locc.*)

Rhymed decasyllable couplets are used to close a scene or a speech; and Hamlet occasionally breaks into doggerel rhyme in moments of excitement.

### § 2. Form of Blank Verse.

Our study of versification is commonly restricted to that of Latin and Greek. When we examine English verse-structure, a distinction at once appears. In the classical verse the governing element is quantity; in English it is *stress*. And inasmuch as stress is much less definite than quantity, the rules of English verse cannot be given with the same precision as those of Latin and Greek. But we may begin with certain explanations as to what stress is *not*. A 'stressed' syllable is not the same as a long syllable; nor is stress the same as *sense*-emphasis. Any strong or prolonged dwelling of the voice on a syllable, for whatever reason, is stress. So, while a syllable must be either long or short, there are many shades of gradation between the unstressed and the strongly stressed. And as in Greek tragic verse a long syllable may, in certain positions, take the place of a short one, so a moderately stressed syllable may often in English take the place of an unstressed one.

To start with, then,—to get at the basis of our metre—we will take no account of weak stress, but treat of all syllables as if they must either have no stress or a strong stress; and throughout, the word stress, when used without a qualifying adjective, will mean strong stress. The acute accent (') will be used to mark a stress, the grave (`) to mark a weak stress, the ˇ to mark a syllable sounded but not stressed.

The primary form of the Shakespearian line is—five feet, each of two syllables; each foot carrying one stress, on the second syllable; with a sense pause at the end of the line, and generally a slight pause, marked by a comma perhaps, after the 2nd or 3rd foot. This is called a cæsura.

But look' | the morn', | in rus' | set man' | tle clad' (i. 1. 166).

### § 3. Normal Variations.

But if there were no variations on this, the effect would be monotonous and mechanical after a very few lines.

*(i) The first* variation therefore is brought about by the stress in

one or two of the feet being thrown on the first instead of the second syllable, which is known as an 'inverted' stress.

| | |
|---|---|
| 1st foot. | Cost'ly \| thy ha' \| bit as' \| thy purse' \| can buy' (i. 3. 70). |
| 2nd foot. | The wind' \| sits' in \| the shoul' \| der of' \| your sail' (i. 3. 56). |
| 3rd foot. | But this' \| most foul' \| strange' and \| unna' \| tural (i. 5. 28). |
| 4th foot. | Why thy' \| canon' \| ized bones', \| he'arsed \| in death' (i. 4. 47). |
| 5th foot. | Affec' \| tion! pooh'! \| you speak' \| like' a \| green' girl (i. 3. 101). |

The stress is thus thrown back much more commonly in the first foot of the line than elsewhere: and in the other cases the stressed syllable usually follows a pause.

(ii) Secondly, variety is introduced by the insertion of an extra unstressed syllable which is not extra-metrical, analogous to the use of an anapaest instead of an iambus.

| | |
|---|---|
| 1st foot. | I ăm more' \| an an' \| tique Ro' \| man than' \| a Dane' (v. 2. 352). |
| 3rd foot. | Of im' \| pious stub' \| bŏrnnĕss; 't is' \| unman' \| ly grief' (i. 2. 94). |
| 3rd foot. | Let' it \| be te' \| năblĕ in' \| your si' \| lence still' (i. 2. 248). |
| 4th foot. | The light' \| and care' \| less li' \| vĕry that' \| it wears' (iv. 7. 80). |
| 5th foot. | How wear' \| y, stale', \| flat' and \| unpro' \| fītăble (i. 2. 133). |

As a general rule, however, such extra syllables are very slightly pronounced; not altogether omitted but slurred, as very often happens when two vowels come next each other, or are separated only by a liquid (see § 6).

(iii) The converse of this is the (very rare) omission of an unstressed syllable. This is only found where the stress is very strong, or when the omission is really made up for by a pause.

For'ward, \| not per' \| manent', \| —swe'et, \| not la'st(ing) (i. 3. 8).

(iv) Extra-metrical unstressed syllables are added after a pause, sometimes after the second foot, rarely after the third.

| | |
|---|---|
| 2nd foot. | Till' the \| last trum'(pet): \| for char' \| ita' \| ble pray'ers (v. 1. 252). |
| 3rd foot. | That can' \| denote' \| me tru'(ly): \| these' in \| deed' seem (i. 2. 83). |

More frequently an extra-metrical syllable comes at the end of a line, and this is common in this play. It is only in quite early plays that it is at all unusual, only in the later ones that it is the normal rhythm.

Whe'ther \| 't is no' \| bler in' \| the mind' \| to suf'(fer)
The slings' \| and ar' \| rows' of \| outra' \| geous for'(tune)
Or' to \| take arms' \| against' \| a sea' \| of trou'(bles) (iii. 1. 57–9).

The increasing frequency of extra-metrical syllables is a useful approximate guide to the date of a play. But they are never so frequent in Shakespeare as in some of the younger dramatists.

(v) The variation which perhaps most of all characterizes the later plays is the disappearance of the sense-pause at the end of the line. At first, a clause running over from one line to the next is very rare: in the last plays, it is extremely common. (The presence of a sense-pause is not necessarily marked by a stop; it is sufficient for the purpose that the last word should be dwelt on; the pause may be merely rhetorical, not grammatical.) The proportion of overflow to end-stopped lines in *Hamlet* is considerable.

### § 4. Weak Stresses.

The basis of scansion being thus settled, we may observe how the rules are modified by weak or intermediate stresses, which are in fact the chief protection against monotony.

(i) Lines in which there are not five strong stresses are very plentiful; *e.g.*

> Absent' | thee from' | feli' | city' | awhile' (v. 2. 358).

In the fifth foot particularly, the stress is often extremely slight; such 'light' or 'weak' endings are particularly characteristic of the later plays.

(ii) On the other hand, lines in which there are two stressed syllables in one foot are common.

> His ca' | non gainst' | self'-slaugh' | ter! O' ¡ God'! God'! (i. 2. 132).

A foot with a double stress is nearly always preceded by a pause, or by a foot with a very weak stress only.

(iii) It will be observed that there are never fewer than three strong stresses, and that any foot in which there is no strong stress must at any rate have one syllable with a weak stress, and that very often such a foot has two weak stresses; preventing the feeling that the line is altogether too light. Thus a syllable which is quite unemphatic acquires a certain stress merely by length, as in some of the above cases. And, speaking broadly, a very strong stress in one foot compensates for a weak stress in the neighbouring foot.

### § 5. Irregularities.

(i) Occasionally lines occur with an extra foot; *i.e.* an additional stress after the normal ten syllables.

> A wor | thy pi | oner. | Once more | remove | good friends (i. 5. 162).
> Had he | been van | quisher: | as by ¡ thĕ sāme co' | venant (i. 1. 93).

And sometimes there is even an extra syllable added (§ 3 (iv)).

> 'T is sweet | and com | menda | ble in | your na | ture Ham(let) (i. 2. 87).

But perhaps this should be scanned—

> 'T is sweet | and com | mend'bl' in | your na | ture Ham(let).

Cf. § 6.

But this does not often occur in the course of a speech, and when it does there is usually a break in the middle of the line. It is, however, decidedly common in broken dialogue.

> *Ham.*   Go on; | I 'll fol | low thee |
> *Mar.*                You shall | not go, | my lord (i. 4. 79).

And this is probably often to be explained by the second speaker *breaking in* on the first, so that one or two syllables are pronounced simultaneously.

(ii) Short incomplete lines of various lengths are also found, especially in broken, hurried, or excited dialogue, and at the beginning or end of a speech. They are especially common in this play. Sometimes the gap may be filled up by appropriate action, or a dramatic pause.

(iii) Interjections and proper names (especially vocatives), even short questions or commands, are frequently extra-metrical.

And shall | I cou | ple hell? | (O, fie!) | Hold, hold, | my heart (i. 5. 93).

In nearly every instance observe that an unusual stress or an irregularity comes either after a pause, whether at the beginning of a line or in the middle; or at the end of a line in which there is a break.

### § 6. Apparent Irregularities.

(i) Difficulties occasionally arise from the fact that words in Shakespeare's day were sometimes accented in a different way from that of the present day, and sometimes even bear a different accent in different places in Shakespeare's own writing. Thus, we say 'por'tent', Shakespeare always 'portent'. On the other hand, we say 'complete'', Shakespeare has sometimes 'complete'' sometimes 'com'plete' (i. 4. 52). In effect we must often be guided by the verse in deciding on which syllable of a word the accent should fall, because custom had not yet finally decided in favour of a particular syllable. Speaking broadly, the tendency of the modern pronunciation is to throw the accent far back.

(ii) Similarly, when two vowels come together (as in words ending with -ion, -ius, -ious, and the like) we are in the habit of slurring the first, and sometimes of blending it with the preceding consonant; so that we pronounce 'ambit-i-on' 'ambishon'. In Shakespeare the vowel in such cases is sometimes slurred and sometimes not, in the same word in different places; usually the former in the middle of a line, often the latter at the end. In such cases we must be guided simply by ear in deciding whether the vowel is slurred or sounded distinctly. And we have to decide in exactly the same way when we are to sound or not sound the terminal -ed of the past participle.

So, too, 'prayer' is sometimes a monosyllable, sometimes a dissyllable.

And what's | in pray | er but | this two- | fold force,
To be forestalled ere we come to fall,
Or pardon'd being down? Then I'll look up ;
My fault | is past. | But, O, | what form | of prayer
Can serve my turn? (iii. 3. 48).

(iii) So again in particular words, a vowel seems to be sometimes mute, sometimes sounded. Thus we have mem'ry (i. 5. 96) and memory (i. 5. 98); or again, unnat'ral (i. 4. 25) and unnatural (i. 4. 28).

(iv) In a large number of words where a liquid (l, m, n, and especially r) comes next to another consonant an indefinite vowel sound is sometimes introduced between the two letters (just as now in many places one may hear the word 'helm' pronounced 'hellum'), which may be treated as forming a syllable, and sometimes the vowel is actually inserted, as in *thorough* = 'through'.

A somewhat exceptional instance is

> Lends the | tongue vows: | these bla | zes *daug* | *hter* (i. 3. 117).

(v) Conversely, a light vowel sound coming next a liquid is often sounded lightly and in effect dropped; so that such words as *spirit* (i. 1. 138), *peril, quarrel,* are practically monosyllables. (Hence such a form as '*parlous*' = '*perilous*'. Cf. i. 3. 102.)

> *Ham.*  Perchance | 't will walk | again |
> *Hor.*              | *I warrant* ⟨Q 2 *warn't*⟩ | it will (i. 2. 244).

(vi) *th* and *v* between two vowels are often almost or entirely dropped and the two syllables run into one: as in the words 'whether', 'whither', 'other', 'either', 'ever', 'never', 'even', 'over'. 'Heaven' generally, 'evil', 'devil' sometimes, are treated as monosyllables. Q 2 prints *deale* in ii. 2. 628.

Vowels separated by a *w* or an *h* are habitually slurred and pronounced practically as one syllable.

(vii) 'Fire' and similar words which in common pronunciation are dissyllables ('fi-er', &c.) are commonly but not always scanned as monosyllables.

(viii) Other ordinary contractions, such as 'we'll' for 'we will', *th'* for *the* before a vowel, &c., though not shown in the spelling, are frequent.

### § 7.  General Hints.

(i) Often there are many possible ways of scanning a particular line, and the one adopted must depend on the individual taste of the reader.   Thus he can frequently choose between § 3 (ii) and § 6.

(ii) Irregularities are most common,
- (*a*)  In passages of emotional excitement.
- (*b*)  Before or after pauses.
- (*c*)  Where proper names are introduced.

# GLOSSARY.

**a-**, a degenerate preposition; (1) **a-making** (i. 3. 19), **a-gaming** (ii. 1. 58), for 'at'; cf. 'at gaming' (iii. 3. 91); (2) **John-a-dreams** (ii. 2. 596), for 'of'; cf. *Richard II.* i. 3. 76, 'John a Gaunt'.

**absolute**: (1) (v. 1. 148), precise; (2) (v. 2. 111), Osrician for 'faultless'.

**abuse** (iv. 7. 51), deception.

**addition** (i. 4. 20; ii. 1. 47), that which is added to a man to distinguish him, name, title; and so, reputation; cf. *Merry Wives*, ii. 2. 312, "devils' additions, the names of fiends".

**admiration** (i. 2. 192; iii. 2. 339, 342), astonishment.

**aery** (ii. 2. 354), an eagle's nest or brood; from the Low Latin *area*.

**affront** (iii. 1. 31), come face to face with.

**alarm** (iii. 4. 120), sudden attack; from the Italian cry *all' arme*, to arms!

**amiss** (iv. 5. 18), mischief.

**an**: (1) (i. 5. 19; iii. 4. 122), a form of 'on', in the phrase 'an end'; (2) (i. 5. 177; iv. 6. 8; v. 2. 184), *and*, in the special sense of 'if'. The form *an* was rarely used in Shakespeare's time. Except in *an 't*, it only occurs once in F 1; but modern editors have appropriated it to the conditional sense of the word. *And* or *an* is often strengthened, as in i. 5. 177, by the addition of *if*.

**anchor** (iii. 2. 229), anchorite, hermit.

**anon** (ii. 2. 490), immediately; from the A.S. *on ân*, lit. 'in one' *(moment)*.

**antic**: (1) (v. 2. 352), ancient; (2) (i. 5. 172), fantastic. Probably the second sense is derived from the first, but Murray connects it with the Ital. *antico*, a cavern adorned with grotesques.

**appointment** (iv. 6. 16), equipment.

**approve** (i. 1. 29), justify.

**argal** (v. 1. 13), a clownish corruption of the Latin *ergo*, therefore.

**argument** (ii. 2. 372; iii. 2. 149, 242; iv. 4. 54), subject, especially the subject of a drama.

**arrant** (i. 5. 124; iii. 1. 131), scoundrelly, lit. cowardly; from M.E. *arghen*, A.S. *eargian*, to be cowardly.

**arras** (ii. 2. 162; iv. 1. 9), tapestry, so called from Arras in Artois in the north of France.

**arrest** (ii. 2. 67; v. 2. 343), legal restraint.

**article** (i. 1. 94), clause in an agreement.

**assay**: (1) (ii. 1. 65), test; (2) (ii. 2. 71), attempt.

**assume** (iii. 4. 160), acquire.

**at**: (1) (iv. 3. 46), used by Shakespeare for the earlier *a*, a contraction of the A.S. *on*; (2) (iv. 3. 56), near.

**avouch** (i. 1. 57), acknowledgment.

**audit** (iii. 3. 82), final account.

**bar** (i. 2. 14), exclude.

**batten** (iii. 4. 67), grow fat: cf. *Coriolanus*, iv. 5. 35, "batten on cold bits", and Milton, *Lycidas*, i. 29, "Battening our flocks with the fresh dews of night".

**be**, a form of *by*, used as a prefix, intensifies and modifies, in various ways, often very slight, the sense of the word it is attached to. Often it simply serves to form a verb, as in **berattle** (ii. 2. 357), belabour; **beshrew** (ii. 1. 113), curse; **beteem** (i. 2. 141), allow; **bespeak** (ii. 2. 140), speak to, address.

**bear** (i. 3. 67; iv. 3. 7), carry on, administer: cf. *Cæsar*, ii. 1. 226, 'bear it as our Roman actors do'.

**beaver** (i. 2. 229), the movable part of the helmet covering the face, the visor.

**bedded** (iii. 4. 121), laid flat.

**beetle** (i. 4. 71), hang over.

**bent** (ii. 2. 30), inclination; so **at bent** (iv. 3. 47), inclined.

**bias** (ii. 1. 65), inclination to one side; from Low Latin *bifax*, 'one who looks askew': (1) of a bowl, (2) any preventing tendency. Cf. *John*, ii. 1. 574, "commodity, the bias of the world".

**bilboes** (v. 2. 6), iron fetters; from Bilboa, correctly Bilbao, a place of steel manufacture in Spain.

**bisson** (ii. 2. 529), blind, blinding: probably from A. S. *bi-*, near, and *séon*, to see; cf. *Coriolanus* (ii. 1. 70), "your bisson conspectuities".

**blank** (iv. 1. 42), the white mark in the centre of a target.

**blazon** (i. 5. 21), proclamation.

**blench** (ii. 2. 626), start.

**bodykins** (ii. 2. 554), diminutive of *body*, used in the oath, 'God's bodikins'.

**bore** (iv. 6. 26), importance; lit. the calibre, or size of shot.

**bourne** (iii. 1. 79), boundary.

**brainish** (iv. 1. 11), brainsick.

**brave** (ii. 2. 611), befitting, used ironically.

*bravery* (v. 2. 79), ostentation.

**bruit** (i. 2. 127), announce noisily. Cf. *Macbeth*, v. 7. 22, "By this great clatter one of greatest note [ Seems bruited".

**bug** (v. 2. 22), bugbear, bogy.

**button** (i. 3. 40), bud.

**can** (iv. 7. 85), are able, can do.

**canker**: (1) (i. 3. 39), a worm that destroys blossoms; (2) metaphorically (v. 2. 69), destructive element.

**capable**; (1) (iii. 2. 13), able to receive; (2) (iii. 4. 127), susceptible.

**cap a pe** (i. 2. 200), from head to foot; Old Fr. *de cap a pie*. Cf. *Winter's Tale*, iv. 4. 771, "I am courtier cap a pe".

**card** (v. 1. 149; v. 2. 114), either a 'chart', or the face of a compass, or a card with rules for etiquette, or a player's 'part' or 'plat': see notes *ad locc.*

**carriage** (i. 1. 74), Osrician for the 'hanger' of a sword.

**cast**, noun (iii. 1. 85), surface colouring; cf. 'roughcast,' the plaster surface of a wall.

**cast**, vb. (ii. 1. 115), seek for a lost scent—a hunting metaphor.

**cataplasm** (iv. 7. 144), plaster.

**cautel** (i. 3. 15), deceit.

**cease** (iii. 3. 15), death.

**censure** (i. 3. 69; i. 4. 35; iii. 2. 82), opinion.

**cerement** (i. 4. 48), a shroud of waxed linen; from the Lat. *cera*, wax.

**choler** (iii. 2. 315), anger, literally 'bile'.

**chopine** (ii. 2. 447), a high-heeled shoe used by women in Italy.

**chough**: (1) generally a crow or jackdaw; (2) (v. 2. 89), here only, a clown, spelt *chuff* in *1 Henry IV.* ii. 2. 94. Cf. Cotgrave's *Dictionary*, s.v. *Maschefouyn*, "A chuffe, boor, lobcocke, lozell; one that is fitter to feed with cattell, than to conuerse with men".

**circumstance** (i. 5. 127; iii. 1. 1; iii. 3. 83), a roundabout course.

**clepe** (i. 4. 19), call, name. A.S. *cleopian*. The word, so common in Chaucer, is rare in Elizabethan English. Cf. *Macbeth*, iii. 1. 93; *Love's Labour's Lost*, v. 1. 24; *Venus and Adonis*, 995.

**climature** (i. 1. 125), country. *Climate* is similarly used in *Cæsar*, i. 3. 32, "They are portentous things | Unto the climate that they point upon".

**coil** (iii. 1. 67), either that which is wrapped round, like a coil of rope, a covering; or turmoil, bustle; cf. *Much Ado*, v. 2. 98, "Yonder's old coil at home".

**collateral** (iv. 5. 206), indirect.

**compass** (iii. 2. 384), the extent of a voice, the notes which it can take.

**competent** (i. 1. 90), equivalent.

**complexion** (i. 4. 27; v. 2. 102), temperament, disposition.

**comply** (ii. 2. 39; v. 2. 195), be courteous: in the usual sense of *compliment*.

**compost** (iii. 4. 151), manure.

**conceit**: (1) (ii. 2. 579, 583; iii. 4. 114), imagination; often in the sense of (2) (iv. 5. 145; v. 2. 160) fantastic imagination.

**confine** (i. 1. 155; ii. 2. 252), prison.

**congrue** (iv. 3. 66), agree, be suitable.

**conjunctive** (iv. 7. 14), closely united.

**conscience** (1) (iv. 7. 1), the moral consciousness; (2) (v. 2. 67), morality; (3) (iii. 1. 83), consciousness generally, especially self-consciousness, speculation.

**consonancy** (ii. 2. 295), agreement.

(885)

**continent**, that which contains: (1) (iv. 4. 64), literally, 'cover'; (2) (v. 2. 115), metaphorically, 'inventory'.

**contraction** (iii. 4. 46), marriage contract.

**conversation** (iii. 2. 60), intercourse; the sense of the Latin *conversari*.

**cope** (iii. 2. 60), encounter.

**cote** (ii. 2. 329), pass by, outstrip; a technical term in coursing. Cf. Drayton, *Polyolbion*, xxiii. 1115—

"Each man notes
Which dog first turns the hare, which first the other cotes";

and Turberville, "In coursing at a deer, if one greyhound go endways by another, it is accounted a cote". From the French *côtoyer*, to coast along.

**counter** (iv. 5. 110), in the wrong direction; another technical term of venery, used when a dog follows the scent backwards; cf. *2 Henry IV.* i. 2. 102, and *Comedy of Errors*, iv. 2. 239, "a hound that runs counter, and yet draws dry-foot well". From the Latin *contra*, opposite to.

**cozen** (iii. 4. 78), **cozenage** (v. 2. 67), trick, trickery; lit. 'call cousin', and so 'sponge upon', 'beguile'; the French *cousiner*.

**crants** (v. 1. 255), a garland, in the especial sense of a maiden's funeral garland, the German *krans*. The word is connected with the Latin *corona*, crown; cf. stage-direction to Chapman's *Alphonsus*, "Enter Saxon Mentz, like Clowns with each of them a Mitre with *Corances* on their heads".

**cry** (iii. 2. 289), company; lit. the noise of hounds, and so, a pack of hounds; cf. *Midsummer Night's Dream*, "a cry more tuneable | Was never holla'd to", and *Coriolanus*, iii. 3. 110, "you common cry of curs".

O

**cue** (ii. 2. 60), hint, motive; lit. in stage terminology, the catchword by which an actor knows his turn to speak; cf. *Henry V.* iii. 6. 130, "now we speak upon our cue".

**curb** (iii. 4. 155), bow, bend; the French *courber*.

**dear** (i. 2. 182) is used of anything that touches deeply, even if it yields pain rather than pleasure; cf. *Richard II.* i. 3. 151, "my dear exile"; *King John*, i. 1. 257, "my dear offence"; *Macbeth*, v. 2. 3, "their dear causes".

**defeat** (ii. 2. 598), destruction.

**delate** (i. 2. 38), convey, intrust; Bacon appears to use the word in this sense, but it generally means 'accuse'.

**design** (i. 1. 94), point out, mention, designate.

**die** (i. 3. 128), colour, character.

**dild** (iv. 5. 41), in the phrase 'God dild you', probably a corruption of 'God yield you', possibly of 'God shield you'. This form occurs in *Sir John Oldcastle* (1600), but 'God 'ild you' is more usual; cf. *e.g. Macbeth*, i. 6. 13.

**disclose**, noun (iii. 1. 174); vb. (v. 1. 310), hatch.

**document** (iv. 5. 178), lesson, object-lesson; from the Latin *docere*, teach.

**dole** (i. 2. 13), grief; from the Latin *dolere*, grieve.

**dout** (iv. 7. 192), extinguish; a contraction of *do out*, just as *don* is of *do on*; cf. i. 4. 37, note.

**down-gyved** (ii. 1. 80), of stockings, pulled down over the ankles like gyves or fetters. Cf. **gyves**.

**drossy** (v. 2. 197), pinchbeck, imitative. The *dross* is the refuse of an ore from which the pure metal has been extracted.

**ducat** (iii. 4. 24), a gold coin, the Italian *ducato*, from *ducatus* (Duchy of Apulia) in the legend upon it.

**eager**: (1) (i. 5. 69), acid, sour; (2) (i. 4. 2), keen, biting; from the O. F. *egre* (French *aigre*), Latin *acer*, sharp.

**ecstasy** (ii. 1. 102; iii. 1. 168; iii. 4. 74, 138, 139), excitement, madness; any state of being beside oneself; from Gr. ἐκ = out, στάσις = standing.

**edge** (iii. 1. 26), keenness, desire.

**effects** (iii. 4. 129), actions; cf. *Macbeth*, v. 1. 12, "do the effects of watching".

**eisel** (v. 1. 299), either the corruption of the name of a river, as the Yssel or Weissel; or vinegar. Cf. *Sonnet* cxi., "I will drink potions of eisel 'gainst my strong infection"; cf. Chaucer, *Romaunt of the Rose*, 217, "Breed | Kneden with eisel strong and egre"; and the eighth prayer in the *Salisbury Primer*, 1555, 'O blessed Jesu!... I beseech thee for the bitterness of the aysell and gaul that thou tasted".

**emulate** (i. 1. 83), emulous, jealous.

**enacture** (iii. 2. 207), action.

**encounter** (ii. 2. 164; v. 2. 199), meeting, behaviour, dialogue.

**entertainment**: (1) (ii. 2. 329), reception, treatment; (2) (i. 3. 64; ii. 2. 392; v. 2. 216), in the special sense of kindly treatment, courtesy.

**envious** (iv. 7. 174); **enviously** (iv. 5. 6), spiteful, spitefully, petulantly.

**escot** (ii. 2. 362), paid, maintained; from O.F. *escotter*; A.S. *scot* = payment, money shot into a common fund, *scéotan* = to shoot.

**eterne** (ii. 2. 512), eternal. Cf. *Macbeth*, iii. 2. 38, "But in them nature's copy's not eterne".

**exception** (v. 2. 242), dislike; as in the phrase, 'to take exception'.

**excrement** (iii. 4. 121), hair. Cf. *Comedy of Errors*, ii. 2. 79, "Why is Time so niggard of hair, being as it is so plentiful an excrement?"

**expostulate** (ii. 2. 86), converse, expound.

**express** (ii. 2. 317), expressive, significant.

**extent** (ii. 2. 390), behaviour. Cf. *Twelfth Night*, iv. 1. 57, "In this uncivil and unjust extent | Against thy peace".

**eyas** (ii. 2. 355), nestling; a term of falconry for a young hawk just taken from the nest. French *niais*.

**fantasy** (i. 1. 23; iv. 4. 61), imagination, caprice.

**fardel** (iii. 1. 76), bundle, burden; said to be from the Arabic *fardah*, through the French *farde*.

**fay** (ii. 2. 271), faith.

**fee**: (1) (iv. 4. 22), land held as private property; (2) (i. 4. 65; ii. 2. 73), payment, value; from A.S. *feoh*, cattle, property, connected with Latin *pecus, pecunia*.

**fell** (v. 2. 61), cruel.

**felly** (ii. 2. 517), the rim of a wheel.

**fetch** (ii. 1. 38), stratagem. Cf. *Lear*, ii. 4. 89—
"Deny to speak with me? They are sick? they are weary?
They have travell'd all the night? Mere fetches".

**figure** (i. 1. 41, 109; i. 2. 199; iii. 4. 104), form, shape.

**flaw** (v. 1. 239), a gust of wind. Cf. *2 Henry IV*. iv. 4. 35—
"As humorous as winter and as sudden
As flaws congealed in the spring of day".

**flushing** (i. 2. 155), either a rush of water or a redness.

**foil** (v. 2. 265, 266, &c.): (1) a blunted rapier, from 'foil', defeat; (2) the gold-leaf used to set off a jewel; from Latin *folium*, 'leaf'. Hence whatever serves to set off anything else by contrast.

**fond** (i. 5. 99; v. 2. 200), foolish.

**fordo** (ii. 1. 103; v. 1. 244), destroy.

**forgery** (iv. 7. 89), invention, imagination.

**fret**: (1) (iii. 2. 388), vex, chafe, with an allusion to the *fret* or stop in a musical instrument; from A. S. *fretan*, short for *for-etan* (*for*, 'entirely'; *etan*, 'eat'), 'to eat away', 'wear away'. Cf. *Lear*, i. 4. 307, "fret channels in her cheeks": (2) (ii. 2. 313), ornament; from A. S. *frætwian*. Cf. *Cymbeline*, ii. 4. 88, "The roof of the chamber | With golden cherubins is fretted".

**function** (ii. 2. 582), bodily activity.

**fust** (iv. 4. 39), grow mouldy; lit. 'taste of the cask', from O.F. *fuste*, a stick, a cask; Latin *fustis*, a stick.

**gain-giving** (v. 2. 226), misgiving, the sense of 'gain' being adverse, as in 'gainsay'.

**gentry** (ii. 2. 22; v. 2. 114), courtesy.

**gib** (iii. 4. 190), a tom-cat; cf. *1 Henry IV*. i. 2. 83, "As melancholy as a gib-cat".

**goblin** (i. 4. 40; v. 2. 22), a mischievous spirit, from L. L. *gobelinus*, dimin. of *cobalus* = demon.

**gorge** (v. 1. 207), stomach.

**grained** (iii. 4. 90), ingrained, dyed in grain, *i.e.* of a fast colour. M. E. *engreynen*, coined from F. *en* (Lat. *in*), and O.F. *graine*, "the seed of herbs, also grain, wherewith cloth is died *in grain*.

scarlet die, scarlet in graine", Cotgrave. From L. *granum.*

**green** (i. 3. 101), **greenly** (iv. 5. 83), foolish, foolishly.

**gules** (ii. 2. 479), red, an heraldic term. Cf. *Timon,* iv. 3. 59, "With man's blood paint the ground, gules, gules"; probably from the open mouth of the heraldic lion, Lat. *gula*=throat.

**gyves** (iv. 7. 21), fetters; a Celtic word. Cf. Irish *gabh* = take; con. with Lat. *capere*=to take.

**harbinger** (i. 1. 122), forerunner; M. E. *herbergeour,* O. F. *herberg-er,* one who provided lodgings for a man of rank.

**hatchment** (iv. 5. 213), a coat of arms hung up as a sign of the death of the owner.

**haunt** (iv. 1. 18), publicity. Cf. *Antony and Cleopatra,* iv. 14. 54—
" Dido and her Æneas shall want troops,
And all the haunt be ours".

**hautboy** (iii. 2. 145, stage-dir.), a wooden wind-instrument resembling the modern oboe.

**havoc** (v. 2. 375), slaughter; said to be from A. S. *hafoc,* hawk, so that ' Cry havoc!' is literally ' Cry ware hawk!'

**head** (iv. 5. 101), armed force.

**hectic** (iv. 3. 68), fever.

**hent** (iii. 3. 88), grip; or perhaps 'way', 'course'. The word is used in western counties for the course of a ploughshare.

**heyday** (iii. 4. 69), wildness, wantonness.

**honesty**: (1) (ii. 2. 204), becoming, befitting; (2) (iii. 1. 108), chastity.

**hoodman blind** (iii. 4. 78), blindman's buff.

**hugger-mugger** (iv. 5. 84), secrecy.

*humour* (ii. 2. 12), disposition. *The four chief types of disposition,*

the sanguine, choleric, phlegmatic, melancholic, were supposed to depend on the preponderance of various humours in the blood.

**husbandry** (i. 3. 77), thrift. Cf. *Macbeth,* ii. 1. 4, "There's husbandry in heaven, their candles are all out".

**impartment** (i. 4. 59), communication.

**impasted** (ii. 2. 481), made into paste, clotted.

**imperious** (v. 1. 236), imperial

**implorator** (i. 3. 129), one who implores or solicits.

**impone** (v. 2. 155, 171), lay upon; Osrician for ' wager'.

**import**: (1) (i. 2. 23), purport; (2) (iv. 3. 65; v. 2. 21), imply; (3) (iii. 2. 149, &c.), signify.

**imposthume** (iv. 4. 27), abscess.

**impress** (i. 1. 75), enforced service. Cf. modern ' press-gang'.

**incapable** (iv. 7. 179), unable to understand. Cf. **capable.**

**incorporal** (iii. 4. 116), immaterial.

**indenture** (v. 1. 119), agreement, a legal term. Agreements made in duplicate were cut with indented edges to fit one another.

**index** (iii. 4. 52), explanatory prologue.

**indifferent** (ii. 2. 3), of moderate estate, neither high nor low.

**indue** (iv. 7. 180), furnish.

**ingenious** (v. 1. 271), belonging to the intellect, wise.

**inhibition** (ii. 2. 346), prohibition; used technically for a prohibition of theatrical performances by authority.

**inoculate** (iii. 1. 119), graft, bud.

**instance** (iii. 2. 192), motive.

**instant**, adj. (i. v. 71), immediate; adv. (i. v. 94), immediately.

**investment** (i. 3. 128), dress.

**jealousy** (ii. 1. 113; iv. 5. 19), suspicion.

**jowl** (v. 1. 84), thrust, throw.

**jump** (i. 1. 65; v. 2. 386), exactly.

**kibe** (v. 1. 153), a sore on the heel, chilblain. Cf. *Lear*, i. 5. 9, " If a man's brains were in 's heels, were 't not in danger of kibes ".

**kindless** (ii. 2. 609), unnatural.

**lard** (iv. 5. 37; v. 2. 20), enrich; lit. fatten.

**learn** (v. 2. 9), teach.

**let**: (1) (iv. 5. 54), allow; from A. S. *lættan*; (2) (i. 4. 85), hinder; from A. S. *lettan*.

**liberal** (iv. 7. 171), licentious, free-spoken.

**list**, noun: (1) (i. 1. 98; i. 2. 32), catalogue, number; (2) (iv. 5. 99), border, boundary. The idea common to both meanings appears to be that of a strip.

**list**, vb.: (1) (i. 5. 177), desire, conn. with *lust*; (2) (i. 3. 30; i. 5. 22), listen.

**loggats** (v. 1. 100), a game, something like bowls, in which wooden logs are thrown at a ' jack'; cf. Jonson, *Tale of a Tub*, iv. 6, " Now are they tossing of his legs and arms | Like loggats at a pear tree".

**luxury** (i. 5. 83), lust.

**mallecho** (iii. 2. 147), mischief, the Span. *malhecho*. Cf. Shirley, *Gentleman of Venice*, " Be humble, thou man of mallecho, or thou diest ".

**marry** (i. 4, 13, &c.), an exclamation denoting indignation, scorn, or vehement assertion; originally an invocation of the B. V. Mary, of whose name the word is a corrupt form. Cf. *Richard II.* i. 4. 16; iv. 1. 114.

*mart* (i. 1. 74), traffic.

**mass** (v. 1. 62), the communion service in the Catholic church; from the concluding words of the priest, *Ite, missa est*.

**matin** (i. 5. 89), morning.

**mazzard** (v. 1. 97), head, skull; used again in *Othello*, ii. 3. 155.

**miching** (iii. 2. 147), secret; lit. sneaking; cf. Florio, *Ital. Dict.*, " *Acciapinare*: to miche, to shrug or sneak in some corner"; and *Prompt. Parv.* "Mychyn, or stelyn pryuely".

**milch** (ii. 2. 540), moist; not confined to milk; cf. Drayton, *Polyolbion*, xiii. 171, "exhaling the milch dew".

**mineral** (iv. 1. 26), a mine or vein of metal; cf. Hall, *Satires*, bk. vi.—
" Shall it not be a wild fig in a wall, Or fired brimstone in a mineral?"

**mobled** (ii. 2. 525), muffled, wearing a mob-cap or ' clout' (line 529); cf. Shirley, *Gentleman of Venice*, "The moon does mobble up herself".

**moiety** (i. 1. 90), portion, lit. half.

**mole** (i. 4. 24), blemish.

**mope** (iii. 4. 81), be dull, without activity.

**mortal**: (1) (iv. 4. 51; iv. 5. 60), subject to death; and so (2) (ii. 2. 539; iii. 1. 67), human; (3) (iv. 7. 143), causing death.

**mortise** (iii. 3. 20), fasten. A *mortise* is a hole in a piece of wood into which a projecting part of another piece is fitted.

**mountebank** (iv. 7. 142), quack; the Ital. *montambanco*, lit. one who mounts a bench to proclaim his wares.

**mow** (ii. 2. 301), grimace.

**muddy-mettled** (ii. 2. 593), sluggish-natured. *Mettle* is 'substance', 'temper': another form of *metal*; no distinction is made between the two words in old editions, either in spelling or use.

**mutine** (v. 2. 6), mutineer, rebel.

**napkin** (v. 2. 299), handkerchief.

**native** (i. 2. 47), at home, in the place of one's birth.

**nerve** (i. 4. 83), muscle, the 'sinew' of modern English, whereas the Elizabethan *sinew* often corresponds rather to our *nerve*.

**nonce** (iv. 7. 16), always in the phrase **for the nonce**. This is the A. S. *for then anes*, where *then* is the dat. of the article, and *anes =* once. Thus 'for the once, for the occasion'. (Skeat.)

**occurrents** (v. 2. 368), occurrences, events.

**o'erreach**: (1) (iii. 1. 17), overtake; (2) (v. 1. 87), outwit, with a punning allusion to the literal sense.

**o'ersized** (ii. 2. 284), smeared over.

**omen** (i. 1. 123), a fatal event foretold by a sign; more usually the word means the sign itself, but not in Shakespeare.

**operant** (iii. 2. 184), operative, active.

**ore** (iv. 1. 25), a mineral containing precious metal.

**orisons** (iii. 1. 89), prayers; from Fr. *oraison*, Lat. *oratio*.

**ostentation** (iv. 5. 209), display, pageant.

**paddock** (iii. 4. 190), toad. Cf. *Macbeth*, i. 1. 9. The word is also used in various parts of England for a frog.

**pajock** (iii. 2. 295), probably peacock. Dyce states that in the north of Scotland a peacock is popularly called a 'peajock'. Skeat, however, would derive the word from *patch*, a motley fellow, a fool. Or it may be merely ragamuffin, tatterdemalion, the 'king of shreds and patches' of iii. 4. 102. Mr. Ingleby quotes *patchocke*

as applied by Spenser to a ragged Irishman.

**palmy** (i. 1. 113), glorious: the palm being an emblem of superiority; cf. v. 2. 40, and *Timon*, v. 1. 12, "You shall see him a palm in Athens again and flourish with the highest".

**paragon** (ii. 2. 320), model, pattern; from Span. *para con*, in comparison with.

**parle** (i. 1. 62), parley, conference. From Fr. *parler*, speak, a military term. Cf. *Richard II.* i. 1. 192; iii. 3. 33.

**partisan** (i. 1. 140), halberd, battle-axe; perhaps from the O.H.G. *partá*, axe.

**pass**, noun (iv. 7. 139; v. 2. 61, 173), thrust, bout, at fencing. So the vb. **to pass** (v. 2. 309).

**periwig-pated** (iii. 2. 10). A periwig is false hair; the Fr. *perruque*, Ital. *perucca*; conn. with Ital. *piluccare*, pull out hair. Lat. *pilus*, a hair.

**perpend** (ii. 2. 105), consider.

**peruse** (iv. 7. 137), examine closely.

**petard** (iii. 4. 207), a case or shell filled with explosives.

**picked** (v. 1. 151), refined, dainty.

**pioner** (i. 5. 163), military engineer.

**pitch** (iii. 1. 86), importance, lit. height: a metaphor from falconry, in which the word denoted the height to which a hawk soared before it swooped. Cf. *2 Henry VI.* ii. 1. 5—

"But what a point, my lord, your falcon made,
And what a pitch she flew above the rest".

**plausive** (i. 4. 30), plausible.

**plurisy** (iv. 7. 118), properly *pleurisy*, an affection of the lungs, from the Gk. πλευρά, but treated as if it meant a 'plethora' or fulness of blood, and spelt as if from Lat. *plus*, more.

**point** (i. 2. 200), summit of perfection, in the phrase *at point*, *i.e.* perfectly ready. Cf. *Macbeth*, iv. 3. 135.

**porpentine** (i. 5. 20), porcupine.

**posset** (i. 5. 68), a hot thick drink, generally made of curdled milk; the phrase 'eat a posset' occurs in *Merry Wives*, v. 5. 180. Cf. also *Macbeth*, ii. 2. 6.

**posy** (iii. 2. 162), motto on a ring, a corruption of *poesy*; cf. *Merchant of Venice*, v. 1. 148—
'A ring . . . whose posy was
For all the world like cutler's poetry
Upon a knife ".

**power** (iv. 4. 9), armed force.

**practice** (iv. 7. 66. 139), stratagem.

**precurse** (i. 1. 121), forerunning, omen.

**pregnant** (ii. 2. 212), ingenious, full of subtle meaning.

**present** (iv. 3. 67), immediate.

**pressure** (i. 5. 100; iii. 2. 27), impression, character.

**prevent** (ii. 2. 305), anticipate.

**primy** (i. 5. 7), in its prime, spring-like, youthful; cf. *Sonnet* iii., "the lovely April of her prime ".

**process**: (1) (i. 5. 37; iii. 3. 29), proceeding, course of events; cf. *Richard III.* iv. 3. 32, "tell the process of their death "; (2) (iv. 3. 65), order, decree.

**proof**: (1) (iii. 2. 179; iv. 7. 113, 155), trial; (2) (ii. 2. 512), strength. Cf. *Macbeth*, i. 2. 54—
" Bellona's bridegroom, lapped in proof".
So too the adj. (iii. 4. 38), and the participle **unapproved** (i. 1. 96).

**puffed** (i. 3. 49; iv. 4. 49), inflated.

*pursy* (iii. 4. 153), fat and breathless.

**push** (v. 1. 318), impulse, setting in motion.

**quality** (ii. 2. 263), profession.

**quarry** (v. 2. 375), a heap of dead game; Fr. *curée*, the entrails given to the hounds; a technical term of sport. Cf. *Macbeth*, iv. 3. 206.

**question** (ii. 2. 356), conversation; cf. notes *ad loc.* and *As You Like It*, iii. 4. 39, "I met the duke yesterday, and had much question with him ".

**quick**, noun (ii. 2. 626; iv. 7. 124), sensitive flesh.

**quick**, adj. (v. 1. 137, 274, 302), alive.

**quiddity** (v. 1. 107), subtlety; from Med. Lat. *quidditas*, the 'whatness' or nature of a thing, a scholastic term; and so 'a subtle scholastic distinction'.

**quietus** (iii. 1. 75), discharge; a legal term for the acquittance given by the exchequer at the settlement of an account. Cf. *Sonnet* cxxvi.—
"Her audit, though delayed, answered must be,
And her quietus is to render thee".

**quillet** (v. 1. 108), trick, esp. in argument; from Lat. *quidlibet*, anything you will.

**quintessence** (ii. 2. 321), an extract of a thing containing its chief qualities; so, the purest part of a thing; cf. *As You Like It*, iii. 2. 147—
" The quintessence of every sprite Heaven would in little show ".
From Lat. *quinta essentia*, fifth essence, the first four being the four elements.

**quit** (v. 2. 68, 280), requite.

**quote** (ii. 1. 112), observe; cf. *Troilus and Cressida*, iv. 5. 233—
" I have with exact view perused thee, Hector,
And quoted joint by joint".

**rack** (ii. 2. 506), cloud.

**rank** (iv. 4. 22), great, literally luxuriant. Cf. iii. 4. 152.

**ravel** (iii. 4. 186), loosen; woven or twisted things are said to 'ravel' when the strands part; cf. *Richard II*. iv. 1. 288—"Must I ravel out | My weaved up folly?" and cf. *Macbeth*, ii. 2. 37—"Sleep that knits up the ravell'd sleave of care".

**razed** (iii. 2. 288), streaked, slashed. Cf. Holme, *Academy of Armory*, bk. iii. ch. i. p. 14: "Pinked or raised shooes, have the over leather's grain part cut into roses, or other devices".

**reck** (i. 3. 51), care for, mind.

**recorder** (iii. 2. 303, 360), a kind of small flute. Cf. Chappell, *Popular Music of the Olden Time*, p. 246.

**rede** (i. 3. 51), counsel.

**reechy** (iii. 4. 184), stinking, lit. smoky.

**regard** : (1) (iv. 7. 76), estimation, opinion; (2) (iii. 1. 87), consideration ; (3) (ii. 2. 79), in the phrase 'on such regards', on such conditions.

**region**, noun (ii. 2. 509), the sky, properly a division of the sky according to the science of the Roman augurs; so too the adj. (ii. 2. 607); cf. *Sonnet* xxxiii., "The region cloud hath masked him from me now".

**replication** (iv. 2. 13), reply.

**requiem** (v. 1. 260), a hymn sung for the dead; from the Lat. *requies*, rest.

**respect** (iii. 1. 68; iii. 2. 193), consideration.

**retrograde** (i. 2. 114), contrary.

**return** (i. 1. 91), fall to, without any idea of previous possession.

**rhapsody** (iii. 4. 48), a collection of meaningless words. Cf. Florio's *Montaigne*, p. 68, ed. 1603, "This concerneth not those mingle-mangles of many kindes of stuffe, or, as the Grecians call them, rapsodies ". The Gr. ῥαψῳδός is properly 'one who strings songs together, a reciter of epic poetry'.

**rival** (i. 1. 13), associate. Cf. the use of *rivality* in *Antony and Cleopatra*, iii. 5. 8, " Cæsar having made use of him in the wars against Pompey, presently denied him rivality ".

**robustious** (iii. 2. 10), sturdy, Cf. *Henry V*. iii. 7. 159.

**romage** (i. 1. 107), bustle.

**rood** (iii. 4. 14), cross, crucifix, the same word as 'rod'.

**round** (iii. 1. 191; iii. 4. 5), plain-spoken. Cf. *Othello*, i. 3. 90, "A round unvarnished tale ".

**rouse** (i. 2. 127; i. 4. 8; iii. 1. 58), revel, noisy mirth: the German *rausch*, a flare up. See the passage from Howell on 'the Danish rousa' quoted in the note to i. 4. 8. The word has no connection with *carouse*.

**rub** (iii. 1. 65), obstacle, lit. roughness or inequality in the ground, especially on a bowling-green. Cf. *Richard II*. iii. 4. 4, " 'T will make me think the world is full of rubs ".

**sallet** (ii. 2. 462), spiciness, indecency. The same word as 'salad'.

**sans** (iii. 4. 79), without ; a French word.

**saw** (i. 5. 100), maxim. Cf. *As You Like It*, ii. 7. 156, " wise saws and modern instances ".

**scarf**, vb. (v. 2. 13), fling on like a scarf. Cf. *Macbeth*, iii. 2. 47, 'Sealing night | scarf up the tender eye of pitiful day ".

**scope** (i. 1. 68; i. 2. 37), extent, range of action. From the Greek σκοπός, 'mark to aim at'.

**scrimer** (iv. 7. 101), fencer; the Fr. *escrimeur*.

**season**: (1) (i. 2. 192; ii. 1. 28), qualify, by throwing in an ingredient; (2) (iii. 2. 219; iii. 3. 86), mature, ripen.

**seize** (i. 1. 89), a legal term, to take *seisin* or possession.

**sere** (ii. 2. 337), the catch in the mechanism of a gun which prevents it from going off until it is released by the trigger.

**sergeant** (v. 2. 347), bailiff.

**set** (i. 3. 122; iv. 3. 64), value.

**shard** (v. 1. 254), fragment of pottery.

**shark** (i. 1. 98), gather together without selection, as a shark collects every kind of fish into its maw.

**shent** (iii. 2. 416), reproached, put to shame.

**short** (iv. 1. 18), in the phrase **keep short**, restrain. So *take up short* in *Henry V*. ii. 4. 72.

**siege** (iv. 7. 77), rank; cf. *Othello*, i. 2. 22, "men of royal siege".

**simple** (iv. 7. 145), medicinal herb; orig. a single element in a compound medicine. Cf. *As You Like It*, iv. 1. 16, "a melancholy of mine own, compounded of many simples".

**sith** (iv. 4. 45), since; both forms are short for 'sithence'.

**slander** (i. 3. 132), disgrace, waste, spoil. Cf. *Much Ado*, ii. 3. 47, "Tax not so bad a voice | To slander music any more than once".

**sledded** (i. 1. 63), either 'borne on sleds or sledges', or 'heavily weighted'. Cf. *sledge-hammer*.

**sliver** (iv. 7. 174), small branch, twig. Cf. the use of the verb in *Macbeth*, iv. 1. 28, "Slips of yew, slivered in the moon's eclipse". From A.S. *slifan*, to cleave.

**sort** (i. 1. 109), either 'suit', 'befit', or 'turn out', 'fall out'.

*station* (iii. 4. 58), attitude, bearing.

**statist** (v. 2. 33), statesman; used again in *Cymbeline*, ii. 4. 16.

**still** (ii. 2. 42; iv. 7. 117), always, constantly.

**stithy** (iii. 2. 79), anvil, smithy.

**stop** (iii. 2. 76, 376, 381), the mechanism for regulating the passage of air in a wind-instrument.

**stoup** (v. 1. 68; v. 2. 278), a drinking vessel.

**stuck** (iv. 7. 162), a thrust in fencing; the Italian *stoccado*.

**supervise** (v. 2. 23), inspection, reading.

**suppliance** (i. 3. 9), diversion, pastime, that which supplies or fills up a vacant moment.

**table** (i. 5. 98; ii. 5. 107), tablet, or memorandum-book; so **table-book** (ii. 2. 136).

**take** (i. 1. 163), enchant. Cf. *Winter's Tale*, iv. 4. 118, "daffodils that . . . take the winds of March with beauty".

**tarre** (ii. 2. 370), set on, originally to incite dogs to fight. Cf. *Troilus and Cressida*, i. 3. 392, "Pride alone must tarre the mastiffs on".

**temper** (v. 2. 339), mix.

**tend**: (1) (iii. 1. 170), have a tendency; (2) (i. 3. 83; iv. 3. 47; iii. 2. 216), attend.

**tender**, noun (i. 3. 99, 103, 106), offer; vb. (1) (i. 3. 107; iv. 3. 43), treat tenderly, take care of; (2) (i. 3. 109), show. Cf. *Winter's Tale*, iv. 4. 826, "I'll . . . tender your persons to his presence".

**tent** (ii. 2. 626), search, prove, try; so the noun in *Troilus and Cressida*, ii. 2. 16, and elsewhere.

**tetter** (i. v. 71), a thickening of the skin in disease.

**thews** (i. 3. 12), muscles, strength.

**tickle** (ii. 2. 337), unstable, easily moved.

**top**, vb. (iv. 7. 89), surpass.

**toward** (i. 1. 71; v. 2. 376), at hand.

**toy**: (1) (iv. 5. 18), trifle; (2) (i. 3. 6; i. 4. 75), idle fancy.

**travel** (ii. 2. 343), go on tour in the provinces; used technically of theatrical companies.

**trick**, noun (iv. 4. 61), plaything. Cf. *Winter's Tale*, ii. 1. 51, "A very trick for them to play at will".

**trick**, vb. (ii. 2. 479), adorn, properly an heraldic term; "a *trick* being a delineation of arms, in which the colours are distinguished by their technical marks, without any colour being laid on" (Dyce).

**tropically** (iii. 2. 247), metaphorically, from Gr. τρέπω, a figure of speech.

**truepenny** (i. v. 150), true, honest fellow.

**truncheon** (i. 2. 104), staff.

**tyrannically** (ii. 2. 356), violently, as the part of the tyrant was played in the mysteries. Cf. iii. 2. 15, "It out-herods Herod", and note *ad loc.*

**unaneled** (i. 5. 77), without the rite of extreme unction or anointing, a sacrament in the Catholic Church. Cf. Sir T. More, "The extreme unction, or anelynge, and confirmacion, he sayed, be no sacraments of the church".

**unbated** (iv. 7. 39; v. 2. 328), unblunted, without a button (cf. *foil*); to *bate* is to 'abate, diminish', and so to 'blunt'; cf. *Love's Labour's Lost*, i. 1. 6, "bate his scythe's keen edge".

**unhouselled** (i. 5. 77), without the sacrament; *housel* is from A.S. *húsel*, lit. sacrifice.

**union** *(v. 2. 283, 337)*, an especially fine pearl; probably from Lat. *unus* in the sense of 'unique'.

**unsifted** (i. 3. 102), untried.

**use** (i. 2. 134; iii. 4. 163, 168), habit, custom.

**vail** (i. 2. 70), lower; cf. *Merchant of Venice*, i. 1. 28, "vailing her high-top lower than her ribs".

**valanced** (ii. 2. 442), fringed, lit. with drapery; metaphorically 'with a beard'.

**ventage** (iii. 2. 373), a hole in a musical instrument for the passage of air.

**very**: (1) (ii. 2. 49), veritable, real; (2) (iii. 4. 137; iv. 7. 78; v. 1. 119), mere.

**virtue** (iv. 5. 155; iv. 7. 145), power, efficacy.

**wake**, vb. (i. 4. 8), revel by night; cf. *Sonnet* lxi., "For thee watch I while thou dost wake elsewhere". A *wake* is properly the Vigilia, or eve of the dedication of a church, during which watch was kept in it; then the annual feast of dedication.

**wassail** (i. 4. 9), revelry; from A.S. *waes hael*, be of health, a formula used in drinking a toast.

**windlass** (ii. 1. 65), a winding, circuitous course; so, a subtle stratagem; cf. Golding, Ovid, *Met.* bk. vii.—

"like a wily fox he runs not forth
    directly out,
Nor makes a windlasse over all
    the champion fields about";

and *Mirror for Magistrates*, "Which by slie drifts and windlaces aloof, | They brought about".

**woundless** (iv. 1. 44), invulnerable.

**writ** (ii. 2. 420), writing, especially dramatic writing; cf. note *ad loc.* and *Titus Andronicus*, ii. 3. 264, "This fatal writ | The complot of this timeless tragedy".

**yaw** *(v. 2. 120)*, stagger, move unsteadily; used especially of ships. Massinger, *Very Woman*, iii. 5, has the substantive, "O, the yaws that she will make! Look to your stern, dear mistress, and steer right". From the Scand. *gaga*, to bend backwards, probably a reduplicated form of *go*.

# INDEX OF WORDS.

(The references are to the Notes *ad locc.* Other words will be found in the *Glossary.*)

# GENERAL INDEX.

Lightning Source UK Ltd.
Milton Keynes UK
13 February 2011

167420UK00001B/44/P